Give it to Moore,
He Will Score!

Stuart Humphreys & Richard Harrison

Give it to Moore, He Will Score!

The Authorised Biography of

Ian Storey-Moore

The Man Clough Couldn't Buy

Foreword by

Martin O'Neill

pitch

First published by Pitch Publishing, 2023
Reprinted, 2023
2

Pitch Publishing
9 Donnington Park,
85 Birdham Road,
Chichester,
West Sussex,
PO20 7AJ
www.pitchpublishing.co.uk
info@pitchpublishing.co.uk

A CIP catalogue record is available for this book
from the British Library.

ISBN 978 1 80150 510 9

Typesetting and origination by Pitch Publishing

Printed and bound in Great Britain by
TJ Books Limited, Padstow, Cornwall

Contents

In memory of our fathers, Dennis Humphreys and Harry Harrison, for introducing us to the delights (and despair) of following Nottingham Forest, and to our wives, Erika and Marina, for patiently tolerating the lifelong obsession that has ensued.

Foreword

by Martin O'Neill

It is 27 December 1971. A cold wind blows over the River Trent and cuts through the City Ground, home to Nottingham Forest. Despite the weather, 42,000 fans make their way to the stadium hoping for some festive cheer. Arsenal, last season's Double-winning team, are today's opposition and with Alan Ball making his debut for the Gunners, having signed from Everton only a few days earlier, there is much to be excited about this afternoon. What happens not many minutes after kick-off has passed into City Ground folklore.

An Arsenal attack is repelled with a headed clearance. The ball falls at the feet of Forest's left-winger, just outside his own penalty area. He sets off at a blistering pace, leaving Arsenal players in his wake. Advancing towards the Gunners' penalty box, he weaves his way between an avalanche of lunging tackles and then, with incredible poise, the red-shirted sorcerer slides the ball past the advancing Bob Wilson and into the net. It is a goal of sublime beauty, scored by a supreme artist and still talked about over 50 years later. Perhaps the greatest individual goal ever scored on that hallowed turf.

The scorer is a 26-year-old footballer from Scunthorpe, Ian Storey-Moore. The goal just scored is proof, if indeed proof is needed, that he is one of the most outstanding footballers not just in Britain but in all four corners of Europe.

Grainy archive footage of this magnificent goal shows another red-shirted player trying desperately to keep up with the flying, goalscoring winger. That is me, a 19-year-old and a professional footballer with Nottingham Forest for all of two months. What Ian has just done is sensational but, honestly, no surprise to me. I have witnessed such runs and goals like this on the practice ground almost on a daily basis. Ian would hardly be aware that I am, along with another young Nottingham Forest footballer, John Robertson, in total awe of both the man and his talent.

Ian Storey-Moore first came into my consciousness in early April 1967. I was a boarder at a college back in Northern Ireland. The teleprinter on Saturday afternoons was our only *entrée* into the English league. When Forest beat Everton in the quarter-final of the FA Cup with a late goal to win 3-2 and that double-barrelled surname appeared as the hat-trick hero, I became an immediate fan from quite some distance away. Sunderland were still my favourite team but such an effect had this 22-year-old footballer had on me that I exchanged my treasured Len Ashurst and Jim Baxter bubblegum cards for one of Storey-Moore. And now I find myself playing alongside this winged magician.

I think Ian took a liking to me almost from the start perhaps because I tried, often unsuccessfully, to imitate his dribbling prowess. In fact, when being interviewed by a national journalist (as he often was) he invited me along to the Bridgford Hotel close to the City Ground where the meeting was being conducted just to get the flavour of a big national interview. At the time Nottingham Forest were struggling and the decline of the club from those heady days just four years earlier was an unpleasant watch for the supporters. Ian had almost single-handedly kept Forest in the top flight with his goals and powerful wing play. He could do no more.

If ever there was a footballer who showed incredible loyalty to a club and who deserved to play for a club with annual European ambitions, it was surely Ian Storey-Moore. And when he left to join Manchester United not long after the interview, Forest's hopes of staying in the First Division evaporated completely. I was incredibly sad to see him leave but realised that his chances of silverware with George Best, Denis Law and Bobby Charlton as his team-mates would be enhanced a thousand-fold. After all, United were getting more than just a gifted winger. Ian could ghost past the opposition with consummate ease, go on the outside of defenders to deliver a left-footed cross and was incredibly dangerous when he cut in on the edge of the penalty area and unleashed right-footed thunderbolts on the opponents' goal.

What made him special, his *pièce de resistance*, was his ability to score goals, and lots of them. This priceless quality made him the stupendous footballer he was. Indeed, early goals for United evinced great days ahead. Surely success with the Old Trafford elite was just round the corner. After all, United had been crowned champions of Europe on an emotional evening at Wembley only four years ago. Unfortunately, within two seasons his professional career would be cut painfully short and those medals he craved and richly deserved eluded him.

I got to know Ian well when he and his lovely wife Carol came back to live in Bingham, a village about ten miles outside Nottingham. Invitations to have tea or coffee at his house were taken up with relish, although Ian hid his frustration with me when he had to put Laska, his pet Alsatian, into another room when I was in the house. Despite assurances from both Ian and Carol that the dog was indeed very friendly, his barking from that other room didn't exactly send out well-disposed signals of benevolence to this visitor. I was, to put it bluntly, terrified of this affectionate creature.

There was, of course, natural disappointment and dispiritedness that a career which surely would have seen him earn more than the one solitary England cap gained in 1970 should end so abruptly. I know from personal experience that there is a void in your life which takes a long, long time to fill. Only occasionally would

Ian talk about those dark moments, preferring mostly to be infuriatingly modest about his career and even shying away from compliments pushed in his direction. Self-effacement can be an endearing quality, of course, but in Ian's case too much of it can be irritating because I have no doubt that he knew just how good he was. However, unlike many footballers of vastly inferior talent, he just didn't boast about it all the time. Hopefully I have gone some way to rectifying that.

Ian and Carol even made it to my wedding. My fiancée Geraldine and I were in seventh heaven when they accepted the invitation, even though Ian had a 14-hour flight to South Africa the following day. I think it was the first Irish wedding they had attended!

Naturally we stayed in touch with each other through the years and in 2006, when I became manager of Aston Villa, I asked Ian to become chief scout at Villa Park. But this was not a 'job for the boys'. I had enormous regard for Ian's judgement of a player and as importantly, of course, his commitment, energy and enthusiasm for the task ahead. He set up a network of scouts both in Britain and abroad. However, regardless of how strongly a player might be recommended, Ian wanted to see the player in action himself before passing on information to me. There would be no dereliction of duty with Ian at the helm. This necessitated quite a number of overseas trips which, more than occasionally, proved fruitless. Either the player in question wasn't good enough or was beyond our budget. These unavailing journeys did irritate Ian and – I appreciate this is a bit rich coming from me, the dressing room's 'moaner in chief' – he would grumble about them for longer than one would consider necessary. But Ian did like a moan, if truth be told, even if it was only to his friends.

As you will read in this compellingly excellent biography, Derby County, managed by the charismatically brilliant Brian Clough, try desperately to sign Storey-Moore in early 1972. The move falls through and the flying winger heads to Old Trafford instead. Nottingham Forest are relegated and Derby County win the championship. But within six years, Forest will undergo an unbelievable transformation, gaining promotion, winning the Football League immediately and following up by twice winning the European Cup. The manager guiding the Reds to all of these triumphs is none other than the aforesaid Brian Clough. And one of the major reasons for this on-field success is a Scottish left-winger, John Robertson. Yes, the same John Robertson who, like me, was in thrall to Storey-Moore those seven years earlier. The irony of it all.

Nottingham Forest has, in its rich history, unearthed an abundance of wonderful footballers who have worn the Garibaldi Red with distinction. And of course there has been many a pub discussion about who is the best player to have represented the club. I was privileged to play with, in my judgement, the two finest footballers to grace the City Ground, John Robertson and Ian Storey-Moore. A difficult decision to separate these two very special talents. John's exploits have been well documented over the years, with Forest's European glory at the forefront. I am so pleased that, for Ian Storey-Moore, the story of this wondrous footballer is now being told.

Preface

by Ian Storey-Moore

Over the years I had been asked many times to write my autobiography but had always declined. After all, during my long career with Nottingham Forest and regrettably much shorter spell with Manchester United I didn't win any silverware. Three weeks after my debut for England, I suffered a season-ending injury and missed out on going to the 1970 Mexico World Cup. Rather embarrassingly, two years later Brian Clough and Peter Taylor paraded me as their 'new signing' at the Baseball Ground, only for me to end up at Old Trafford. And within a year poor medical care following a freak training ground injury meant the end of my professional career. For these reasons, I have always considered myself just another of football's many 'nearly men'.

So, when Stuart and Richard approached me, quite by chance, and offered to write my story, my initial response was to suggest that I was perhaps a little long in the tooth to be extolling distant memories of my 'so near yet so far' football career. Fortunately, they persevered and I realised this would be an opportunity for me to thank all of the remarkable, dedicated and talented people who helped a shy, skinny young lad from a council estate in Scunthorpe achieve so much in the game.

In agreeing to do this book I had just one condition. My friend the late, great Jim Baxter said that his autobiography was 'as frank as I can make it, without losing any of my friends'. While I don't think any of my stories could ever be as wild as Slim Jim's, it's a sentiment I share and the authors have done all they can to respect my wish to avoid giving offence to friend or foe, living or dead.

The first person I would like to thank is a wonderful gentleman called Joe McCormack. He was a scout who watched me playing schoolboy football and saw something in me. Joe recommended me to a friend of his from the wartime RAF who was the coach at Nottingham Forest. When Forest invited me for a trial, Joe spent many an hour with me on the park helping me improve my technique and instilling some confidence in me. Basically, he started my career.

That coach at Forest was Joe Mallett. He was a nice man, quiet and measured. In the early 1960s most coaches were really just fitness trainers but Joe was an innovator, ahead of his time. Even after I had a completely disastrous trial match for Forest, he had the faith in me to invite me back for a second try. I always remember him saying to me, 'In a game just start by keeping everything simple. Don't try and do anything too clever. If you see a pass just give it. Don't try and beat two or three people when it's not on. Just ease yourself into the game and give yourself confidence.' That was such good advice and still resonates with me.

The next person to thank would be Forest's 1959 FA Cup-winning captain, Jack Burkitt. Jack was as hard as nails. When I joined Forest as an apprentice I was seven stones wet through. He helped build my strength and physique by really putting me through the mill in afternoon training sessions, making me run up and down the terraces and lift weights. I cursed him at the time, of course, but he soon made me stronger, quicker and fitter and helped me become a better player, for which I'm forever grateful.

So, the two Joes and Jack were a massive help to me. It was thanks to them that Andy Beattie, Forest's manager, selected me for my debut in 1963.

Then Johnny Carey took over; another nice, measured man. I'm not sure he took to me initially but eventually I won him round. With him in charge we came agonisingly close to winning the Double in 1966/67. 'Gentleman John', as he was known throughout the game, deserved better than to have many of the best players in that team sold from under him. He was possibly the first Forest manager to suffer that fate but, sadly, not the last.

When I started at Forest I made many good friends, some of whom have remained just that for over 60 years now, in particular two Nottingham lads.

Henry Newton, who was already an apprentice at Forest, helped me get through that torturous first trial match. My feet were covered in blisters and I could hardly walk but Henry asked if I was all right and looked after me. He developed into a top midfield player and was desperately unlucky not to be capped by England. He was as tough as old boots, strong and won a lot of tackles, invariably passing me the ball. I still see Henry a lot, especially down at Burton Albion.

David Pleat also started a year before me at Forest but we immediately became good friends. Christmas 1961 was the first I had spent away from home and David and his parents were kind enough to invite me over for Christmas dinner. If you had asked me at that time who was going to go on and become a top-class player, it was David. He had everything – technically very good, could go past people, score goals, right foot, left foot. But somehow he drifted out of the playing side and went into management where he did very well at Luton Town and Tottenham Hotspur. David is hugely knowledgeable about the game and we talk all the time on the phone.

Of course, I owe a great deal to all my team-mates over the years. Throughout the 1960s Peter Grummitt was as fine a shot-stopper as any keeper and would have been destined for a successful England career had he not been playing in the same decade as Gordon Banks. In defence Bob McKinlay made over 600 appearances for Forest yet never won a single cap for Scotland. Terry Hennessey was pure class: a hard but fair tackler, he had tremendous positional awareness. John Winfield never let us down. Alongside Henry in midfield, Alan Hinton was technically very gifted, Barry Lyons was full of energy, and John Barnwell knew how to pick a pass. Up front Frank Wignall was always a handful and set up all three goals for my hat-trick against Everton in the FA Cup quarter-final. Big Frank was unlucky to break his leg when well set to be part of Sir Alf Ramsey's plans for the 1966 World Cup. Sammy Chapman started out as a forward but later switched to central defence where he became an integral part of the team that won promotion back to the First Division in 1976/77. And 'Zigger Zagger' Joe Baker, with his ability to turn a defender and accelerate towards goal, will always be, undisputedly, 'The King'.

A special mention goes to Peter Hindley, or 'Tank' as Forest fans nicknamed him. I shared digs with him. Peter had a big heart and was tough, resilient and quick. In the afternoons we used to put on spikes and just do sprints for about half an hour. I was quicker off the mark but Peter was so powerful that once he got into his stride after about 20 yards he was unbeatable. Poor old Peter died from dementia in February 2021, a sad end for someone who was a wonderful asset to that great Forest team under Carey.

Also, there was our coach Tommy Cavanagh, about whom the BBC's Kenneth Wolstenholme said, 'If you can survive a training session with Tommy Cavanagh, you can survive anything.' He certainly put us through hell, but he made us as fit as any team.

Towards the end of my time at Forest I was privileged to play alongside two youngsters who were just establishing themselves in the first team, John Robertson and Martin O'Neill.

I remember watching Robbo when he was in the youth team. In my column for the *Nottingham Guardian Journal* I wrote, 'I think this lad John Robertson will become a top-class player.' I definitely got that right! Robbo's remained a good friend to this day.

When Martin came over from Northern Ireland we became friends straight away. He was a tremendous player. He wasn't just a passer of the ball but was prepared to take people on, which you don't see so much in midfielders these days, and could score goals, most of them from 25 yards out, or so it seemed!

Although I only played around a dozen matches with each of them, it was nice to see Robbo and Martin go on to fulfil their potential and play such an important part in Forest's incredible success in the late 1970s. A couple of decades later I enjoyed working with them as chief scout when they were managing Aston Villa. I still enjoy their company.

When I was chief scout at Forest I got on particularly well with Paul Hart, the best coach I had ever worked with, and Dave Bassett. Both of them had a really strong work ethic and were a huge help to me. It was such a disappointment when the outstanding teams they built were dismantled against their wishes. They deserved far better than that.

In my playing days at Manchester United it was a privilege simply to be in the same dressing room as all those legends – George Best, Denis Law and Bobby Charlton. George was a complete one-off, of course, and he showed me the sights of Manchester. David Sadler was a lovely, down-to-earth guy. I still remember how surprised he was when I scored an unbeaten half-century in a charity cricket match against Everton. 'Blimey, you've played a bit!' was his reaction. Martin Buchan became a very good friend – another wonderful player who had a fantastic career at United. In the weeks and months following my career-ending injury, Paddy Crerand was brilliant – he went out of his way to train with me to try to help me get fit again. Tommy Docherty was good to me also and had really taken to me. It was just so disappointing how it ended.

I would like to acknowledge some of the tremendous players I came up against. Robbo always says that the 1960s and early 1970s was the hardest time to play football because the pitches were so awful and bad tackles went unpunished. A squad of the best opposition players I came up against would be more than a match for any era.

In goal it is impossible to choose between Gordon Banks and Peter Shilton, while Peter Bonetti always seemed to save his best performances for games against Forest. The right-back spot would be between Paul Reaney and Billy Bonds. Both were dogged competitors, Billy being as strong as an ox and Paul really quick for a defender. Without doubt the best left-back I played against was Tony Dunne – quick, strong, a really difficult opponent. At centre-back the outstanding partnership of Colin Todd and Roy McFarland might even keep the great Bobby Moore out of my fantasy starting XI.

My four across the middle of the park would be George Best, Bobby Charlton, Colin Bell and Peter Thompson. Billy Bremner and Johnny Giles were good players and fine off the pitch, but they really weren't very nice to play against. It was just how Leeds were.

Up front the only question would be who to play alongside the great Jimmy Greaves. Denis Law was in many ways a similar player. Martin Chivers and Geoff Hurst played with Jimmy, of course. Mick Jones and Allan Clarke were excellent. Jeff Astle was a handful and his team-mate Tony Brown was a terrific goalscorer. Probably the best foil for Jimmy would be Peter Osgood. He had a nasty streak in him but he could make goals, score goals and was good with his back to goal.

All in all they would make quite some team – if we were ever on the same side I might have to settle for a place on the bench!

After I was forced to retire from the Football League, Ben Robinson was kind enough to hire me as player-manager of Burton Albion. We have been good friends ever since. What Ben has achieved at Burton over the last five decades has been phenomenal. I go to as many matches at the Pirelli Stadium as I can and am generously looked after by the club.

Over the years Manchester United have been very hospitable to former players like Jeff Whitefoot and me and we have always been well treated by the club.

I should, of course, mention the present-day Nottingham Forest. When people like Nick Randall, the chairman, and director Jonny Owen got involved at the City Ground they really embraced the old players and have been absolutely fantastic to me. The club invites me to every home game, which I really enjoy, and always look after me and the other former players extremely well. Jonny also helps organise the regular luncheon club where we meet up with the likes of Robbo, Frank Clark, Colin Barrett, Garry Birtles, John O'Hare and, occasionally, Paul Hart and Sean Dyche. It is a real pleasure to spend time with such a great bunch of players – nice humble people, whose company I really enjoy.

Forest's manager, Steve Cooper, has been brilliant. He has really taken the old players on board, inviting us to visit the training ground, attend club barbecues and so on. After every match he invites us down to his office for a drink. He's a really nice guy, a really good coach. What he has done at Forest has been amazing. I'm sure that with him in charge, the club will keep going forward.

Forest fans have always been extraordinarily kind to me. They never bore any ill will over my involvement with Derby County or for leaving as relegation loomed. I am truly humbled to be stopped in the street by those old enough to have seen me play, to see one of my goals on the pre-match video montage, and to hear hearty renditions of 'When Ian Moore scores a goal …' at supporters' club evenings. They are the best.

Of course, I should thank my parents, Vic and Lily. My father was football-mad and used to take me to Roker Park and Ayresome Park, where I marvelled at the wonders of Sunderland's Charlie Hurley and Len Shackleton and Middlesbrough's Brian Clough. Dad was always very encouraging, took me everywhere, and watched me play on the park behind our home in Scunthorpe.

With my sister Anne, my parents used to come and watch every game I played at the City Ground until they were unable to do so because of ill health. I couldn't have asked for more.

Last, and very definitely not least, I thank the love of my life, Carol, for putting up with me. When we first met in 1963 she was more into Paul McCartney and Mick Jagger, but she took pity on the shy teenager standing by the dancefloor and we've been together ever since. Not long after we first met, we were watching a football match on the television at her house and she said, 'What's that bit of paper on the pitch?' It was the penalty spot! She enjoyed coming to the games and mixing with the other players' wives and girlfriends. Carol has supported me steadfastly, lovingly, through all the highs and lows of my playing career and the adventures in and out of football we've had since then.

I hope you enjoy reading my story – our story.

Ian Storey-Moore
May 2023

Introduction

Where it all began

August 1970. Nottingham Forest versus Coventry City, the first match of a new season. An excited young Forest supporter is on his way to the City Ground with his father and brother. It's Richard's birthday and he is decked out in a new red shirt and white shorts. As they join the crowds walking through The Meadows towards Trent Bridge an excited teenage female voice exclaims, 'It's Ian Moore gone little!' The seven-year-old has never felt so proud. Forest win 2-0 and his favourite player scores one of the goals. This has been a good birthday.

December 1971. Forest versus Double-winners Arsenal. As a Christmas treat, Stuart's father has bought seats for him and his brother in the East Stand, in line with the edge of the penalty area at the Trent End. They watch the crowds of supporters making their way over Trent Bridge towards the ground. A quarter of an hour into the match, their favourite player receives the ball right in front of them and runs at the Arsenal defence. And runs. And swerves, swerves again, shoots and scores. Along with almost 43,000 others, they have just witnessed one of the greatest goals ever scored by a Garibaldi Red.

Down the years, Stuart and Richard, friends since their first day at school, would discuss Ian Storey-Moore's remarkable footballing career and regret that his story had not been told in print.

February 2022. A chance encounter in a coffee shop. Stuart takes the opportunity to thank the trim 77-year-old for some of his best childhood memories and, seizing the moment, raises the subject of a biography. And, well, you have the result in your hands.

Heroes

They say 'never meet your heroes' for fear that the person you have worshipped from afar, perhaps for a lifetime, will turn out to be a crushing disappointment in the flesh. Happily, Ian Storey-Moore is a wonderful exception, as kind and unassumingly gentle off the pitch as he was exhilarating and supremely talented on it. He took quite some persuading to agree to us writing this book. Indeed, he did so on the understanding we would give full credit to all those who helped him not only shine as a professional footballer but also navigate his way through the vicissitudes of an enforced early retirement. Essentially, Ian is a humble and modest man who has absolutely nothing to be humble or modest about.

Moore's career at Nottingham Forest truly spanned the club's postwar successes. As a 16-year-old he was mentored by 1959 FA Cup winners and, a decade later, he inspired future mainstays of Brian Clough and Peter Taylor's all-conquering team of the late 1970s.

His breathtaking hat-trick goal in the last minute of the 1967 FA Cup quarter-final to knock out holders Everton prompted Sir Alf Ramsey to pick him for England, his mother to faint and the majority of the 47,500 crowd to go 'completely and utterly bonkers'.

At the height of the Swinging Sixties and continuing into the 1970s Moore was a pin-up: legions of female fans regularly voted him top of the popularity charts, ahead even of George Best.

His England debut pitted him against Johan Cruyff and the birth of Total Football.

Moore scored over 100 top-flight goals for Forest, averaging one every two games. He was the club's top scorer in five seasons out of six.

He scored arguably the greatest goal ever seen at the world-famous City Ground and became the most sought-after striker in the country. His sensational on-off transfer to Derby County filled the front and back pages for months and left Clough unable to speak to him (at least without expletives) for 20 years.

At Manchester United he played alongside European Cup winners including the peerless Best, Denis Law and Bobby Charlton. Starring for one of the most glamorous clubs in the world, he was well-placed to add to that single England cap and had hopes of racking up another century of goals with his second club.

However, at the height of his playing career, Moore would fall foul of cruel bad luck (and crude foul play) which has, quite unfairly, left him with melancholy thoughts of being a 'nearly man'. On the contrary, Ian Storey-Moore was – and will always remain – an iconic, once-in-a-generation footballer, a 'legend' long before that term became utterly over-used in the modern age.

What's in a name?

As his career at Forest blossomed, Ian Storey-Moore would often be asked about his double-barrelled name. How did that fit with his roots on a council estate in Scunthorpe? Eventually, he asked – pleaded – to be called simply Ian Moore. That he preferred to drop the 'Storey' was somewhat ironic as that is actually his paternal family name. Only when Ian's great grandfather died a few weeks before his grandfather was born did 'Moore' enter the equation, his widowed grandmother marrying a Tyneside publican by that name. Henceforth, Ian's grandfather adopted his stepfather's name and 'Storey-Moore' was born.

Throughout the book we have generally used 'Moore' to make it easier going for the reader.

As for the title of the book, we quickly brushed aside Ian's self-deprecating suggestion of 'The Nearly Man' and decided to opt for one of the many songs and chants dedicated by the Trent End to their swashbuckling hero. It was an era unmatched for fans' inventiveness in transforming chart hits and movie theme tunes into serenades from the terraces, so we had a lot to choose from. We describe many of them in a chapter towards the end of the book.

Never forgotten

This book is intended as an appreciation of and 'thank you' to one of Forest's greatest ever players and a tribute to the team he almost helped to the Double a decade before the club's 'glory years'. It is also a love letter to a wonderful era that is long lost but not forgotten. The Nottingham of the 1960s when the Beatles played 'upstairs at the Co-op' and football fans made their way to the City Ground and Meadow Lane along Arkwright Street, lined with its kaleidoscope of small shops and restaurants. When three o'clock on a Saturday afternoon brought longed-for relief from the factories and pits.

A time before home and away supporters were segregated, when the world-class talents of George Best, Jimmy Greaves and Bobby Moore could be marvelled at for a few shillings at the turnstile. A time when football pitches often resembled ploughed fields, when bone-shattering tackles were legitimised by outdated rules and lenient referees, and when footballers, while well-paid by the standards of the day, usually finished their playing careers not knowing how they would make ends meet.

Moore also spent a decade as a player-manager in non-league football and we are delighted to shine the light on this essential part of the nation's footballing fabric.

These are the ingredients of the fascinating life and career of Ian Storey-Moore. We thank him for refreshing our cherished memories of him, his team-mates and his era, and for allowing us to tell us his story. And we thank you for reading it.

Stuart Humphreys and Richard Harrison
May 2023

1

War baby

'All day long all we could see
were German bombers.'

Lily Storey-Moore, Ian's mother

In September 1939 Vic and Lily Storey-Moore took in a lodger at their rented house on Mersey Road, Ipswich, a short walk from the docks. Elsie Bonnett had been sent by the authorities to the Suffolk town to help organise the evacuation of schoolchildren should the expected air raids start. They duly did.

In the summer of 1940 the Luftwaffe bombed Ipswich incessantly, devastating the dockyards and surrounding areas. Also, each day vast formations of German bombers flew overhead towards their targets in London and the Midlands. On their return journey back across the North Sea, those that had escaped the attention of the ack-ack guns and RAF fighters would jettison surplus fuel over the town. Soon Vic and Lily were forced to move to Felixstowe Road, a mile or so further away from the docks.

Before long, with no let-up in the bombing raids, the order to evacuate was given. Lily, by now heavily pregnant with her first child, escaped to the relative safety of Cheltenham.

A few months later Lily and her daughter, Anne, were allowed to return home. Along with her baby's gas mask and favourite rag doll, Anne was put on the first available train and entrusted to the care of a soldier. Lily followed on the next train. At Ipswich railway station they were met by Vic, all happily reunited.

In 1942 the family moved again, this time to a three-bedroomed semi in Beechcroft Road in Ipswich's Castle Hill district. There they were joined for the rest of the war by Vic's mother, Annie, who had moved down from Sunderland, itself a prime target for the Luftwaffe.

In later years Lily would reflect that, strange as it may seem, the war had been an enjoyable time to live through: no one locked their front doors, and everyone got on well together and looked out for each other.

On 17 January 1945, a few months before VE Day, Lily gave birth to a son, Ian.

The immediate postwar years were austere, with petrol, clothes and most foodstuffs rationed as the country struggled to get back on its feet. But Vic, an architect with Ipswich Town Council, successfully applied for a new job – a promotion – and in the middle of the harsh winter of 1947 the Storey-Moores moved to Ashby, a suburb of Scunthorpe. And with that, two-year-old Ian would enjoy the most tremendous piece of good fortune.

2

Boom town

'Not bad for a lad from a council house in Scunthorpe.'

Ian Storey-Moore

Field of dreams

Ashby had been one of five villages amalgamated to form the borough of Scunthorpe in the 1930s. Vic's new position as chief architect of Scunthorpe Borough Council meant he had the pick of council houses to choose from on the rapidly expanding Lincoln Gardens estate.

To young Ian's delight, 107 Lincoln Gardens was situated right next to playing fields that extended as far as the eye could see. This was where he would spend his schoolboy years acquiring and developing his footballing skills – that is, when he wasn't playing cricket.

When the Storey-Moore family arrived in Ashby the midwinter snow was several feet deep and for weeks it just kept snowing. This did little to endear the place to Lily, who had really not wanted to move away from Ipswich, but Vic's new job had been too good to turn down. Moreover, Scunthorpe really was a boom town as its three steelmakers – Redbourn, Appleby-Frodingham and Lysaght's – worked flat out to make their vital contribution to Britain's postwar reconstruction.

Number 107 was a three-bedroom semi on what was colloquially known as 'NALGO Avenue' as most of the residents worked for the council and, thus, were members of the white-collar trade union that represented local government officers.

By no means affluent, the Storey-Moores didn't go short of anything. Vic's job was well-paid and he was always able to pay his bills. Household affairs were very organised. Vic kept a box in which he set aside money for the coal, gas and rent. Everything was paid straight away – there was no credit, no getting into debt. Vic's oft-repeated mantra to his son was, 'Ian, if you can't afford it, don't buy it.' Each week he would give his wife a 'white fiver' – a large £5 note printed in black on white paper – for the housekeeping. Lily spent this wisely and rarely bought anything new: if the children needed a jumper, she would knit it, if a sock had a hole in it, she would darn it. For Ian's parents the wartime ethos of 'make do and mend' lasted a lifetime.

Vic would come home for his dinner at lunchtime, and the whole family sat down for tea in the evening. They had a busy social life, with Christmas and birthday parties a particular highlight. Although Lily missed Ipswich she got on well with her friendly, community-spirited neighbours, who soon helped her settle in.

In other words, the Storey-Moores lived a typical 1950s suburban life.

Ian grew up a happy boy, was popular and had lots of friends, but was quite shy. If he was invited to a birthday party he would protest, 'I don't want to go because there will be aunties there.' (Ian didn't have any aunts.) Unlike his more rebellious sister, Ian was relatively quiet and always seemed to do the right thing.

Football, football, football (and cricket)

From the moment he was old enough to kick a ball, Ian Storey-Moore's life revolved around football. At every opportunity he would play on the park just over the back fence, kicking a football around with Graham Kemshall and Michael Hewson, two friends he remembers fondly. These games would last well into the evening, right up until bedtime.

As Moore remembers it:

> 'Every day was football, football, football and, in the summer, cricket, cricket, cricket. Otherwise, a bit of bike riding with sandwiches packed up by my mother. You had to make your own amusement in those days. We used to walk up to the Ashby Road, catch the bus into Scunthorpe and go to the swimming baths – that was a bit of a treat. But other than the odd visit to the cinema, that was about it. My parents always used to take us for a ride out somewhere on a Sunday afternoon, often for an ice cream or candy floss by the seaside at Cleethorpes.'

The park had two football pitches for local amateur teams, tennis courts and a cricket pitch. In the summer groundsmen would put the cricket nets up at the back of the field and Moore and his friends would play in them. Like football, cricket came naturally to him and he captained the school team. In the evenings he would go along and watch his father play for the NALGO first XI.

Moore's ability with bat and ball – he batted high up the order and bowled off-spin – came despite the best efforts of his pet dog:

> 'We always had a dog when I was young. They were always mongrels; the last one was called Timmy, a smashing dog. Whenever we were playing cricket on the field, he loved chasing the ball and we couldn't get it back off him! We used to have to get the stumps in his mouth to prise the ball out.'

Moore's father was mad about football and encouraged his son's growing obsession. Even when Moore was just having a kick-about with his mates, he used to see his father watching admiringly from the upstairs window.

As Moore got older, ever larger groups of children would congregate to play football on the park: pullovers and jackets down for goalposts, 15-a-side. He remains a firm believer that this was how he honed his inherent football skills, 'Just playing amongst your mates, controlling the ball, passing the ball, dribbling, having a shot. That's how you developed your natural ability. In those days there were few, if any, coaches around.'

From the age of six Moore attended Lincoln Gardens Junior School, a stone's throw from home. The football team was run by Mr McClurkin, a Scot, and played in a strip of blue and white quarters. Every Monday morning Moore would be embarrassed to hear the headmaster inform the school assembly how the team had fared at the weekend and how many goals Master Storey-Moore had scored. That was despite the fact that in those early years he actually played centre-half: it was only later, when he began playing for Scunthorpe Boys, that he switched to inside-forward.

In no time at all, Moore became captain and the first name on the team sheet. So much so that one Friday afternoon, after Moore had been in bed all week thanks to a flu epidemic, Mr McClurkin knocked on the front door and persuaded Moore's mother to let him play on the Saturday morning. That wouldn't be the last time in his career that Moore would play while ill or injured.

Although his mother wanted him to take his studies more seriously – Moore liked geography and history but hated maths – all he ever wanted was to be a footballer. That said, academically he was no slouch and passed the dreaded 11-plus exam to go to the local grammar school. Before being accepted for entry, however, he had to attend a daunting interview with the headmaster. His shyness led to him being rejected, his mother being informed, 'He's not going to have the confidence to take everything on board.' So, instead, he ended up going to Westcliffe Secondary Modern School.

It was there that Moore acquired the nickname 'Mugsy' for no particular reason other than it allowed his friends to call him 'Mugsy Moore'. The nickname stuck and remains in use to this day, somewhat to his regret.

Otherwise, things actually worked out rather well at Westcliffe. In his first year at the school the scrawny 11-year-old was put in an intermediate football team comprising bigger, second-year pupils. They used to play on Saturday mornings and Moore's parents never missed a match. Before his first game for them Moore's father promised him a sixpence for every goal he scored. 'We won 17-0 and I scored 12 of them! So that soon stopped – he didn't make that offer again!' Once again, he was made team captain.

Boyhood heroes

Quite naturally Moore became a Scunthorpe United fan. He was lucky enough to get the job of putting the half-time scores up against the giant letters alongside the pitch (the key to the letters being set out in the matchday programme) which meant he got to watch the games for free at the Old Show Ground.

Those were exciting times for Scunthorpe supporters. In the 1952/53 season they took Sunderland to a replay in the FA Cup third round after drawing 1-1 at Roker Park before narrowly losing the second match 2-1. In 1957/58, in addition to winning the Third Division North, the Iron had another memorable cup run, beating Newcastle United 3-1 away before losing 1-0 at home to Liverpool in the fifth round. In January 1961, as a Second Division team, they beat Stanley Matthews' Blackpool in the third round. Moore was one of over 19,000 packing out the Old Show Ground as Scunthorpe – 2-1 down at half-time – scored five goals without reply in the second half. The final score was 6-2, with hat-tricks by Joe Bonson and Barry Thomas.

Like most schoolboys of that era, Moore collected cigarette cards of well-known footballers. Similarly, on Sunday mornings he would update his football league ladders, wondering, when it came to the Scottish divisions, where on earth Cowdenbeath, Stenhousemuir and Stranraer were.

During the summer holidays Moore and his sister would stay for a couple of weeks with their paternal grandmother in Seaburn on the north-east coast. At the start of the football season in August, Moore would excitedly go to watch Sunderland play at Roker Park. He loved being part of the crowd of more than 50,000 giving full voice to the 'Roker Roar'.

Two of his heroes were centre-half Charlie Hurley – later voted Sunderland's Player of the Century – and forward Len Shackleton. Moore saw that Shackleton was different from most of the other players and marvelled at the eye-catching tricks the 'Clown Prince of Soccer' would perform on the pitch, sometimes while looking at an imaginary wristwatch.

Of course, being a football fan means pain inevitably follows pleasure. When, in March 1955, the Rokermen lost 1-0 to Manchester City in the semi-final of the FA Cup, ten-year-old Moore, who had been listening to the commentary on the wireless, burst into tears and had to be consoled by his mother.

But it wasn't just Scunthorpe and Sunderland that held Moore's attention. Regular family trips to see his maternal grandmother in Middlesbrough gave him the opportunity to see another of his footballing heroes in action, a prolific striker called Brian Clough. Their paths would cross again – in sensational circumstances – several years later.

Joe McCormack

In addition to playing for Westcliffe Secondary Modern on a Saturday morning, Moore also played for Ashby Juniors in the afternoon. It was there that he first came to the attention of Joe McCormack, a scout for several league clubs including Nottingham Forest, with whose reserve team coach, Joe Mallett, he had served in the RAF during the war.

McCormack recognised Moore's raw talent and took him under his wing. On the playing field behind Moore's house he would do football drills with the youngster, showing him how to control the ball and beat a player, and instilling confidence in a shy teenager.

McCormack would speak with Moore's father, making him aware that he knew people at Forest and that they were keeping an eye on young Ian. Moore's ability to score goals at every level he played at meant that McCormack had no hesitation in recommending to Mallett that he should invite him for a trial.

Only one thing stood in his way: Moore's mother insisted that he finish school first before going to any football trials, just in case things didn't work out. Moore duly passed his exams but without ever feeling that he had learned anything useful.

Before the eagerly anticipated trial at Forest, Moore had trials with a couple of other clubs. The one at Grimsby Town didn't go particularly well and they didn't ask to see him again. He played two trial games for Blackpool, staying in a seaside boarding house with another schoolboy trialist from Scunthorpe. Blackpool liked what they saw but told him, 'You've got the ability but you're too small.'

In fact, Moore's slight build had counted against him once before. One of his team-mates in the Scunthorpe Boys team had been full-back – and future England manager – Graham Taylor. Both had been hopeful of being invited to a trial for England Schoolboys. Only Taylor, a strapping 15-year-old, got the call.

Although he was not on their books, Moore also played a couple of games for Scunthorpe United's youth team in the Northern Intermediate League. Nothing came of it, but it is worth recalling that this is where, a few years later, the talents of future Liverpool and England stars Kevin Keegan and Ray Clemence would be nurtured. Anyway, knowing that Forest were interested meant that was where Moore set his sights.

Second chance

By the early 1960s, competition among clubs for young players was becoming quite fierce. All the top teams had networks of scouts across the country watching schoolboy matches. Any young footballer showing signs of potential, coupled with the right attitude and physical attributes, would quickly be snapped up. For their part, Forest would organise full-scale trials at regular intervals, giving a total of some 300 boys a year the opportunity to prove their worth. Football League rules meant that clubs were allowed up to 15 apprentices at any one time, so only a lucky few would make it.

With this in mind, early one morning in June 1961 Moore and his father drove the 60 miles or so from Ashby to the RAF's former Fighter Command base at Watnall, north-west of Nottingham, where the trial for Forest was to take place.

A few days earlier Moore's proud father had bought him a brand-new pair of football boots to wear for the occasion. That turned out to be a big mistake: by half-time Moore's feet were covered in blisters and by the end of the game he could hardly walk. To make matters worse, once again he was up against fellow trialists who were bigger and stronger than him, including one who would become an outstanding player for Forest, Everton and Derby County and a lifelong friend: Henry Newton.

Fortunately for Moore, Forest's coaching staff realised he had had problems with his boots and made allowance for that. Moreover, they recognised that what he lacked in size and strength, he more than made up for with speed, skill and courage. They asked him to return in a month's time for a second trial. As his father drove him back to Scunthorpe in the late afternoon, Moore – devastated at how the trial had gone but relieved to be given a second chance – was determined not to make the same mistake again. Immediately upon returning home he retrieved his threadbare old boots from the dustbin – fortunately the dustmen weren't due to empty it until the following day.

The night before the second trial match Moore didn't sleep a wink. He was kept awake by self-doubt: after all, this would probably be his last chance of becoming a professional footballer. For a schoolboy as totally absorbed in football as Moore, failure was not an option.

The second time round at RAF Watnall, on a boiling-hot day in early July, he played a great deal better and, with the aid of his trusty old boots, scored a couple of goals. On the drive home Moore and his father were in better spirits than a month earlier, but still they wondered whether he had done enough.

The answer came a week later in the form of the eagerly anticipated letter from Forest. The letter had been typed – rather poorly, if truth be told – by Tommy Graham, the club's chief scout. At the time he was the last Forest player to have been capped by England, making two appearances back in 1931 when Forest were a Second Division team. To Moore's delight Graham offered him an apprenticeship on the ground staff: the first part of the youngster's dream fulfilled. In the years to come, Moore would follow in Graham's footsteps in more ways than one.

For a weekly wage of £4 10s Moore, along with the dozen or so other apprentices, would be expected to train in the afternoons but not before having spent the mornings doing all manner of menial tasks such as polishing the professionals' boots, sweeping up litter on the terraces and weeding the pitch.

3
Little weed

'You soft bugger, you need to toughen up!'

FA Cup winners Johnny Quigley and
Jeff Whitefoot to 17-year-old Ian Storey-Moore

Hound Road

Early one hot summer afternoon in late July 1961, Vic and Lily Storey-Moore dropped off their son, his belongings in a single brown suitcase, at the City Ground. They were greeted by a familiar face, Joe Mallett, who had just finished taking the first team through their pre-season training routines. Moore's parents wished him good luck and set off back to Scunthorpe. The shy 16-year-old looked around, anticipating living away from home for the first time and embarking on the next step of his cherished dream of becoming a professional footballer.

As Mallett introduced him to several of the first team, Moore was excited at the opportunity to start immersing himself full-time in football. For now, though, his place would be behind the scenes, learning his craft, waiting and hoping for the chance to be an understudy and perhaps, in time, a star in his own right.

Centre-forward Geoff Vowden, just four years Moore's senior, was assigned to make sure he settled in. Brought up in Jersey, Vowden had signed professional terms with Forest at the end of 1959 and since then had been living in the same digs on Hound

Road that would now also become Moore's home from home. Moore recalls Vowden as 'a really nice, pleasant guy, someone who Joe obviously thought was sensible and a good role model even though he was only 20'. Later in his career, with Birmingham City, Vowden would become famous for being the first substitute to score a hat-trick in the Football League.

After the training session had finished Vowden took Moore the short distance to the lodgings. As they walked down Fox Road alongside the Trent Bridge cricket ground, Moore noted how convenient it would be to watch – if time allowed – his other sporting passion.

The boarding house on Hound Road was run by a larger-than-life Yorkshire couple. The landlady, Mrs Tordoff, was 'a kindly, blonde lass'. Her husband, Albert – 'a big, fat Yorkshire lad' – did all the cooking. He turned out to be a bit of a loveable rogue, as Moore, flinching slightly at his own naivety, recalls:

> 'A few weeks after I arrived, Albert and I were, for some reason or other, talking about Christmas presents. He said, "If you give me some money every week, I'll give it back to you at Christmas and you can get some presents for your family." Surprise, surprise but in December, when I asked him for it, I couldn't get it off him. So, I had to tell Joe Mallett and, of course, he came straight round and got my money back for me.
>
> 'Despite that episode, we all liked Albert. One night he took five of us in his car to a match at Leicester City. He just walked straight into the club reception and – without paying – said, "Come on boys, come on boys! These are my boys from Nottingham Forest. Straight through, lads!" Unbelievable, he had some cheek, quite brazen.'

In the digs they each had their own bedroom and shared a bathroom. Forest recognised the importance of building up the young apprentices as quickly as possible, so they were well fed: a full English breakfast; gammon (occasionally steak), egg and chips for tea; always fish and chips on a Friday. At lunchtimes they were given ham or beef sandwiches at the ground.

It didn't take long for Moore to settle in. He got on well with three other apprentices in particular: Bob Chapman, another resident of the Hound Road digs, who was affectionately known as 'Big Sammy' – with calves like tree trunks, at the age of 15 he was as big and strong as somebody twice his age – and two Nottingham lads who lived with their parents: Henry Newton from Wollaton (who had helped Moore during that first trial match) and David Pleat from Clifton.

Before being signed by Forest, Pleat had played for the renowned Clifton All-Whites. In the 1950s the Pleat family had been one of the first to move to the new council housing estate at Clifton, destined to become the largest in Europe. Apparently, by the late 1960s one in four schoolboys in Nottingham would live on Clifton Estate. It was (and remains) a hotbed of footballing talent.

At Christmas 1961, his first in Nottingham, Moore was unable to go home to Scunthorpe because he had work to do as one of the ground staff. Upon hearing of this, Pleat's parents invited him over for Christmas dinner at their house on Farnborough Road. Ian and David have remained friends ever since.

Another occasion from that same period provides a somewhat embarrassing memory for Moore. A Christmas party was held in the Hound Road digs and a few girls were invited round. Lacking confidence, the perennially shy Moore thought he should have a drink for 'Dutch courage'. For the first time in his life he downed a whisky and then another. He spent the next half an hour with his head in the toilet, violently sick. An early night beckoned and the fairer sex would have to wait until a later date.

Moore and his mates used to walk over Trent Bridge and catch the bus down Arkwright Street into town. Nightlife in

Nottingham city centre in the 1960s was lively, to say the least, with fights regularly breaking out around closing time in Yates's Wine Lodge and other hostelries. The Forest apprentices would steer well clear. 'To be fair, we didn't have enough money to cause any problems,' recalls Moore. They would go to the pictures once a week and to a dance hall on a Saturday night. They couldn't afford to go out every night of the week, though that would change when they turned professional and had more money.

An early encounter with one of the natives of Nottingham was a bit of an eye-opener for young Moore:

> 'On just my second day at Forest I was on Arkwright Street and had to get back to the digs. I was standing at the bus stop and this bus came along, the conductress standing at the bottom of the stairs. I said, "Excuse me, does this bus go over Trent Bridge?" She said, "No, me duck, we're going under it today!" "Me duck"; I'd never heard anything like that before!'

While enjoying his new-found freedom, Moore stayed in regular contact with his parents. Every Monday morning he would wrap Saturday's *Football Post* in brown paper and post it to his father. He would also include clippings from the *Nottingham Evening Post*, *Guardian Journal* and *Evening News* – these were halcyon days for Nottingham newspapers – of reports on the youth team games he played in.

Most Saturday evenings, Moore would catch the train to Scunthorpe where his father would collect him from the station. On Sundays he would make the return journey to Nottingham. On passing his driving test he bought a treasured pale green Triumph Herald and would drive the 60 miles or so home via the scenic country route of Newark, Gainsborough and then on to Ashby. On one such occasion he was delighted to be able to return the Pleats' favour and took David with him for Sunday lunch and a tour of the Lincoln Gardens playing fields that had shaped his schoolboy footballing exploits.

There was only one problem with the Hound Road digs. As a member of the ground staff Moore's weekly pay packet was £4 10s yet his board and lodging cost £4 a week, leaving him just ten shillings of spending money. Before long, Moore was steeling himself to ask Forest's quiet, sternly officious manager, Andy Beattie, for a rise, quite an ordeal for a mere apprentice. Entering Beattie's office, Moore pleaded his case, 'Excuse me, Mr Beattie, but I've only got ten shillings for the week.' He needn't have worried. In his harsh Scottish accent Beattie replied, 'I'll give you another two pounds a week.' And with that, Moore's first – but certainly not last – contract negotiation was settled: £6 10s a week.

As hard as nails

As part of the ground staff, Moore spent his mornings undertaking various unglamorous chores. Like all the apprentices he hated this part of his job: when he wasn't tending to the terraces and the pitch, he was helping tidy the dressing rooms or spending hours in the boot room, cleaning the boots of first-team players such as FA Cup winners Jack Burkitt, Johnny Quigley and Jeff Whitefoot. None of them had enough money to be able to tip him for his efforts but these three became hugely influential in Moore's development.

Although some of the senior pros didn't particularly like the idea of 'an upstart from a council estate in Scunthorpe' threatening to break through and take their place, he got on well with Quigley and Whitefoot. Two 'dirty bastards', in the nicest sense of the term, they helped toughen Moore up – both mentally and physically – by creating an environment where the youngster had to learn to look after himself. 'You soft bugger, you've got to be tougher!' they would yell at him. Both of them knew very well what it took to succeed in the game. Prior to joining Forest in 1958, Whitefoot had been Manchester United's youngest ever league debutant and twice won the First Division title under Matt Busby's inspired management. Quigley had once given Bobby Moore, playing just his second game for West Ham United, such a runaround that the future World Cup-winning England captain was swiftly consigned back to the Hammers' reserves.

Ever since his very first trial match for Forest, Moore had realised how puny he was compared with well-built contemporaries such as Chapman, Newton and Pleat. Indeed, photographs of Moore as an apprentice in the summer of 1961 show a skinny figure in a rather loose-fitting red shirt – 'scraggy, scrawny, seven stones wet through'. Actually, he weighed nearer nine stones. In addition to learning his trade as a fleet-footed winger, the slight teenager would need to work on his strength and fitness.

In just 18 months Moore added two and a half stones and grew three inches. The man Moore credits with this remarkable transformation in his physique is the legendary Burkitt, Forest's victorious captain from that 1959 FA Cup Final.

A one-club man, in a 15-year career Jack Burkitt had made over 500 appearances for Forest by the time he retired from playing. By a curious twist of fate the guest team in Burkitt's testimonial match in November 1961 were Swedish champions – and Forest's opponents one balmy night in Munich's Olympic Stadium 18 years later – Malmö. Atrocious weather on the night of the testimonial – incessant rain followed by fog that actually forced the game to be abandoned late in the second half – restricted the attendance to fewer than 8,000, meaning that the match receipts only just covered the Swedes' travel expenses. Showing the high esteem in which Burkitt was held, Forest's governing committee came to the rescue and gave the great man £1,000.

Burkitt was now the club's reserve team trainer and he saw the potential in the weedy young winger. As 'hard as nails', like most footballers of his generation, Burkitt knew that Moore would need to bulk up if he were to survive in the professional game.

As part of the typical afternoon training regime, Burkitt would work Moore hard with weights and have him running up and down the steps of the Bridgford End 'Kop'. The monotony of this left the youngster cursing Burkitt at the time, but Moore would forever be indebted to him:

> 'Jack was from the Black Country and was a hard man – he really put me through the mill. He was as honest as the day is long: if you played poorly, he would tell you – he wouldn't beat around the bush. What he did for me was top drawer. He was a big part of me being successful. He gave me the desire, the will and, most importantly of all, confidence in my own ability.'

Burkitt, who as a player himself had never taken any prisoners, showed Moore how to tackle and look after himself in the face of defenders trying to kick lumps out of him. Such instruction certainly came in handy when Moore, playing with fellow teenagers for Forest Colts in the Thursday League, faced the law enforcers of Nottingham City Police, miners of Shirebrook Byron, and soldiers of Chilwell Royal Ordnance depot.

Despite hating the tiresome hours spent running and weightlifting, Moore took Burkitt's advice to heart and trained as hard as he could, so much so that within a few years one football reporter would describe him as having the physique of a boxer.

Panic stations

Moore became a prolific scorer for Forest's youth teams and was soon given his chance to make an impression at senior level with an away fixture in the Football Combination against Crystal Palace reserves on 4 April 1962.

The team coach arrived at Selhurst Park in the midst of a thunderstorm which lasted for half an hour and made the pitch almost unplayable. Forest took to the field with one of their youngest ever reserve teams – Moore, Pleat and David Wilson were all 17 years old, Trevor Hockey just a year older. Despite what Andy Beattie described as a 'slushy' pitch, a good game of football broke out. Moore put in a great display and scored the only goal of the match. Accepting a pass from Hockey, he beat three Palace defenders in the penalty area before whipping the ball into the corner of the net. 'The goal scored by young Ian Moore was one that he will always remember,' Beattie (correctly) predicted after the match.

Moore was also chosen to represent the county as a member of the Nottinghamshire FA youth team. In that 1961/62 season they had a great run in the FA County Youth Challenge Cup. In the home leg of the semi-final against Durham FA, played at the ground of Newark ball bearings manufacturer Ransome & Marles, Moore scored all the goals in a 5-0 win. Playing Middlesex FA in the final, Notts FA won the away leg 3-1. The second leg, played at the City Ground on 12 May 1962, should have been a formality. Whether it was because the game came at the end of a long season or because Pleat – an integral part of the Notts team – had been called up to play for an England Youth XI on the same day, the home side put in an abject performance and Middlesex went on to win 5-0 after extra time, 6-3 on aggregate.

A few days after that disappointment, Moore faced the ordeal that awaited all the youngsters after they had served their apprenticeship: the wait to be called in, one by one, to the manager's office to be told if they were going to be offered a professional contract.

As he walked to the City Ground that morning, Moore could hear the faint, rumbling sound of a bulldozer, its driver hard at work levelling a field at nearby Lady Bay that would become the club's new training ground to reduce the wear and tear on the matchday pitch at the City Ground. Moore thought that was great news but wondered whether he would ever get the chance to train there.

He recalls his date with destiny:

> 'Those early years were happy years, except it was "panic stations" when you were 17. If you weren't given a professional contract, that was it, you were gone. They wouldn't say, "Well, he's small but he's got lots of ability, let's give him another year to develop." There was none of that: if they didn't deem you good enough, you were out. I lost a lot of good mates at Forest like that – I never saw them again.
>
> 'We were all playing cricket in the car park as we waited with great trepidation to be called in. My turn came: fortunately, it was good news. The manager, Andy Beattie, simply said, "We're going to give you a professional contract." And that was that.'

Moore immediately telephoned his father in his architects' office at Scunthorpe Borough Council to give him the news. Needless to say, he was delighted and more than a little relieved.

Moore's wages were boosted to £17 a week basic pay plus the same again for each first-team appearance. Although his basic wage was lower than that of the more senior professionals, the potential appearance money was more generous, although the youngster wasn't expected to feature much for the first team for quite a while. In addition, he received a £20 signing-on fee and duly deposited the two £10 notes into his account at the National Westminster Bank on Trent Bridge. Best of all, turning professional meant Moore no longer had to sweep the terraces and do all those other menial chores: a blessed relief.

Even with his professional contract, however, Moore continued to suffer from self-doubt and worried that Forest would at some point dispense with his services. Hence, when one day in November 1962, Bob Davies, Forest's physio, greeted Moore with the words 'you're going home', it was a heartstopping moment for the young man.

Fortunately, Davies was merely referring to Forest's youth team having been drawn away against Scunthorpe United in the second round of the FA Youth Cup. A couple of years earlier Moore had played at their home, the Old Show Ground, for Scunthorpe Boys and on 10 December 1962 he marked his return with two goals in a 4-0 win, much to the delight of his watching parents and the man who had scouted him, Joe McCormack. His first goal that night, on 78 minutes, was typical of what was to come in later years as he weaved his way through United's stubborn defence before unleashing an unstoppable right-footed drive into the net. His second goal was from the penalty spot – he rarely missed from 12 yards.

Summer of '62

With his professional contract secured and the football season over, Moore was able to devote the summer months to his second love, cricket. He spent June and most of July back at home in Ashby, turning out for local steelmakers Lysaght's in the Grimsby League. Moore played alongside another talented young footballer and more-than-handy cricketer, his former Scunthorpe Boys team-mate Graham Taylor, who was now on the books of Grimsby Town.

Back in Nottingham for pre-season training, Moore was one of several local footballers to play in amateur cricket's half-day Thursday League. Together with goalkeeper Peter Grummitt (a slow bowler who would keep wicket if needed) and David Pleat, he played for Victoria Embankment Cricket Club and, occasionally, Nottingham Taxis Cricket Club, which was captained by 'colourful' local businessman Derek Pavis.

Pavis was well connected at Forest, seemingly knowing all the management and players. In 1964 he admitted in court to having offered a £500 bribe to Jeff Whitefoot to play badly in a game against Stoke City. Whitefoot had replied, 'I am not interested, not for £500 or £5,000,' and he duly reported the matter to his employers. Despite this, Pavis would eventually be made a director of Forest during their late-1970s heyday and later became the long-standing chairman of Notts County.

Also playing for Nottingham Taxis was a Nottingham-born goalkeeper by the name of Peter Taylor. Taylor had been on Forest's books at the end of the war but never played for the first team. He spent ten years at Coventry City before joining Middlesbrough. Moore had watched him play at Ayresome Park in the same team as Brian Clough, who was now knocking the goals in for Sunderland.

Apparently, Clough himself hadn't taken much persuading to turn out for Nottingham Taxis whenever he could. 'Brian thinks the world of Nottingham and has spent part of his holidays down here,' Taylor told the *Nottingham Evening News*. 'Next season he has promised that he will be available for the first three weeks. He even thinks he may be able to manage it more regularly.'

Earlier that summer Taylor had made a guest appearance for the cricket team of the Nottingham branch of the Inland Revenue, scoring a quickfire century against Notts Unity. To raise money for charity the Revenue had now asked Taylor to organise a team for a celebrity fixture to be played at the Civil Service ground at Wilford. Taylor's side included Moore, Grummitt and Pleat, together with Notts County's ace strikers Tony Hateley and Jeff Astle, and wing-half Gerry Carver, plus Pavis and Clough.

Despite Taylor nominally being the captain, when the All-Stars fielded Clough soon took charge of proceedings. Many years later, Pleat recalled in an interview with the *Daily Mail*, 'I loved cricket and could keep wicket a bit … Cloughie asked me, "What do you do, then?" I told him I was a "stumper" and he promptly sent me to field at third man!'

For Moore, who was 'chuffed' to be playing in such esteemed company, it was the first time he had met Clough and Taylor in person. It wouldn't be the last.

First-team debut

By the time the 1962/63 season was under way, Moore had graduated from the junior teams to become a regular for the reserves. He soon found that with the step up in quality of the opposition came an increased physicality – even brutality – from the defenders he faced as he sped down the wing or made an attempt on goal.

Indeed, the rough treatment meted out to him at the Police Training Ground or Annesley Miners' Welfare in the Thursday League would almost become a fond memory. In one match he faced one of Chelsea's tough-tackling Sillett brothers at right-back. History doesn't record, and Moore doesn't recall, whether it was Peter – apparently once described by Stanley Matthews as his most difficult opponent – or John, later the joyous FA Cup-winning manager of Coventry City. Either way, Moore soon found himself being unceremoniously booted over the touchline, his muscular nemesis snarling, 'Don't worry son, there's a lot more of that to come!' It made Moore ponder whether such brute force violence was all that football was about but he would always come back for more.

Moore's turn of speed and courage in front of goal meant that he soon started to attract attention and garner headlines as a skilful frontman and brave goalscorer.

Nonetheless it still came as a bit of a surprise when, towards the end of that season, he was selected to make his debut for the first team. The team sheets for the first team and the reserves were always put up in the dressing rooms on Friday lunchtime after training. Burkitt would burst in, shout 'Runners and riders!', stick the lists on the noticeboard, and all the players would gather round to see whether or not they were playing.

On this occasion, Thursday, 9 May 1963, the team sheets were put up a day earlier than usual. Forest's home game against Ipswich Town had been brought forward to the Friday night so the England Schools FA Victory Shield match against Scotland could be played at the City Ground on the Saturday. As was his habit, Moore looked at the reserve team list first but, not seeing his name on that, looked across to the first-team line-up – he had been picked to make his debut against his home-town club. (To be precise, although he was born in Ipswich, Moore would consider Scunthorpe to be his real home town, having lived there from the age of two.)

During January and February constant snow, deep frosts and, as pitches thawed, thick mud had forced the postponement of all but three of Forest's games. The winter's 'Big Freeze' had left all clubs with a huge fixture backlog towards the end of the season. In April alone Forest played ten times – including an inexplicable 5-0 defeat to Second Division Southampton in an FA Cup quarter-final second replay at White Hart Lane. With a further five league matches to be played in May, manager Andy Beattie had necessarily started rotating his squad. Billy Cobb had won many plaudits when deputising for the otherwise ever-present Dick 'Flip' Le Flem in Moore's preferred left-wing position. Therefore, it is reasonable to assume that Beattie intentionally chose Ipswich as the team against which Moore should make his debut.

Moore's mother and father travelled down from Scunthorpe for the match and he received good luck telegrams from his friend and fellow young hopeful David Pleat, and Victoria Embankment CC, among others.

Moore lined up on the left wing in a Forest XI that included two of the FA Cup-winning team in centre-half Bob McKinlay and inside-left Johnny Quigley, as well as Cobb, who had scored Forest's first-ever goal in European competition in the Inter-Cities Fairs Cup against Valencia the previous season; Peter Grummitt, Doug Baird, Dennis Mochan, Cobb, McKinlay, John Winfield, Trevor Hockey, Colin Addison, Len Julians, Quigley and Storey-Moore were the names on the list.

Forest won 2-1, having gone behind early in the game. After a quiet start, 18-year-old Moore made a telling contribution, floating in a cross from way out on the left for leading scorer Julians to head home the equaliser at the far post. According to the *Nottingham Evening Post*, Moore 'showed some nice touches and he looks a good prospect'. The *Evening News* reflected, 'Moore, in his first game, finished up with a winner's bonus. He could look back on a useful performance ... he used the ball to advantage and sent over some dangerous crosses.'

Hard taskmaster that he was, Forest's trainer, Moore's mentor Burkitt, said, 'You've done all right but you should have done better.'

Disappointingly, the unusual kick-off time meant that Moore's debut was witnessed by the season's lowest home attendance of just over 13,000. By contrast, the schools international the following day drew over 21,000. England's under-16s won by a single goal: their line-up included winger Jimmy Husband from Newcastle-upon-Tyne. Four years later he would be back at the City Ground to play an important role in Moore's greatest day in the Garibaldi Red.

The Beatles (and Stones) come to town

On 7 March 1963 an up-and-coming pop band, the Beatles, played 'upstairs at the Co-op'; that is, in the popular Elizabethan Ballroom at the Co-operative department store on Upper Parliament Street. They were being showcased alongside Gerry and the Pacemakers and Billy J. Kramer and the Dakotas, among others, as part of the new wave of Merseybeat bands. Beatlemania hadn't yet gripped the nation and, together with their fellow Merseyside musicians, John, Paul, George and Ringo unloaded their instruments from their van parked outside the Co-op and carried them upstairs.

With their recently released second single 'Please Please Me' selling 50,000 copies a week, the Beatles were just breaking through. No one in Nottingham really knew who they were at the time and, despite tickets being reasonably priced at just 6s 6d, the venue was only half full. As they waited backstage for their turn, Paul McCartney – possessor of a 'round baby face' according to the *Nottingham Evening Post* – shared a cigarette with teenager

Carol Ann Griffiths, who had been given a ticket by a friend who helped organise the show.

A couple of months later, on 23 May, the Beatles were back in town on a tour with Gerry and the Pacemakers and Roy Orbison. This time the Odeon Cinema on Angel Row was the venue and, with 'From Me to You' top of the charts, the concert was a 2,500 sell-out. The Fab Four had taken over from Orbison as the headline act and, according to the *Evening Post*, 'took the rapturous Odeon audience by storm'.

This was as nothing compared with their next appearance at the Odeon on 12 December. Thanks to 'She Loves You', Beatlemania had well and truly broken out. All police leave was cancelled, a fleet of ambulances stood by in case teenage fans were overcome by hysteria, and ticket touts were selling even the cheap seats at the back of the cinema for five times their face value.

Moore remembers going into Nottingham that night just to soak up the atmosphere:

> 'Pleaty, Sammy Chapman, David Wilson and I went into town to try and catch a glimpse of the Beatles. Of course, they were smuggled into the cinema via the back door. We tried but couldn't get tickets. The scenes outside the theatre were amazing though.'

It was around this time that Moore met the girl who would become his wife, a certain Carol Ann Griffiths, former brief acquaintance of Paul McCartney. This was at the Lacarno nightclub, the former Victoria Ballroom, on St Ann's Well Road.

Before the Palais de Danse, complete with revolving dancefloor, opened on Lower Parliament Street, the Lacarno was the place to go on a Saturday night. No alcohol was allowed – which suited Moore – but at the end of the evening there would always be a 'bloody great fight'. With Moore being so shy ('I wouldn't say boo to a goose in those days'), Carol, apparently feeling rather sorry for him, made the first move. For the next few weeks they saw each other every now and again, not yet at the 'courting' stage.

Vying with the Beatles at the top of the charts were the Rolling Stones. Moore managed to get tickets for the Stones' concert at Nottingham's Albert Hall on 2 March 1964 and was in the audience with Carol. Of the concert, Moore recalls, 'I had heard of them, naturally, and they were just starting to make their mark. They were fantastic and I've liked them ever since.' The Stones' set list mostly comprised their versions of Chuck Berry and Bo Diddley songs but also included a raunchy cover version of the Beatles' 'I Wanna Be Your Man'.

Whereas the recent Beatles concerts had been drowned out by screaming audiences, the noise at the Stones gig was generated by the band themselves – the loudest thing most of the audience had ever heard.

Moore unsuccessfully tried to get tickets – allocated by public ballot – for what would turn out to be the Beatles' last appearance in Nottingham, on Bonfire Night 1964, again at the Odeon. Although he had missed out on seeing the Beatles, he was, by that time, 'going steady' with the girl who had once 'shared a fag with Macca' – more than adequate compensation.

4

Lift-off

'Feared by the bad, loved by the good.'

The Adventures of Robin Hood TV show theme song

'Gentleman John' arrives

The summer of 1963 saw builders hard at work at the City Ground, demolishing the old wooden Main Stand and starting to erect a modern, steel-framed one in its place. The car park was full of rubble when, on 8 July, Forest announced that Andy Beattie had left to concentrate on 'business interests' and with their grateful thanks for his three years in charge. The fact that three months later he took the manager's job at Second Division Plymouth Argyle came as something of a surprise but didn't harm his good standing with Forest's hierarchy and most of the supporters.

Indeed, Forest had finished the 1962/63 First Division season in a highly encouraging ninth place, their equal-highest league position in 55 years. However, towards the end of the season the tide had rather turned against Beattie. In March Forest were booed off after adopting a new defensive formation in a heavy away defeat at Goodison Park. In April the humiliating cup exit to Southampton had been swiftly followed by a depressing home defeat against Birmingham City. Afterwards fans had gathered in the Main Stand car park, chanting 'Axe Beattie' and 'Resign' before being removed by the local constabulary.

In one of his last acts at the City Ground, however, Beattie had done the club a great service by signing striker Frank Wignall from Everton for £20,000, equalling Forest's record transfer fee.

In Beattie's place, Forest persuaded Johnny Carey to leave the relative peace and quiet of Leyton Orient. A self-deprecating, unassuming Irishman, he had had an illustrious playing career with Manchester United, captaining them to FA Cup glory in 1948 and the First Division title in 1952. After retiring as a player, he had become a successful manager, guiding Blackburn Rovers to promotion to the First Division in 1958, Everton to their highest postwar finish – fifth place – in 1961, and unfancied Orient to promotion to the top flight in 1962. Widely admired throughout the game, Carey was known as 'Gentleman John' on account of his softly spoken, gentlemanly good manners.

Carey arrived at the City Ground at the start of August, the first time he had set foot there since before the war. In December 1937 the 17-year-old inside-left had scored his first goal for United in a 3-2 win that helped secure their promotion from the Second Division. When interviewing him for the job, Forest's committee had impressed on Carey the importance of restoring both the Reds' reputation for their attractive style of football and the good atmosphere at the City Ground on matchdays. Carey's first remarks to the press were diplomatic and measured:

> 'Forest have every right to be a First Division club. By tradition, by the size of the population to support it, by any standards, they are First Division material and are of First Division quality.'

With a new training ground and the new Main Stand being built, Forest were making their ambitions clear. The club's finances were helped by the fact that – in this era long before the Premier League – gate receipts were shared between the home and away clubs rather than being pocketed by the hosts. Provincial clubs like Forest relied heavily on receiving their share of the higher attendances at away games in the big cities such as Manchester, Liverpool and London. For instance, the trip to Anfield on Wednesday, 28 August 1963 yielded not only a 2-1 win courtesy of goals by Quigley and Wignall, but a cheque for £1,225 15s 6d – a record amount – as Forest's share of the receipts from the near-50,000 crowd.

Investment in the City Ground was also partially funded by the supporters' club, the Nottingham Forest Sportsmen's Association. It donated £12,000 to the club in 1962/63 and over £15,000 in 1963/64, the money being spent specifically on developing the ground rather than strengthening the team.

As the 1963/64 First Division campaign began, Carey kept faith with the two wingers who had played in most of the previous season's games, Trevor Hockey on the right and Flip Le Flem on the left. Completing the forward line, new signing Wignall quickly formed an effective partnership with Colin Addison, at the expense of the unfortunate Len Julians.

Forest's early season form saw them start slowly but soon spring into life, briefly topping the table towards the end of September following a fifth successive win. Moore appreciated that it would be hard to break into a settled and successful side. In the meantime, he played regularly in the reserve team and, under the tutelage of Burkitt and Mallett, scored a goal every other game.

Forest's good start didn't last. After that five-match winning run they won only two of their next 15 and, as he looked to arrest the club's slide down the table, Carey began to ring the changes. Hockey was sold to Newcastle United for £25,000, a healthy £10,000 profit on what Forest had paid for him two years previously. Pleat, who had turned professional not long before Moore, was finally given a few starts in the number seven shirt. Addison also wore it a couple of times before it was the turn of Mike Kear, signed from Newport County, who made his debut in a 2-1 home defeat to Tottenham Hotspur which saw Jimmy Greaves notch one of his 24 career goals against the Reds.

First goals

Forest were now drifting aimlessly in mid-table with 22 points from 23 games. When Sheffield United visited on Boxing Day 1963, Carey switched things around again. The talented but erratic Le Flem lost his place on the left wing and Moore finally got his chance in the coveted number 11 shirt. And he made the most of it, playing his part as Forest flew out of the traps, racing into a three-goal lead after just 17 minutes.

Wignall and Geoff Vowden had already netted by the time Moore's volley from 25 yards flew into the net to open his account for the first team. For a while it seemed a case of how many Forest would score, but half-time came with no further goals. The Blades fought back to gain an unexpected share of the points, levelling the scores at 3-3 in the last minute. Three months after topping the table, Forest were now languishing in 14th place.

As was the seasonal tradition at the time, the teams met again two days later in the return fixture. Thanks to Moore, Forest finally ended their run of eight matches without a win. United dominated the first half and took a deserved lead a few minutes before the break, but the Reds came back with two goals in three minutes just before the hour mark. First Moore created an opportunity for himself and, despite the keeper getting a hand on his shot, the ball dropped under the bar before a defender could clear it. Then Kear broke quickly and found Moore, who dribbled past two defenders and slotted the ball past the keeper for the winner.

The headlines rightly belonged to teenagers Kear and Moore, the *Football Post* describing how the latter had taken his chances 'with the assurance of a veteran'. In that same edition one of the paper's correspondents had written an article looking forward to the new year with the headline 'Forest's 1964 need is [a] star to score and attract crowds'. If Moore thought his match-winning performance at Bramall Lane had put him in prime position to be that star, he was soon reminded of the realities of 'modern' football.

In addition to the ongoing investments in the physical infrastructure, Forest needed to refresh and strengthen the first-team squad. Emerging home-grown talent such as Moore, Newton, Pleat and Chapman was all well and good, but Forest's committee wanted the club to demonstrate its ambition by participating in the increasingly competitive transfer market for proven talent.

Carey set about this task with alacrity. In no time at all he had sold Trevor Hockey, Calvin Palmer, Doug Baird, Billy Cobb and Len Julians for a total of £80,000. The committee gave him the freedom to use this 'war chest' to bring new talent to the City Ground. Carey's first major move came in January 1964 when he signed England international left-winger Alan Hinton from Wolverhampton Wanderers in a straight player exchange with Le Flem, who was disappointed to be moving in the opposite direction. Sadly, the move to Wolves didn't work out well for Le Flem, serious illness restricting the number of appearances the England under-23 international would make for the Molineux club. Hinton soon displaced Moore in the left-wing position, with Kear preferred on the right.

With Carey favouring the Hinton–Kear combination, between mid-January and mid-March Moore played in only one game, a disappointing single-goal reversal at relegation-threatened Blackpool. Eventually, the versatility Moore showed for the reserves in being able to play – and score – in any of the forward positions helped him return to the first team. Wearing the number seven shirt, he played in seven of the final eight league games of the season.

This included Moore's first professional appearance in the town of his birth with Forest's visit to Ipswich on 28 March 1964. He marked the occasion by scoring two goals and playing a key part in another. After 28 minutes Moore saw his header come back off the keeper's knees to give Wignall an easy finish to equalise Ipswich's opening goal. Then he gave the Reds the lead with a fine first-time shot from a half-cleared corner. In the second half, with the scores level at 2-2, Moore restored Forest's advantage with an easy finish when the keeper could only parry John Barnwell's shot after the Reds' inside-left had advanced some 40 yards with the ball. Moore's efforts were in vain, however, as Ipswich completed the scoring with two goals in ten minutes to win 4-3.

That match was the first of three defeats in four days over Easter, as Forest twice lost to Chelsea by a single goal, with Moore sitting out the second of them. The following week they were back on form, though, thrashing Birmingham City 4-0. Addison scored a first-half hat-trick and Moore added the fourth near the end, a simple finish after the Birmingham defence failed to clear a corner.

That was Moore's final goal of the season, though he did net the seventh of the eight the Reds put past a New Zealand XI in a friendly at the City Ground, played on the Monday between the final two league games. Before the match the visitors had performed the traditional haka, more usually associated with the All Blacks.

Forest finished 13th, a considerable disappointment after their good early season form. As well as Moore adding to his previous solitary first-team appearance, 1963/64 had seen the debuts of no fewer than five players who would play a part three years later in what would be one of the most successful seasons in the club's history – Alan Hinton, John Barnwell, Henry Newton, Mike Kear and Sammy Chapman.

With a return of six goals in 12 league games, Moore had proven his ability to both create and score from either wing. His record certainly stood comparison with those he was competing with for a place in the first-team starting line-up; Hinton had scored twice in 15 league starts, while Kear failed to net in his 11 games.

Surely the teenager had done enough to ensure his was one of the first names on the team sheet for the 1964/65 season. However, not for the last time in his career, Moore's progress would be cruelly disrupted by injury. What made this particular injury doubly frustrating was that it was inflicted – intentionally – by a team-mate.

'Desperate Dan'

Joe Wilson was a tough-tackling, no-nonsense defender (somewhat in the Stuart 'Psycho' Pearce mould) whose uncompromising approach had made him a firm fan favourite since joining the club in March 1962. His craggy looks and square jaw gave him a resemblance to *The Dandy*'s comic anti-hero, Desperate Dan.

Andy Beattie had had no hesitation in signing Wilson for £8,000 from Fourth Division Workington just a few weeks after Forest had narrowly won a hard-fought FA Cup third round tie at Borough Park. Wilson had been the Cumbrian side's standout player that day and his robust play had apparently 'frightened to death' Forest's left-winger, Le Flem.

A fine defensive performance on his home debut – a 1-0 win against Manchester United – had removed any doubts that Wilson could handle the transition to the First Division. But towards the end of the 1963/64 season Wilson's position had come under threat from Peter Hindley, another uncompromisingly physical player who came to be known affectionately as 'Tank' by the Forest faithful.

As the squad started pre-season training in July 1964 the desire to gain or maintain first-team status was as strong as ever; with appearance money and win or draw bonuses, a player could earn double his basic weekly wage.

Each week at the new training ground at Lady Bay there would be a practice match between the first team and reserve team – the 'probables' versus 'possibles'. In one such match Moore (hoping to cement his place in the first team) came up against

Wilson (fearful of losing his). As the two players lined up against each other, 'pleasantries' were exchanged.

Moore picks up the story:

> 'Joe wasn't the quickest but he was tough. I was playing on the left wing for the first team, he was at right-back for the reserves. After about ten minutes I received a pass, went past him, and crossed the ball into the penalty area. The next thing I knew, I was flat out on the deck, in a lot of pain. Joe had come in about five minutes late with a tackle and broken my ankle. He stood over me with his big ugly face and said, "I told you not to take the piss out of me!"'

Moore missed the first four months of the new season. Hinton took full advantage of his opportunity, playing in 41 of the 42 First Division games and scoring a creditable 13 goals.

Moore's recovery saw him return to reserve team action in late September. At the end of October he was joined in the team to play Colchester United by a certain Joe Wilson. Indeed, Forest opened the scoring when Wilson's shot was blocked and Moore fired home the rebound. Moore then provided the crosses for two more goals before the visitors rescued a point with three late goals. The unlikely duo continued to play together in the reserves for the next couple of months as Moore regained full match fitness.

Wilson had, in fact, been in the starting line-up for Forest's first 11 games of the season but strained his groin in a 1-1 draw at Stoke City. Substitutes would not be introduced until the following season, so with characteristic toughness he played the full 90 minutes and, improbably, scored Forest's equaliser with a diving header. For the next match his place at right-back was taken by Hindley and Wilson never played for the first team again.

A few months later, in March 1965, Beattie, who was by then managing Wolverhampton Wanderers, bought Wilson for a second time. He helped Wolves win promotion from the Second

Division in 1966/67, though in his three seasons at Molineux the fans dubbed him 'Joe (own goal) Wilson'.

Stop-start

For the first half of the 1964/65 season, with Moore working his way back to full fitness in the reserves, Alan Hinton was ever-present in the number 11 shirt. But when Hinton needed eight stitches in a wound to his forehead sustained in a draw at Birmingham City, Moore took his place for the visit of West Ham United on the Saturday before Christmas. With injuries to Addison and Wignall further depleting Forest's regular forward line, Sammy Chapman and Johnny Quigley were also given rare starts. Both scored in a fine 3-2 win against the FA Cup holders and retained their places for the next match, unlike Moore, who was replaced by a fit-again Hinton.

On 9 January 1965 Norwich City were the visitors to the City Ground in the third round of the FA Cup. Flu victim Chris Crowe was a late withdrawal and Moore replaced him on the right wing in a 1-0 win. Moore retained his place for the next two games. He gave a good account of himself against well-regarded left-back Tony Dunne in a 2-2 thriller with Manchester United and his cross set up Barnwell for Forest's goal in a 4-1 defeat at Craven Cottage.

Although his form was promising, Moore hadn't scored in five appearances and he sat out the next two matches, Crowe taking his place. This meant that he missed Forest's 3-1 FA Cup fourth round win over Sunderland at the end of January in front of almost 42,500 at Roker Park, scene of many happy childhood memories.

The next game was a creditable but dour goalless draw with league leaders Leeds United which left Forest in an encouraging sixth place, though with 31 points from 29 games they were way off the pace – joint leaders Leeds and Chelsea both had 42 points.

The following Saturday's home match against Stoke City saw Moore make the first of ten consecutive starts, his longest run yet in the first team. He scored against the Potters and then notched the winner as Forest came from behind to beat near neighbours Leicester City 2-1, his goal coming as something of a relief after he had earlier blazed a golden opportunity wide and seen an effort cleared off the line.

In an eventful match against reigning champions Liverpool on 1 April 1965, Moore opened the scoring and was on the receiving end of some rough (and unpunished) challenges. He had the last laugh though, with Forest 2-1 down in the 90th minute, being brought down and earning a penalty. John Barnwell dispatched the spot kick to earn his team a point.

The final goal of Moore's curtailed campaign came in a comfortable 2-0 win against Blackpool. He only featured in one of the remaining four league games as Forest – who had been in the top six all season – finished fifth, their highest top-flight finish since achieving the same placing in 1902. Moore had played his part in Forest's success despite the 'desperate' pre-season attentions of his over-zealous team-mate Wilson.

Moore also scored in the 5-0 thrashing of Mansfield Town in the final of the Nottinghamshire FA County Cup, in which Frank Wignall broke his leg. To mark the start of their centenary year, Forest then embarked on a somewhat ambitious tour of the United States and Canada. Coming at the end of a demanding campaign the itinerary was punishing, with 11 matches in 32 days. Forest won nine of them, though, scoring freely until the last few games, when the extended season was perhaps beginning to fatigue the players. Moore only played in three of these games and shared centre-forward duties with David Wilson and Chris Crowe – to good effect, as he scored four times in an 8-2 thrashing of American Soccer League champions Hartford and twice in a 4-2 win against Boston Metros.

Breakthrough

The 1965/66 season marked Forest's centenary as they became only the second league club in England – after neighbours Notts

County – to reach an unbroken century. The actual anniversary was marked in September 1965 with a friendly match against Valencia, a mark of the cordial relations between the clubs since their Inter-Cities Fairs Cup encounter earlier in the decade.

The City Ground was an upbeat place to be as the new season dawned. The new £110,000 Main Stand was nearing completion, season ticket sales had increased and there was optimism that Forest could match or improve on that impressive fifth place in the First Division table. The club had reported a £60,000 profit, though no new signings had been made.

Moore found himself having to fight for his place again at the start of the new campaign. Manager Carey's wing options were once more a case of 'perm two from three' and – to the surprise of many supporters – he opted to start the season with the Crowe–Hinton combination. Moore was back playing for the reserves in the Football Combination, but rumours that he might be leaving the club to get more regular first-team football were quickly quashed.

Despite the exhausting post-season tour and the resultant short close-season, Forest made a good start, taking six points from their first four games. Most notably, in their first home game they were four up just after the hour mark against champions Manchester United before conceding twice late on, the 4-2 result flattering a well-beaten United side.

The first defeat of the season came by the odd goal in three at Leeds and the match marked Forest's first use of a substitute, young forward Barry McArthur making his debut when Addison went off injured.

Moore finally made his first appearance of the campaign when he replaced Crowe for the visit of Arsenal, but it was not a happy return to the team. Forest played poorly in a single-goal defeat and were slow-handclapped by the crowd at the end, unfortunately not for the last time that season. The dip in form continued with three more defeats and an ill-deserved last-minute draw against struggling Northampton Town, with Moore getting no nearer to the action than the odd place on the bench, despite appeals from some fans for him to be given his chance.

He did return to the team for the centenary friendly against Valencia, who had beaten Real Madrid 3-0 just two days earlier. Before the game, Arsenal chairman Denis Hill-Wood presented Forest with a ceramic gun and a set of red shirts in recognition of the part the club had played in the Londoners' foundation in 1886. Two Forest players who had gone to work at the Woolwich Arsenal had set up a football team and asked their former club for a set of shirts. Forest duly obliged and Arsenal have worn red ever since.

Heavy rain no doubt influenced the slightly disappointing attendance of just under 19,000. Those who braved the elements eagerly awaited the appearance of the Brazilian forward Waldo, who had so impressed them when scoring twice in the visitors' thumping 5-1 win at the City Ground in that Fairs Cup tie four seasons earlier.

The teams served up plenty of entertainment in a 1-1 draw, a result the visitors felt was 'most diplomatic'. Chris Crowe put Forest ahead from the spot after a handball offence in the fifth minute and Guillot equalised a quarter of an hour later. While Crowe's contribution was particularly outstanding, the *Nottingham Evening Post* also praised Moore's 'highly impressive' performance.

He had evidently caught Johnny Carey's eye and, after scoring twice in the reserves' 4-0 win at Chelsea he was back in the first team for the next league match at home to West Ham. Forest picked a good time to rediscover their form against the Hammers, easing to a 5-0 win in front of the BBC's *Match of the Day* cameras. Moore scored the third goal just before half-time and two minutes from the end David Wilson became Forest's first substitute to score. Forest's dominance was such that West Ham's Geoff Hurst and Martin Peters spent the evening planning where they would go on holiday in the summer of 1966 rather than playing for England in the World Cup.

Transfer activity

Despite that big win Forest needed more firepower and fans were clamouring for some big signings. Among the names they were linked with were Wyn Davies at Bolton Wanderers, Chelsea's Barry Bridges (for whom a bid was rejected) and Aston Villa's former Notts County star, Tony Hateley. The latter, who was thought to be keen on the move, soon scored against Forest in a game that flu victim Bob McKinlay missed, ending a remarkable run of 265 consecutive appearances for the Reds.

Moore was finally getting a run of games, with Crowe initially missing out, but Forest's form remained a worry, especially away from home, where they lost six successive matches before picking up a point at Fulham. To make matters worse, in the last of those defeats, a 4-0 thrashing at Liverpool that left Forest third-bottom of the table they had led in August, Wignall suffered another fracture in his leg and was sidelined for two months.

While the team as a whole struggled for consistency, there was repeated praise for the performances of Peter Grummitt in goal and Henry Newton in midfield. Some fans even suggested they should be considered for England's squad for the following summer's World Cup, though more dispassionate observers conceded there were players in their positions who would take some displacing.

Rumours came and went about the possible signing of a goalscorer, but in November 1965 one significant transfer Forest did make was the purchase of Welsh international half-back Terry Hennessey for a club record £50,000 from Birmingham City. He had a debut to remember when Forest beat Blackpool 2-1, with the visitors managing to score all three goals.

One of the low points of the season came with a dismal 5-0 thumping on an icy pitch at Blackburn Rovers at the end of

November. While Moore could hardly be blamed for the team's defensive shortcomings, he found himself a victim of the changes that followed, losing his place in the side. As luck would have it, his team-mates responded with four wins and two draws from the next six matches and it would be mid-February before Moore returned to the first XI.

Back in the reserves, Moore refused to sulk and got on with the job in hand. He scored regularly, attracting interest from Newcastle United, but manager Carey was adamant he was not for sale.

The first team's improvement was short-lived and they soon lost three successive league games, in one of which, against Newcastle, the luckless Wignall's season came to a premature end when he broke his leg for a third time in eight months. Forest had beaten Northampton Town in the third round of the FA Cup, but 8,000 travelling fans witnessed a poor performance from them in a 2-0 defeat at Third Division Hull City in the fourth round. The week before, Moore scored four goals in the reserves' 8-1 drubbing of Shrewsbury Town; he had earned another chance in the first team and it came with the visit of Leeds.

Although he was the liveliest of Forest's forwards, Moore was helpless as Leeds built a three-goal cushion before half-time, prompting more slow handclaps from the frustrated supporters. Forest limited the damage to one more goal after the break but were outclassed by a Leeds team that would again finish runners-up.

The mood was soon lifted – and the gap at centre-forward caused by Wignall's misfortune filled – by the signing of striker Joe Baker from Arsenal for another club record fee, this time £65,000.

Baker's arrival brought the best out of Moore, who struck three times in four games. On 8 March 1966 his goal seven minutes from time was enough to beat Burnley on Baker's league debut. He was on the scoresheet again when Baker bagged his first two goals for the club in a 3-3 draw at Northampton. He also got an assist, Baker prodding home the rebound after the keeper found

Moore's shot too hot to hold but, true to Forest's season, they were pegged back at 3-3 with the last kick of the game. After a defeat at Everton Moore scored again in a 4-3 win against Stoke City.

By now the transfer deadline had passed without Forest making further additions to their squad, but the deadline was not as absolute as it is now. Players could still be signed on condition that they were not fielded in games that might affect promotion or relegation. Supporters were perhaps more concerned about the possibility of players leaving, though.

Forest actually came quite close to selling Moore at this time. Former coach Joe Mallett had left the City Ground to become the manager at recently relegated Birmingham City. As the one who, on his friend Joe McCormack's recommendation, had invited Moore to those trial matches at RAF Watnall four years earlier, he was keen for Moore to join him at St Andrew's. With Moore just breaking through into the Forest side but struggling to cement his place, Mallett could guarantee him first-team football.

Although Birmingham themselves never spoke directly to Moore, they let it be known to him via contacts in the press that they were interested. Negotiations with Forest reached an advanced stage and a transfer fee of £30,000 was agreed, not an insignificant amount for an unproven player. But at the last minute, for whatever reason, Forest decided against selling. And if he had been given the choice – admittedly unlikely in those days – Moore may well have declined to go despite the debt of gratitude he owed Mallett.

Meanwhile, Blackpool and Bolton Wanderers were said to be interested in Alan Hinton and John Winfield had been on the transfer list for months. So it was a relief when manager Carey said Forest neither needed nor wanted to sell any players, adding, 'I'd be content to keep them all and have them fit and ready for next season.'

Transfer rumours around Moore persisted, however, and Carey felt obliged to issue a more specific statement – in the face of inquiries from Newcastle and Fulham – that Moore was definitely not for sale.

In the meantime, trainer Jack Burkitt had left to manage neighbours Notts County, leaving Carey in the unfamiliar position of having to train the players as well as manage them until a successor was found.

Inconsistency

Moore was consistently putting in good displays, with his strong running and willingness to shoot with either foot. He was becoming increasingly popular with the fans, among whom the first comparisons were being made with a certain George Best. While Moore flourished, the unfortunate Hinton was getting the attention of the boo boys, his form and consistency not helped by finding himself in and out of the side as Carey took advantage of the ability of both Moore and Crowe to play at inside-forward as well as on the wings. Forest remained inconsistent, their performances ranging from winning 3-2 at Tottenham Hotspur to losing 3-0 at home to bottom club Blackburn.

The win at White Hart Lane on 2 April 1966 was all the more remarkable for injury-hit Forest fielding several reserve players, with rare starts for Geoff Ball at right-back and David Stainwright and Mike Kear in the forward line. Despite the makeshift line-up, after a quarter of an hour Forest were three up and had also hit the post, with a panicky Tottenham defence making unforced errors and Moore giving 17-year-old right-back John Collins a torrid time. Tottenham pulled a goal back and Forest were further weakened when Hennessey had to be replaced at half-time. They resisted the inevitable second-half onslaught – for once even keeping out Jimmy Greaves, thanks to the close attentions of substitute John Winfield – until Spurs scored five minutes from time, but the Reds held on for a 3-2 win.

Forest were still losing more often than winning, sometimes unluckily, as was the case when they were applauded off the pitch after an unfortunate 2-1 defeat at home to Chelsea, who scored from their only two attempts at goal and had a magnificent display from keeper Peter Bonetti to thank for coming out of the game with anything at all.

Forest's survival was all but guaranteed on 30 April when they lost 2-1 at Leicester City – the Foxes' Graham Cross scoring all three goals for an unusual 'hat-trick' – as other results went their way. A week later, Baker's goal to beat FA Cup finalists Sheffield Wednesday made it mathematically certain that Forest would still be a top-flight club the following season.

Despite his impressive form, Moore went nine games without scoring, but he got the Reds' final goal of the season in an entertaining 1-1 draw against champions Liverpool at the City Ground. He could have had a first hat-trick but was unlucky to see two shots bounce off keeper Tommy Lawrence. The goal he did score hinted at a fruitful partnership to come, as Baker played him in with a quality pass and Moore evaded Lawrence and slotted the ball home. In contrast to the groans and slow handclapping that had accompanied some of Forest's home displays, the Reds were again applauded off the field.

Forest finished 18th, a huge disappointment after spending the whole of the previous season in the top six. Many observers felt the exhausting North American tour had had an adverse effect on the team's form and contributed to the generally lacklustre performances throughout the season. The lesson having apparently been learned, Forest contented themselves with three post-season games in Belgium and France, Moore scoring in a 3-1 win against Angers.

With the big-money signings of Hennessey and Baker and the consistent good form of Grummitt, Newton and Barnwell in particular, Forest now had the nucleus of a very good team. With his strong finish to the season making him arguably the club's most exciting player, Moore had established himself as a player feared by his opponents and loved by his fans. He was now firmly among that core of key players on whom the club's fortunes would depend.

After a summer that was to be dominated by England hosting and winning the World Cup, the nation was about to discover just how good that Forest team would become.

5

A new dawn

'The turning point was switching to 4-4-2 with Terry Hennessey as sweeper at the back – he was different class.'

Ian Storey-Moore

World Cup hangover

The start of the 1966/67 season was eagerly awaited in the afterglow of that World Cup victory. With expensive recent signings Terry Hennessey and Joe Baker adding class at both ends of the pitch, Forest fans' hopes were high for a better campaign this time round. Hennessey took over as captain from Bob McKinlay, who felt the role should be given to a younger man. As the players posed for the habitual pre-season squad photograph, McKinlay and Jeff Whitefoot were the sole survivors from the FA Cup winners of 1959.

The Reds had a new trainer in Tommy Cavanagh, a no-nonsense Scouser, and it was hoped the team would benefit from the combination of his motivational skills and manager Johnny Carey's more cerebral approach. Cavanagh certainly worked the players hard, with an intense pre-season fitness programme getting the players into shape and adding necessary steel to the aesthetic footballing style for which the club was well known. Nonetheless, Forest only had three pre-season matches in which to work on their tactics and match fitness.

If the triumph of Bobby Moore and company was to generate a new wave of enthusiasm for football across the nation, there was little sign of it as the season kicked off. With the campaign traditionally beginning in August, it had long been accepted that attendances at the first few games would be adversely affected by fans being away on holiday. Package holidays abroad to sunnier climes were not yet the norm and most people cheerfully made do with a week at the British seaside. Crowds at matches were usually a few thousand down until the schools went back at the start of September. In Forest's case, many a fan will have been on Skegness beach tuning into a transistor radio for the score or scouring the streets of Mablethorpe for a TV rental shop window at 4.40pm to watch the results on the BBC's *Grandstand* or ITV's *World of Sport*.

The modest turnout of just under 22,000 at the City Ground for the visit of Stoke City on 20 August was perhaps slightly disappointing for the start of a new campaign, but it was on a par with the attendance for the final home game of the previous season against champions Liverpool.

After his breakthrough season in 1965/66, Moore felt he had earned the right to be a first-team regular despite the strong competition for forward places. Fortunately, Carey agreed and Moore was in the starting line-up wearing the number 11 shirt, with Alan Hinton nominally taking Mike Kear's place on the right wing. In practice Moore's role was more fluid, giving Hinton the opportunity to play on his preferred left side.

Forest lost 2-1, goals from ex-Red Calvin Palmer and Peter Dobing sealing the points for the Potters. Moore crossed for Baker to score what was little more than a consolation, though the quicksilver striker came agonisingly close to equalising when his lob over Stoke's goalkeeper came back off the post.

In the match programme, chairman Tony Wood had expressed the hope that 'when the time comes for the 1966/67 honours board to be written, the name of our club will boldly appear'.

This might have been a little ambitious, given the previous season's disappointing placing, but even he could not have imagined how close Forest would come to fulfilling that wish. That defeat against Stoke would turn out to be the Reds' only home reverse of the season.

Forest also found themselves two goals behind in their first away game at Chelsea four days later. After a dull first half in which the home side were frustrated by the form of Peter Grummitt, who always seemed to play well at Stamford Bridge, Chelsea took control with two goals from Peter Osgood. Moore was a constant threat, though, and he opened his account for the season, heading home a cross from Hinton.

The two 2-1 defeats made for a disappointing start to the season for Forest and prompted Carey to ring the changes.

A change for the better

For the following weekend's trip to Sheffield United the manager made a tactical switch that would stand Forest in good stead for the rest of the season. John Winfield and John Barnwell replaced Jeff Whitefoot and Colin Addison, with Winfield, who had hitherto played as a half-back on either side of the pitch, moving to left-back. This meant Forest adopted a 4-4-2 formation in which Henry Newton was able to move forward to his preferred position in midfield, where he formed a formidable partnership with Barnwell. Forest never looked back.

After the Bramall Lane side took the lead, Forest were the better team and equalised when Baker took advantage of a defensive slip to convert Moore's ball in from the right. Moore scored the winner after bringing down a high cross from Barnwell. Despite the home side's protests, the officials ruled that he had been onside when the ball was played. The Blades hit the woodwork while Forest also came close through a diving header from Moore. A third successive 2-1 scoreline was in Forest's favour this time and they had their first points of the season.

Next was the return meeting with Chelsea, just a week after the narrow defeat at Stamford Bridge. Not for the last time that season the game was marred by trouble on the terraces. Forest dominated a one-sided affair, but another brave and athletic display in the visitors' goal from Peter Bonetti – like Grummitt, a brilliant shot-stopper – showed exactly why he would go on to play for England.

Even when the outstanding Bonetti was beaten, efforts by Winfield and Hinton were denied by goal-line clearances, and the match finished goalless.

Carey had written in the programme, 'We now have the nucleus of a very fine, talented side worthy of competing with and extending the best,' and Forest were cheered off at the end of what was considered to be their best display for two years. No doubt the home fans' acclaim was also directed at Bonetti after what the *Nottingham Evening Post* described as 'one of the greatest individual displays seen in the city for many years'.

Carey's optimism was not, however, matched by all. 'Forest have a side capable of playing a classic short game on a firm surface, but I fear that as in most seasons their promise will dwindle as the long winter months come along' was the verdict of the *Daily Telegraph*'s David Miller. Time would tell whether Forest would be able to prove him wrong.

On 3 September Forest finally claimed their first home win of the season, beating West Bromwich Albion 2-1. Both teams could consider themselves unfortunate not to have added to their tally, with Forest having no fewer than three goals ruled out for offside (two of them finished by Moore) and Albion hitting the woodwork three times.

Forest took the lead after a break down the left, Baker crossing for Moore to score. The prolific Tony Brown equalised after Forest failed to clear a corner but the winner came from Baker, who rounded the goalkeeper to score after a move involving Hennessey, Barnwell and Wignall. McKinlay kept Albion's other dangerman, Jeff Astle, quiet, while alongside him Hennessey led by example, the additional responsibilities of captaincy clearly not affecting his fine form.

Three days later the visit of Fulham saw the first opportunity for the City Ground to welcome one of England's World Cup winners, with Moore in direct opposition to right-back George Cohen. The visitors' attacking 4-3-3 line-up included future England manager Bobby Robson in midfield. Forest took a grip on the game and scored when Moore half-volleyed a dipping Barnwell cross into the roof of the net from a narrow angle. Although the Cottagers equalised just after half-time, Moore's 88th-minute header from a Baker cross secured the Reds another 2-1 win and two hard-earned points. Fulham's frustration at losing the game so late on saw some of their players reportedly refusing at first to shake hands at the end of the game.

That late winner brought Moore's tally to five in five games and led the *Nottingham Evening Post* to declare that he was 'blossoming … into one of the game's match-winning wingers'.

A tough away trip followed to face a Leeds United side that had been runners-up in the league for the last two seasons. Well drilled by their manager, Don Revie, Leeds were not only one of the fittest sides around but were quite adept at testing the boundary of fair and foul play. Moreover, they had two of the most difficult defenders Moore ever played against, Paul Reaney and Jack Charlton:

> 'Paul was quick, a dogged player to play against, left his foot in – typical Leeds! There were one or two "rabbits" I used to like to play against, but he certainly wasn't one of those. As for Jack, he was a really friendly guy off the pitch, always good fun. But on the pitch he could be a dirty so-and-so, very niggly, always pulling your shirt.'

Colin Addison's last appearance for Forest before completing a club record £45,000 move to Arsenal could have been a high-scoring affair if either team had taken their chances. Addison and Baker for Forest, along with Leeds' Eddie Gray and Peter Lorimer, were among those guilty of wasting opportunities to score. As it was, Johnny Giles set up Gray to give Leeds a half-time lead. Norman Hunter kept goal for four minutes while Gary Sprake received treatment for an injury, but Forest were unable to capitalise on the Welsh keeper's temporary absence. Wignall equalised with his first goal of the season after Sprake fumbled Addison's powerful shot and the points were shared in a bruising encounter that left several Forest players nursing, thankfully, only minor knocks.

Next came the first round of the League Cup, which had received a lukewarm reception from the country's biggest clubs since its inception in 1960, with many simply choosing not to enter it. Indeed, after taking part in the first two years of the competition, Forest hadn't bothered with it for four seasons. The competition was invigorated for 1966/67 by staging the final at Wembley – previously it had been a two-legged affair at the grounds of the finalists. A further incentive was a place in the Inter-Cities Fairs Cup for the winners.

Forest thus resumed their interest in the competition at home against Second Division Birmingham City, the club that, with Hennessey at full-back, had won the competition four years earlier. A more than respectable 19,000 crowd saw Forest renew acquaintances with former players Trevor Hockey and Geoff Vowden. Forest took the lead when Newton beat Birmingham's persistent offside trap to score but Vowden equalised, after which the Reds were unable to capitalise on several good chances. Skipper Hennessey generously conceded that his former club had deserved to take the tie to a replay as Forest had not matched the visitors' work rate.

Forest immediately returned to winning ways with a third successive home league victory, cruising to a comfortable 3-0 win against an admittedly poor Newcastle United side that included future Reds star Frank Clark. Early in the game, Wignall headed down Newton's free kick for Baker to score. Moore made it two just after the hour mark, breaking through after Barnwell's quickly taken free kick to beat keeper Gordon Marshall. In the last action of the game Chris Crowe set up Baker to score his second, but Forest could and should have scored several more. Both Moore and Barnwell hit the post, while Marshall (who would have a brief spell with Forest two seasons later) twice tipped efforts from Wignall over the bar. Incredibly, for the second time in a fortnight, Forest had no fewer than three goals ruled out for offside.

The *Nottingham Evening Post* didn't mince its words in describing Newcastle as 'quite the most unimpressive Division One side to play in Nottingham for a long time'. The paper was more impressed by the potential of its own team, though, astutely observing that 'the Reds could be on the verge of great things' and concluding, 'Forest's investment in quality players, and their insistence that attacking soccer must be their watchword, is beginning to pay off.'

Around this time false reports were circulating that Forest were interested in signing Fulham legend Johnny Haynes. They could have done with some of Haynes's star quality in the League Cup replay at St Andrew's, which ended in a deserved 2-1 win for the hosts, Vowden again scoring against his former team. Moore had a quiet game but this was possibly just as well: Tottenham Hotspur manager Bill Nicholson was in attendance, ostensibly watching the Reds ahead of their forthcoming meeting, but reportedly also having a good look at Moore – who had now scored six goals in eight league games – with a possible transfer bid in mind.

Big-money transfers were becoming more common and at White Hart Lane four days later Spurs demonstrated their spending power by fielding two expensive signings, Mike England (£100,000 from Blackburn Rovers) and Terry Venables (£80,000 from Chelsea). Their line-up also included two future Forest managers in Dave Mackay and Joe Kinnear.

Forest paid the price for playing risky football at the back, conceding two early goals as first Baker and then Hennessey lost possession in their own penalty area. Spurs' second goal was, inevitably, prodded home by Jimmy Greaves, who scored more times against Forest than any other opponents. Forest came back into the game after half an hour when Wignall scored from Moore's low cross and they went on to create numerous chances. Baker, Crowe and Hindley all came close, Baker was cynically pulled back by Alan Mullery after breaking clear, a Venables handball in the penalty area went unpunished and Winfield burst through to hit the bar. At the other end, Greaves crashed a shot against the bar five minutes from time, but the score remained 2-1.

Not for the last time that season, Forest could consider themselves unfortunate to lose to Tottenham by the odd goal in three and some observers felt the Londoners had been lucky to get one point, never mind two. In the opinion of the *Sunday Mirror*, 'Forest emerged as far the better footballing side.'

All Forest had to show for one of their best away performances of the season to date was praise in defeat and the widespread view that this entertaining game had been a credit to English football.

With Forest in ninth place (having won four, drawn two and lost three) the next day Carey took the team away for their traditional early season break in Skegness, allowing Forest's manager and some of the players to enjoy a round or two of links golf.

Manchester United humiliated

At the start of October Forest's increasingly dominant home form would be put to the test in what was always one of the most anticipated fixtures of the season – the visit of Manchester United. With the 1958 Munich air disaster relatively fresh in supporters' minds and a forward line boasting the diverse talents of George Best, Denis Law and Bobby Charlton, the Red Devils were many people's 'favourite other team' in the 1960s and on several occasions their visit drew the biggest crowd of the season to the City Ground.

United's early season form had been surprisingly inconsistent, though. They had won all five home games but had lost three out of four away and crashed out of the League Cup 5-1 at Blackpool. They were fifth in the table, two points and four places above Forest. The programme notes expressed the hope that Forest might 'give this all-star Manchester United side a game they won't readily forget' before confidently predicting 'a fine, thrilling game of football'. These opinions were proved correct on both counts.

Baker turned in what was considered his finest performance to date for the Reds, sweeping past veteran defender Bill Foulkes time and again. Forest ran riot, going four goals up within an hour against an unexpectedly disappointing United, whose ponderous defence had no answer to the speed and invention of the Reds' forward line. Crowe opened the scoring with one of the fastest goals in the club's history, flicking a header past Alex Stepney from Baker's corner after just 15 seconds. United came back strongly but, shortly after the police removed around 20 supporters from the crowd for chanting abusive language, Forest increased their lead. Baker chased a long ball with Tony Dunne and they both collided with Stepney, leaving Wignall a simple finish into an open goal. The pace and tension of the game saw angry clashes between Baker and Best, Wignall and Nobby Stiles, and Baker and Stiles. Crowe made it three before the break, heading in after a poor punch from the unfortunate Stepney.

In the second half United tried to get back into the game, but Forest extended their lead when Baker was fouled by Stiles for the penalty that completed Crowe's hat-trick. Charlton's goal, after a brilliant dribble from Best, was no more than a consolation. United's 4-1 humiliation would prove to be their biggest league defeat of the season and the only time they conceded four goals.

The biggest Football League crowd of the day (almost 42,000) and the audience of ITV's Sunday afternoon highlights programme *World of Soccer* had seen a promising Forest side show they could hold their own among the biggest clubs, outplaying a United XI with eight full internationals. Crowe's starring role was to be something of a swansong for his Forest career, though: those three goals turned out to be his last for the club and he was transferred to Bristol City in the new year.

The one disappointing aspect of the game was the fighting in the crowd after some United fans got into the Trent End, to the considerable displeasure of the regulars there. Eventually the police were able to calm things down and restore order, but this was a growing problem in the game. The youth culture that developed along with the increasing freedoms of the mid-1960s had led to an increase in violence (such as the notorious seaside clashes between Mods and Rockers) alongside a diminishing respect for authority and, particularly, the police. In any case, policing was as yet minimal at football matches, so there were plenty of opportunities for those so inclined to cause trouble. The incidents at the United game prompted the police to ban flags and banners from the City Ground, though that would have been unlikely to pacify any would-be troublemakers.

Forest's next challenge was a trip to fourth-placed Leicester City, who were managed by another future Reds boss, Matt Gillies. Undefeated since the opening day of the season, the Foxes were the leading goalscorers in the division. Quite a rivalry was developing between the clubs. With several thousand Forest fans making the short trip, the battle to be considered the Midlands' best team added 13,000 to Filbert Street's previous highest attendance of the season. With almost 40,000 inside the ground, hundreds of supporters were locked out. Again there was an infiltration of a staunchly 'home' part of the ground, as a section of the Forest following attempted to 'take' the Spion Kop.

With Crowe's future uncertain, a large banner reading 'Crowe must stay' was draped over the Forest coach on its arrival at the ground. Crowe himself was quick to joke, 'I was up half the night making that!' That was where the fun ended for Forest, though.

As they had at Tottenham, they failed to deal with early pressure, the hosts taking advantage of defensive errors to race into a three-goal lead within a quarter of an hour. Having given a head start like that to a team with the great Gordon Banks in goal, Forest were never going to take anything from the game. Indeed, Leicester remained the likelier to score and the game finished 3-0, to chants of 'Champions!' from the gleeful, if rather optimistic, home fans.

On the Wednesday after the rout by Leicester, Frank Wignall put in a shock transfer request, stating, 'My reasons are entirely personal. I just feel that the best thing for me is a change of club … In fact, about three weeks ago I made my worries known to the manager and we had a long chat. I decided then to give it another go, but I find that I still feel the same. The trouble is that I find I am losing interest in the game and I don't want that to happen. I have thought about it a great deal and have come to the conclusion that a move is the only answer.' This was despite the fact that Wignall had started all 13 league and cup games up to that point.

To compound matters, the following day Alan Hinton, dissatisfied with reserve-team football, also handed in a written transfer request. The repercussions of the strong competition for starting places in the forward line were beginning to be felt.

Forest's run of difficult fixtures continued with the visit of reigning league champions Liverpool on 15 October. The Merseysiders were in good form, unbeaten in eight games and having won on their last three away trips. Again there were opposition scouts at the game, this time from Blackpool, who, as well as watching Forest ahead of the game between the sides at the end of the month, were reportedly considering a bid for Wignall. The Seasiders had sold Alan Ball to Everton earlier in the season and the British record £112,000 would undoubtedly have been burning a hole in the club's proverbial pocket.

Unsurprisingly, Liverpool were backed by a sizeable away following. Some of them made their presence felt in the Trent End but there was little trouble once a few of the more boisterous ringleaders had been removed by the police.

After Liverpool had wasted a couple of early chances Forest had the better of the game, with Baker again the pick of the Reds' forwards. He opened the scoring after a mistake by Ron Yeats, who misjudged a high ball, allowing Moore to lob it over him for Baker to head home. Five minutes later, Liverpool equalised when the unfortunate Grummitt slipped as Ian St John headed the ball across for 'Sir' Roger Hunt to head home. Thereafter it was his opposite number, Tommy Lawrence, who kept the visitors in the game, saving from Moore, Barnwell and Baker. With a strong claim for a penalty for handball being turned down, Forest had to settle for a 1-1 draw. It had been a tough game, though, the *Birmingham Sunday Mercury* deeming it 'dull and depressing … [a] deplorable and scrappy apology for football'.

Forest then had an 11-day wait for their next match, at West Ham United on 22 October, one of several moved to midweek from the previous weekend to accommodate international games for the four home countries. West Ham's triumvirate of World Cup winners – captain Bobby Moore and goalscorers Geoff Hurst and Martin Peters – had all played in England's win in Belfast, while Hennessey was in the Wales team that drew with Scotland in Cardiff. The Reds' skipper had generously donated his shirt and half of his appearance money to the disaster relief fund set up after the tragic collapse of a colliery spoil tip at Aberfan the previous day, which killed 116 schoolchildren and 28 adults.

A brace from Hurst gave the Hammers a two-goal lead in the first half an hour as the Forest defence once again struggled against early pressure. With Baker absent due to tonsillitis, Crowe came closest to scoring as Forest briefly rallied, but West Ham dominated. Shortly after Barnwell saw a goal ruled out because Moore had strayed offside, they added a third to make the game safe. Moore made amends four minutes from time, converting Hinton's cross from close range, but overall 3-1 was a fair reflection of the game. Just one point from three games had stalled Forest's momentum.

With Wignall and Hinton on the transfer list, scouts from Aston Villa were at the City Ground for the visit of Blackpool at the end of October. Villa had £100,000 to spend, Tony Hateley having in the end joined Chelsea. Wignall was immediately involved in the action, heading on a Newton free kick for Moore to score in the first minute. Moore then had a goal disallowed for offside, but Forest were not at their best and were indebted to Grummitt for several saves in the first half. Blackpool's spoiling tactics had attempted to blunt Forest's attacking threat, with Moore – the pick of the Reds' forwards – feeling the force of their robust play more than most. The second half was a scrappy affair, but Forest were spared a nervous end to the game when Hinton headed home, with Wignall once again the provider, to seal a 2-0 win.

Rude awakening at Anfield

On 5 November Forest travelled to Anfield for the return game against Liverpool, but the only fireworks would come from the home team's forward line. The Merseysiders were on top throughout and it was largely thanks to Hennessey that after an hour they only had a solitary goal to show for their superiority. However, Liverpool took full advantage of a tiring Forest side, with Newton and Barnwell playing on with injuries and Baker evidently not fully fit after missing two games with his tonsillitis. A Roger Hunt goal midway through the second half was followed by goals in the last five minutes from Hunt again and Peter Thompson. The margin of defeat was greater than Forest deserved; 'a travesty' according to one newspaper. The 4-0 scoreline condemned Forest to what would turn out to be their heaviest defeat of the season.

With just over a third of the campaign gone, Forest were in ninth place, heading a group of four teams on 15 points thanks to a superior goal average, the predecessor to goal difference. Averaging a point per game, this mid-table placing was testimony to the Reds' infuriating inability to replicate their home form on their travels.

	First Division table (extract), 5 November 1966							
		P	W	D	L	F	A	Pts
1	Chelsea	15	8	5	2	32	17	21
2	Stoke City	15	9	2	4	25	14	20
3	Everton	15	8	4	3	25	19	20
4	Manchester United	14	9	1	4	28	22	19
5	Leicester City	14	7	4	3	37	24	18
6	Tottenham Hotspur	15	8	2	5	26	23	18
7	Burnley	14	6	5	3	27	21	17
8	Liverpool	14	6	5	3	26	22	17
9	**Nottingham Forest**	**15**	**6**	**3**	**6**	**21**	**22**	**15**
10	Leeds United	14	5	5	4	17	18	15
11	Southampton	15	6	3	6	25	27	15
12	Sheffield United	15	6	3	6	19	24	15

The resounding win against Manchester United, a battling draw at Elland Road and their unlucky defeat at White Hart Lane had shown that Forest were capable of competing with the best teams of the era, but they would need to respond to this emphatic wake-up call at the hands of the reigning league champions.

Moore and Baker had scored 14 goals between them – in fact, they had either scored or assisted in all but two of Forest's 21 league goals. With winter's muddy and icy pitches approaching, the Reds would be hoping the inventive, deadly duo would be able to maintain their fine form.

6

Climbing the table

'Forest will play football even if the stands fall down.'

Joe Mercer, manager of Manchester City

Unbeaten run begins

The inquest in the dressing room after the defeat at Anfield had lasted over an hour. Coach Tommy Cavanagh's ear-splitting monologue of expletives filled the air and left Moore and his team-mates in no doubt that the following week's training regime would be unusually cruel and harsh.

Each player was asked to have his say on what had gone wrong. Terry Hennessey summed up the mood, 'We only seem to be going away for a day trip, we don't seem to be going away with the determination to win. We have to start winning 50-50 balls.' In the spirit of Brian Clough's mantra a decade later, he continued, 'You can't play football unless you get the ball.'

Classy as ever, manager Johnny Carey calmly concluded matters by saying, 'Just put it to one side. Let's make sure we improve next week.'

Cavanagh wasn't prepared to leave it at that, though. Back at the City Ground on the Monday after the defeat, he gave the players a particularly hard training session, making them run laps on the track round the pitch. Moore takes up the story:

> '"Run, run, run, run!" Tommy shouted. Then he stopped us in one of the corners next to the corner flag. We all gathered round in a semi-circle and he started ranting and raving – he used to foam at the mouth – saying this, that and the other about us not being good enough. He was just about to have a go at John Winfield when John said to him, "Tommy, just a second, do you know you're talking to a top-class professional footballer?" We all fell about laughing. It certainly broke the ice that morning!'

The Liverpool defeat would be a turning point. Forest regrouped and embarked on a long unbeaten run that would see them rapidly climb the table. Incredibly, they wouldn't concede more than a single goal in a league game for another six months.

In his first few seasons at the club Moore had faced competition from several talented forwards as he tried to cement his place in the first team. Now the £45,000 arrival of Barry Lyons from Rotherham United added a fifth winger to Johnny Carey's attacking options, with right-wingers Chris Crowe, Mike Kear and Lyons battling for the number seven shirt and a similar tussle between Moore and Alan Hinton on the left wing. Although Moore usually wore number 11, he was given a free role as he could operate effectively across the front line, being two-footed and a good header of the ball. That versatility would be vital for Forest as injuries took their toll later in the season.

Moore duly took his place on the left wing as Lyons made his debut against Sunderland, in the process becoming the seventh different player to wear the number seven shirt in the first three months of the season. Nobody knew it at the time, but the addition of Forest supporter Lyons – as a child he used to stand in the children's pen at the City Ground – was the catalyst for the Reds' rise from mid-table anonymity to mount an unexpected challenge for silverware. In particular, his mobility and energy made a big difference to the team's work rate.

Sunderland included three future Forest players in mercurial midfielder Jim Baxter, striker Neil Martin (who would score the first goal of Brian Clough's reign on Trentside) and goalkeeper Jim Montgomery.

Forest were on top throughout and made their quality tell with three goals in a 13-minute spell. Baker opened the scoring after Wignall's free kick fell to him in a crowded area, then Moore turned sharply to fire beyond Montgomery. The pick of the goals was John Barnwell's volley from the edge of the area after the keeper punched a corner clear.

Sunderland's frustration at being outplayed spilled into the ferocity of their tackling, with Lyons and Moore targeted in particular, to the extent that Moore had to be replaced by Hinton. Indeed, Baxter, who had been sent off in the corresponding fixture the previous season, was lucky not to be similarly punished for the nasty foul that injured Moore.

A Sunderland goal just after the break gave the noisy away following something to cheer but the result was a comfortable 3-1 win for the Reds. Nonetheless, Carey felt it necessary to make known his displeasure at Baxter's foul play, 'I have always had a great respect for Baxter. He is a wonderful player, but a man with his ability doesn't have to stoop to such fouls.'

Forest's own vociferous away support travelled in numbers to boost the crowd at Villa Park the following week. Generously, the matchday programme stated that if Forest were to one day win the league it would 'give great pleasure to the many folk who admire the sporting way in which they invariably play'.

Baker and Moore were the stars of the show for Forest, each being denied by the woodwork and being the victims (Baker twice) when, yet again, the Reds had three goals ruled out for offside – all in an incident-filled first half. The one goal they did score was Lyons' first in a Forest shirt. He began the move with a pass to Baker, who took the ball forward before finding Moore, whose cross Lyons converted. Forest were all over Villa, so it was a surprise when the hosts equalised before half-time. Lyons was replaced at the interval due to an ankle injury and, not for the first time, Forest faded in the second half, ending up hanging on for a point when they should have had the game won long since.

On 26 November Forest's 2,500th league game saw Nottingham-born Arsenal manager Bertie Mee return to his home city with his struggling team, including September signing Colin Addison, who had been made captain for the day. The Gunners had only won once away from home but took an early lead when they capitalised on a poor back-pass from Henry Newton. Soon after, Baker set up Moore to equalise with a deflected shot. The visitors applied plenty of pressure in the second half, so it was a great relief when former Arsenal man Barnwell scored with a 30-yard free kick to give the Reds a 2-1 win. 'A free kick even Pelé could not have bettered,' drooled the reporter from the *Sunday People*. The margin might have been greater had Moore not dallied after rounding the goalkeeper, enabling Arsenal to clear.

High praise

Despite their indifferent away form, Forest were clearly making a good impression: in the programme for the match at Manchester City the style of play Carey nurtured in his players drew praise from both City manager Joe Mercer and future TV commentator Gerry Harrison. Harrison noted Forest's emphasis on 'the freedom of individual skill rather than the restriction of any particular system', while Mercer felt 'they will play football even if the stands fall down'. Echoing the editorial from the recent game at Aston Villa, there was speculation that 'no doubt one of these days Forest will achieve their ambition and win the First Division championship', while the Reds were also described as 'a very popular club with a reputation for good sporting play'.

Inevitably, after such high praise, Forest – with Hinton taking the place of Moore – failed to live up to their billing. In a poor game played in cold, misty conditions, Forest were unable to capitalise on their chances and had to settle for a 1-1 draw. They still hadn't won on the road since August.

With Hinton unwell, Moore returned for the visit of Sheffield Wednesday, the match only going ahead after a mid-morning pitch inspection following three days of rain. With Baker given precious little space he was forced to go deeper to try to exert an influence on the game and Forest's main threat came more from the flanks. The Owls took the lead after a goalmouth scramble but Bob McKinlay equalised with his first goal for more than two years, diverting Lyons' shot past England goalkeeper Ron Springett. Both Moore and Lyons missed presentable chances and again the Reds had to be content with a 1-1 draw.

Forest finally managed a win on their travels in the return fixture against their opening-day opponents, Stoke City. Yet again the programme was generous in its praise for the 'skilful, creative game' played by a team considered to be 'among soccer's purists' and noted for 'the grace and quality of their play'. After two matches in which the defences had been on top, this was an exciting, end-to-end match.

In the last minute of a goalless first half Wignall, Baker and Lyons combined to create a chance for the onrushing Moore, who could only lift his shot over the bar from close range. The hosts opened the scoring after 65 minutes with a penalty conceded by Winfield.

It looked as though Forest's frustrating away form was to continue, but Baker had other ideas. Just three minutes later he equalised with a typical poacher's finish after a defensive mistake. Seven minutes from time he clinched the points with a goal that echoed Carey's philosophy that 'our players are encouraged to use imagination and to apply this to the game as they see fit. If we stifle individualism completely, the game will suffer in spectator appeal.' A clearance from Hindley found Baker in space and he burst forward, beat three defenders and slotted the ball past Stoke's goalkeeper.

The goal – reckoned to be one of the best ever by a Forest player – was rapturously received by those who had made the 50-mile journey along the A52 from Nottingham and was long remembered by all who witnessed it.

Forest had created much the better opportunities and the *Nottingham Evening Post* hailed the 2-1 win as the team's best display of the season. Presumably in recognition of ending that long run without an away win, the Reds were named Team of the Week in the *Football League Review*, a magazine produced by the competition's governing body and inserted into many clubs' matchday programmes. The prize was for Forest to select a local amateur club to be given a kit and a football supplied by sports clothing manufacturer Uwin. They chose Clifton All-Whites, with whom Forest have had strong connections for many years, with Garry Birtles and Jermaine Jenas among the better-known Reds to have played for them.

Christmas double-header

These were the days when teams would play a double-header against the same opposition either side of Christmas Day and Forest faced tough opponents in seventh-placed Everton, who were above them in the table on goal average. The day before the first match, BBC viewers saw Forest take part in the first edition of a new entertainment show, *Quiz Ball*, a light-hearted sports and general knowledge contest. They were represented by Johnny Carey, Bob McKinlay, John Barnwell, and a guest 'supporter' in pipe-smoking Derbyshire farmer-turned-TV-personality Ted Moult. Their opponents were Arsenal, who, with considerable help from 'referee' David Vine, won the contest 3-2.

At Goodison Park, Forest and Everton had a chance to steal a march on the teams around them, the game having been brought forward to Friday, 23 December. This was another opportunity for Forest to pit their wits against a World Cup winner: the Toffees' record signing Alan Ball.

Forest drew first blood midway through an even, flowing first half. Everton centre-half Brian Labone – who would go on to have a decisive influence on Forest's quest for honours later in the season – hauled Baker down and then failed to deal with the resultant free kick from McKinlay, leaving Moore free to score. Forest's attacking flair of the first half gave way to defensive resilience after the break. Grummitt and his defence had to be on top of their game to prevent Everton from creating clear openings, though McKinlay had to make a headed goal-line clearance. Forest looked capable of adding to their lead when they broke and almost did so when Moore netted again, but he was clearly offside, and 1-0 was the final score.

The following day there was more good news for Forest, with Carey announcing that Wignall had agreed to come off the transfer list:

> 'After the game I had a talk with Frank about his future. The talk was at my instigation and I am happy to say that at the end of it Wignall expressed a wish to have his name removed from the transfer list. He said that the circumstances which prompted him to ask for a change no longer obtained and when I told my committee of the player's decision they were delighted that he wanted to stay with us and immediately agreed.'

On Boxing Day the lack of public transport to the return match at the City Ground restricted the attendance to just over 36,000, when the visit of the FA Cup holders might otherwise have attracted an even larger crowd. The growing connection between the players and the fans was evident before the game, as the players acknowledged their individual chants from the Trent End.

The match itself was less fluent and more physical, with several ill-tempered incidents. The *Liverpool Echo*'s report pulled no punches:

> 'Permitted by weak control to indulge in tactics extremely regrettable and at times disgraceful, Nottingham Forest and Everton carried on vendettas apparently left over from the Goodison Park meeting last Friday ... It was a foul-ridden, no-quarter battle studded with free kicks yet incredibly free from the kind of stern action demanded.'

A case in point was Ball, who had got very little change out of Hennessey and Newton in the first game, giving what the *Evening Post* described as a 'startling display of temperament'. He was lectured by the referee after two early fouls on full-back Winfield, and thereafter was subjected to some crude tackling by Forest players and loud barracking from the Reds' fans every time he touched the ball.

Forest completed a Christmas double thanks to McKinlay heading in Lyons' cross just before the break for his second goal in successive home games. Everton attacked more in the second half but were forced to rely on set pieces and rarely troubled Grummitt. The 1-0 win catapulted the Reds from ninth to fourth place in the table.

These two hard-fought wins and clean sheets against Everton were encouraging evidence that Forest were able to defend resolutely against more physical opponents in games they were unable to dominate through their skilful and attacking play.

In the syndicated column published in his name in the *Football Post*, Ball expressed his wish not to have to face the Reds in the FA Cup and said they 'played like a team already in Europe'.

Forest saw the year out with a visit from Sheffield United. Overnight rain had left puddles on the City Ground pitch, but a morning of wind and sunshine dried the surface sufficiently for the match to go ahead. Lyons turned in his most influential performance to date, creating all Forest's goals as they eased to a 3-1 victory.

Late in the first half, United's keeper was unable to hold Moore's header from Lyons' free kick, leaving Wignall to score from close range. On 54 minutes, after a jinking run along the touchline, the right-winger crossed for Baker to dive and head in the second. Lyons also laid on the third ten minutes later, although there was some doubt as to whether Moore or the goalkeeper got the final touch. Each of the managers felt their player was the last to touch the ball, but with the Sheffield player reluctant to have an own goal against his name, the goal was officially credited to Moore. When Mick Jones, a future England colleague of Moore's, pulled a goal back with a fierce header two minutes from time it was no more than a consolation for United.

Productive new year

Conditions were also difficult at The Hawthorns the following week. In bitterly cold weather, and with the hard pitch covered partly by sand and partly by snow, it was Forest, noisily backed by more than 30 coachloads of fans, who adapted the better. Forest deservedly took the lead after 39 minutes when Hennessey scored from the penalty spot after Baker had been brought down. The Reds' skipper was at his commanding best, teaming up with McKinlay to stifle the threat of Albion's renowned strike force of Jeff Astle, Tony Brown and Bobby Hope, leaving Grummitt little more than a spectator for much of the game.

Forest controlled the midfield, with Barnwell's distribution catching the eye. Newton showed why he was being spoken of as a potential full international, almost scoring when his shot hit the bar and threading the ball through for Moore to score the decisive second goal ten minutes from the end. A 66th-minute goal against the run of play had drawn Albion level, but in better conditions Forest's superiority might have been rewarded with victory by a wider margin than 2-1.

On 14 January 1967 the visit of Leeds United, who were just two points behind Forest, attracted the City Ground's biggest league crowd of the season to date – almost 44,000, producing record receipts, with some 5,000 making the journey from Yorkshire. Forest again showed they could rise to the occasion against the better teams and took the lead after 21 minutes when Gary Sprake touched Wignall's header on to the bar and Moore scored from the rebound. The game continued at a high tempo, but goalscoring opportunities were restricted by the two strong defences. An illustration of Forest's determination and Moore's commitment to the cause came when the left-winger was injured blocking a shot from Eddie Gray – in the right-back position.

This was a game that epitomised Forest's newly acquired ability to 'mix it' with the more physical teams. Leeds were building what would become an enduring reputation for complementing their undoubted footballing abilities with a mastery of the nastier side of the game. One of their leading exponents of the 'dark arts' was combative midfielder Billy Bremner, who enraged Barnwell with a dirty, late and unpunished challenge from behind shortly before the interval. After treatment, Barnwell returned for the second half intent on revenge and soon enough he found an opportunity to give Bremner a whack. The Leeds players and staff were furious, but Wignall and Newton shielded Barnwell from their remonstrations. The 'red mist' duly descended – first Bremner retaliated after a foul by Lyons, then he took a kick at Grummitt as the keeper lay on the ball and was sent off with a quarter of an hour remaining.

The closing stages of the game would later be described by the *Nottingham Evening Post* as 'a shambles full of bad behaviour from both sides and by the fans on the terraces too'. Leeds pressed for an equaliser, but once again McKinlay and Hennessey stood firm. Behind them, Grummitt played his part, turning a late effort from Jimmy Greenhoff over the bar to keep the score at 1-0 as Forest recorded a sixth successive win. After the game Hennessey's opinion of Leeds' physical approach was clear when he said, 'There was never an occasion when they looked like beating us at football.'

The unsavoury scenes in the last 20 minutes drew plenty of comment in the letters page of the *Football Post*. Several writers deplored the 'dirty' play of both teams, with some concerned at the risks to Forest's reputation for fair play of what was seen as a 'win at all costs' approach. However, these letters prompted replies in the following weeks defending the Reds as 'hard' rather than 'dirty' and expressing amazement that fans should complain about the winning formula the club had found.

Forest would have had high hopes of building on that hard-earned win when they visited Newcastle United, having had a four-day midwinter break in Blackpool for relaxation and training. Overnight rain had made the pitch heavy going and a strong wind also meant there was little chance of a free-flowing match. Moore was absent injured, his place taken by Hinton, who was said to be 'in no hurry to leave' despite his recent transfer request.

Hinton had a good game and Forest's threat on the counter-attack made Newcastle's Gordon Marshall the busier of the two goalkeepers. Wignall twice came close to scoring, while Baker and Lyons also missed chances, but Newcastle gained the upper hand as the second half wore on and in the end Forest seemed content to settle for the goalless draw. After the game, Newcastle's former Forest left-half Jim Iley expressed his wish that the Reds would go on to win the championship. Disappointing as the single point was, it meant Forest had equalled their record top-tier unbeaten run of 12 games. Now they turned their attention to the FA Cup.

Forest were given odds of 14/1 to win the cup after being drawn at home to Second Division Plymouth Argyle in the third round on 28 January 1967. Forest took nothing for granted, having been knocked out of the competition by lower-division teams in each of the previous four seasons. Moore was still missing for the Reds and Hennessey, Winfield and Barnwell all played despite illness or injury.

Argyle put in a spirited performance, enjoying a lot of possession and creating most of the early chances. When they took the lead just after the break Forest hardly looked like a side that was among the favourites to lift the trophy. But, urged on by the majority of the crowd of 34,000 – whose noisy backing Newton later described as 'just amazing' – the Reds took their chances when it mattered. It was Lyons who turned the tie Forest's way. First he crossed for Wignall to head the equaliser, then barely a minute later his run and low cross enabled Baker to steer home what proved to be the decisive goal.

Two days later, Forest donated 100 guineas to Southport FC, whose main stand had been destroyed by fire on Boxing Day. Its replacement would be opened in August 1968 – ironically, the very month Forest's own Main Stand would burn down.

Returning to league action, Forest's attempt to extend their unbeaten run faced a stern test with the visit of big-spending Tottenham, whose starting XI had cost £600,000 to assemble. Almost 42,000 headed for the City Ground and the police had to help pack the fans on to the crowded terraces. Moore was still missing after failing a fitness test the day before the match.

Newton was in the thick of the action, crossing for Lyons to go close with a header, shooting narrowly wide and having a header saved by Pat Jennings. Jennings also denied Baker after a long ball had sent him clear, but at the other end Grummitt was in excellent form, saving from Cliff Jones, Jimmy Greaves and, spectacularly, Jones again in rapid succession at the end of the first half. On 56 minutes Cyril Knowles prevented a certain goal by punching clear McKinlay's header and Hennessey sent Jennings the wrong way from the resultant penalty.

Forest pushed for another goal, with Lyons' pace tormenting the visiting defence, and Hinton having a good game in Moore's number 11 shirt, forcing two fine saves from Jennings. But Tottenham also created several chances, and five minutes from time, when it seemed Forest would hold on for a valuable two points, Greaves got the visitors a deserved equaliser after good work from Terry Venables.

Forest's fine run of form had not gone unnoticed. The Tottenham game was featured on *Match of the Day*, while Alan Ball used his newspaper column to sing the Reds' praises, 'I can't help feeling that this could be Forest's year for something.'

The ultimate 'four-pointer'

The draw with Spurs had left Forest in third place, two points behind leaders Liverpool and one behind Manchester United. With 14 games still to go the Reds had already equalled the previous season's tally of 36 points. Their next challenge was as tough as they came – a trip to Old Trafford on 11 February to face a United side that had only lost twice since that 4-1 thrashing on the banks of the Trent in October. The Nottingham press considered this Forest's most important league match since the Second Division promotion decider at Sheffield United a decade earlier. At a time when a win was still worth just two points, it was undoubtedly a real 'four-pointer'.

A huge following from Nottingham (estimated at almost 10,000) swelled the crowd to United's biggest of the season, 62,727, at the time the fourth-largest attendance for a Forest match in any competition. Johnny Carey had enjoyed tremendous popularity as one of the greatest players of his era during a 17-year career with United in which he played in every position, including goal. The match programme welcomed him back to Old Trafford and quoted his assessment of his current charges, 'I consider Forest to be a team in the best sense of the word, combining playing power with the kind of classical football with which the name of the club has always been associated.'

United, with Denis Law and Bobby Charlton to the fore, looked the more dangerous team in attack, but Forest gave as good as they got in an entertaining game played at a frenetic pace. Forest had welcomed Moore back from injury and he produced an energetic, strong-running performance, but the Reds were not helped when Baker had to be replaced by Hinton following a couple of bad challenges. Their best chance fell to Wignall, who was unable to make the most of an opportunity created by Lyons' run.

With both goalkeepers at the top of their game it looked as though the teams would cancel each other out and Forest would claim a well-deserved draw. However, for the second time in eight days, Forest lost a point to a goal in the final five minutes. Grummitt reacted brilliantly to turn Law's close-range shot over the bar, but from Charlton's corner Law acrobatically hooked the ball home for the winner.

Rich entertainment had been provided for the huge crowd and many thousands more savoured the coverage of the game the following day on *World of Soccer*. United's manager, Matt Busby, was clearly impressed by Forest's contribution to the spirit and quality of an absorbing match. Entering the away dressing room, he took the unprecedented step of inviting the Forest players into the boardroom after the game, saying:

> 'That was one of the best games of football I've ever seen – it was a great advert for football. We don't ever do this, but we were so pleased with the display from both sides that we'd like to invite you into the boardroom.'

Despite the defeat ending their 14-game unbeaten run, Forest had put in their best display for several weeks and, with Liverpool a point ahead of United at the top of the table, the *Nottingham Evening Post* considered the Reds 'still a real danger to the big two in the championship struggle'. Forest were in the fortunate position of having no more games to play against the teams in the top six, while that 'big two' still had to meet and Liverpool also had yet to play fourth-placed Tottenham.

	First Division table (extract), 11 February 1967							
		P	**W**	**D**	**L**	**F**	**A**	**Pts**
1	Liverpool	29	16	8	5	52	33	40
2	Manchester United	28	17	5	6	53	35	39
3	**Nottingham Forest**	**29**	**14**	**8**	**7**	**40**	**32**	**36**
4	Tottenham Hotspur	29	15	4	10	52	41	34
5	Leeds United	28	13	8	7	42	34	34
6	Leicester City	29	14	5	10	59	49	33

Just over two-thirds of the way through the season, Moore and Baker had scored 25 goals between them, apparently unaffected by the midwinter pitches and tough-tackling opponents. Importantly, they were being more than ably supported up front by a happy-again Wignall and newcomer Lyons. However, Forest's goal output was much lower than their immediate rivals'.

It was thanks to a miserly defence marshalled by the classy Hennessey and backed up by the superb Grummitt that Forest were now challenging for the title.

When asked to explain Forest's strong defensive record, captain Hennessey was quick to portray it as a team effort prompted by the defeat at Anfield, 'Our forwards do a lot of work to help out our defence. They chase back, they harass, they don't give the opposition time to play the ball around. They are a big part of the success of the defence.' Nowadays that would be called a 'high press'.

He added, 'Peter Grummitt is a great keeper, so we've got every confidence there. Bob McKinlay and myself work together as much as we can at the back. Then we've got Henry Newton who's a dynamo in midfield. So, we've got ideal players and a fairly good system.'

Tellingly, Hennessey concluded, 'Also, last season we played some good football but we weren't as hard as we are now.'

7

Up for the Double

'And the crowd have gone completely and utterly bonkers!'

Kenneth Wolstenholme,
BBC *Match of the Day* commentator

Back on track

The following Saturday, 18 February 1967, Forest had a chance to put that unlucky defeat at Old Trafford behind them by making further progress in the FA Cup with a home tie against Newcastle United. Ticket touts were active on Trent Bridge before the game, though the newly knighted Sir Alf Ramsey would have had no need of their 'services' as he took his place among the large crowd.

Newcastle's support was boosted by numerous Geordies who had moved to Nottinghamshire to work in the pits in the New Ollerton area, though the Magpies returned around 1,000 tickets from their allocation of almost 11,000. Many of these were bought by Forest supporters and the bumper crowd of almost 46,000 meant the receipts surpassed the previous month's record takings against Leeds United. Unfortunately, the tightly packed terraces led to half a dozen spectators being carried away on stretchers after being caught in the crush.

The visitors' main attacking threat, Wyn Davies, was absent with a back injury, but Forest were boosted when both Frank

Wignall and Joe Baker were declared fit to play. Early in the game Peter Grummitt made a fantastic save from a 30-yard piledriver by Bobby Moncur, tipping the shot on to the bar and out for a corner. Otherwise, Newcastle offered little up front and Terry Hennessey was able to show his more creative side, joining midfielders Henry Newton and John Barnwell in laying on chances for Barry Lyons and Moore.

In front of the watching England manager, it was Moore who laid on all three goals, twice with crosses from the left and once from the right. Ten minutes before half-time Wignall headed in his 50th goal for the club. In the second half Barnwell added a second and a close-range finish from Baker put the tie beyond the Magpies' reach. Forest should really have added to their tally, Baker proving particularly wasteful in front of goal. Yet it was Moore, despite his three assists, who was described by one national newspaper as Forest's 'most irritating forward' as he 'time and again … tried to beat half a dozen men'. In the end they had to settle for a second comfortable 3-0 home win that season against the Geordies. Jim Iley sportingly stayed on the pitch at the end to applaud his former team.

Elsewhere in the cup that day, Second Division Norwich shocked Manchester United by beating them 2-1 at Old Trafford. Unfortunately for Forest, that meant United could 'concentrate on the league'.

Forest then resumed their battle with Leicester City for East Midlands supremacy. The Foxes were just three points behind the Reds in the table and averaging more than two goals per game. The crowd of 47,188 was the City Ground's highest league attendance of the season and again brought in record receipts. It remains the biggest crowd for a match between the two teams. When the gates opened there was a rush to get a good vantage point and, in a repeat of the scenes against Newcastle, St John Ambulance volunteers had to treat about a dozen supporters.

The match was a disappointment, dominated by the respective defences. Forest had an opportunity early in a scrappy first half when Gordon Banks deliberately handled outside his area to prevent the onrushing Wignall from scoring – an offence which in those days barely merited a talking-to by the referee, let alone a sending off – but Baker cleared the bar with the resultant free kick.

In the second period the action was mainly in Leicester's half as Forest searched for a breakthrough. Moore forced Banks into a fine save with a smart shot on the turn after skilfully controlling a high ball. It looked as though Forest's winless run in the league would stretch to a fourth game, but this time they were the beneficiaries from a late goal. Six minutes from time, Barnwell's overhead pass was met by Moore, who showed a poacher's instinct in beating Banks with a stooping header and gaining his team a vital second point with the only goal of the game. With league leaders Liverpool drawing and Manchester United winning, third-placed Forest were now just three points off the top.

A trip to Blackpool is usually a popular away day for supporters keen to sample the delights of the famous resort and on 4 March a sparse Bloomfield Road crowd of 14,000 included a large contingent from Nottingham. With Blackpool rooted to the bottom of the table, the travelling fans would have been expecting a comfortable away win. But Forest were without Wignall, ruled out by a thigh strain and replaced by Sammy Chapman, and during the game Baker was affected by a leg injury. Although the Reds dominated the early stages, they were wasteful up front, with Sammy Chapman struggling to make an impact and Moore, who three days earlier had made his England under-23 debut, seemingly out of form. They faded and Blackpool took a surprise lead 15 minutes from the end. Forest's salvation came deep into injury time when Moore's shot – the last kick of the game – deflected in off a defender to earn a valuable point. This was a classic example of the importance of getting something from a game despite not playing well.

Cup marathon

A week later it was back to the FA Cup. The fifth-round draw had seemingly been kind to Forest, giving them a home tie against Swindon Town, who were languishing near the foot of the Third Division. The bookies had Forest second favourites to win the FA Cup; Swindon were at 500/1. No one had told the Robins, though. In the third round they had knocked out West Ham's team of World Cup winners before defeating second-tier Bury in the fourth round. Some 9,000 of their fans made the trip to Nottingham in the hope of witnessing another upset. Once again the crowd was almost 46,000.

Wignall was ruled out, Chapman again filling in for him, while Swindon's main threat came from their answer to Moore, goalscoring winger Don Rogers. After an edgy start the underdogs settled well, defending calmly and posing a threat on the counter-attack. Moore thought he had broken the deadlock with an angled drive from 25 yards that flew into the top corner of the net, only for the goal to be disallowed because Chapman was standing offside in the six-yard box.

In the end the teams cancelled each other out, with Forest again struggling for form and the blustery conditions proving challenging. Forest were using their new loudspeaker system for the first time – but there were no goals to announce over it. Swindon's manager, Yorkshireman Danny Williams, proudly sang the praises of his star player, 'Tha can keep thy Storey-Moore, Don's got more craft and more finish.' Forest captain Hennessey, though, was confident the Robins' chance of an upset had been and gone, 'Swindon had their chance today when we played badly. They weren't able to take it and it won't happen again.'

The replay was held three days later, on Tuesday, 14 March. The previous day's draw for the sixth round had dangled the enticing prospect for the winners of a home tie against holders Everton.

In contrast to the large Swindon following at the first match, the difficulty of taking time off work and arranging transport at

Vic & Lily: *Victor Albert Theodore and Lilian Storey-Moore, Ian's parents*

Field of dreams: *Aerial view of Lincoln Gardens estate in the 1950s with Moore's home (highlighted) backing on to the playing fields. Left: In the back garden of 107 Lincoln Gardens*

Hard as nails: *Three players who would be tremendously influential in Moore's development at Forest: Jeff Whitefoot, Bob McKinlay and Jack Burkitt, seen here in training before the 1959 FA Cup semi-final. Burkitt in particular helped Moore build up his strength and fitness by making him run up and down the terraces and lift weights*

Growing up fast: *The impact of Burkitt's training regime is evident in these photos of Moore in July 1961 (left, with David Pleat) and two years later (centre, with Sammy Chapman, left, and David Wilson, right)*

Breaking into the first team squad: *Nottingham Forest first team squad, 1964/65. Back row (left to right): Ian Storey-Moore, Geoff Vowden, Joe Wilson, Peter Grummitt, Bob McKinlay, Peter Hindley, John Winfield. Middle row: Jack Burkitt (trainer), Johnny Quigley, Colin Addison, Frank Wignall, John Barnwell, Alan Hinton, Bob Davies (physiotherapist). Front row: Jeff Whitefoot, David Pleat, Henry Newton*

City Ground favourite: *Left: Pre-season photo shoot August 1966. Right: At the City Ground during the 1966/67 season*

The 1966/67 'Nearly Men': *Back row (left to right): Henry Newton, Peter Hindley, Sammy Chapman, Peter Grummitt, Bob McKinlay, Mike Kear, Alan Hinton, Joe Baker, Tommy Cavanagh (coach). Front row: Barry Lyons, John Barnwell, Terry Hennessey, Frank Wignall, Ian Storey-Moore, John Winfield, 30 September 1966*

Head-to-head with Manchester United: *Moore shoots in the 4-1 win over Manchester United on 1 October 1966. World Cup winner Nobby Stiles tries to block the shot whilst George Best looks on. Right: Manager Johnny Carey signs autographs before the return fixture at Old Trafford*

Fan club: *Moore signs autographs for young supporters at the City Ground on the day of his England Under-23 call-up, 22 February 1967*

The injury that robbed Forest of their chance of silverware: *Tommy Cavanagh helps Joe Baker off the pitch after a bad tackle by Everton's Brian Labone in the FA Cup quarter-final that ended Baker's season. Moore (No 11) looks on*

FA Cup quarter-final, 8 April 1967, Forest v Everton, City Ground: *Storey-Moore (right) about to slot home the equaliser after goalkeeper Rankin had saved from Wignall (left)*

'Completely and utterly bonkers': *Fans at the Bridgford End celebrate the goal. The children at the front wear scarves embroidered with the names of their favourite players*

Thunderbolt: *Moore (No 11) turns away after putting Forest 2-1 up against the FA Cup holders. This goal is included in Forest's pre-match video montage*

Completing the hat-trick: *At the fourth attempt, Moore scores his hat-trick goal, heading past Rankin in the last minute to give Forest a famous 3-2 victory*

So good they named him twice: *Storey-Moore's contribution to one of the greatest games ever seen at the City Ground, drawn by cartoonist Bob Bond, who also accurately depicts Labone's foul on Baker*

short notice meant only around 2,000 Forest supporters made the journey down to Wiltshire. The replay was more exciting than the game in Nottingham and the first goal of the tie finally arrived shortly before half-time, when Hindley exchanged passes with Barry Lyons and scored from 25 yards.

With nothing to lose, Swindon, with the vociferous backing of the majority of the 28,000 crowd, were on top for most of the second half. With Forest ten seconds away from a place in the last eight, Swindon equalised after Barnwell failed to clear the ball. Extra time failed to produce a winner, so the teams would have to meet for a third time. After the game the two teams shared the champagne Swindon had ordered in anticipation – or at least hope – of having a win to celebrate.

Back in the league, the value of Forest's tight defence was clear to see. Their next opponents, mid-table West Ham, were the division's top scorers, having so far notched up 70 goals in their 30 games. By contrast, Forest had only scored 42 and it was more than two months since they had managed more than a single goal in a league game, highlighting the lack of strength in depth when attacking players were injured. The fact that Forest went into the match in third place was testament to the huge contribution made by their settled back five of Grummitt, Hindley, Winfield, Hennessey and McKinlay.

In the event the Reds' attack dominated, with Baker on the end of most of the game's best chances. His header from Wignall's pass brought the save of the match out of Jim Standen and he finally found the net ten minutes from the end with a shot that deflected over the Londoners' keeper. 'A freak goal' claimed the headline in the *Sunday Mirror*, but the 1-0 win was the least Forest deserved.

With ten games to play, Forest remained in third position, two points behind champions Liverpool and four points behind leaders Manchester United.

On Monday, 20 March, just two days after the West Ham game, Forest had to attend to unfinished FA Cup business with

Swindon, this time at neutral Villa Park. With Forest now at the relatively short odds of 7/1 to triumph at Wembley in May, cup fever was gripping Nottingham and many thousands of fans set out for Birmingham. Some collieries rearranged their shifts, numerous firms let their staff finish early, and most of the bigger companies organised coach trips. Some 200 coaches left the city and many more fans made their own way by road or rail. Swindon were similarly well supported and there was considerable interest in the match from fans in Birmingham itself.

Instead of the expected attendance of around 35,000, the tie was watched by a crowd of 52,000, at least 20,000 of whom were Forest supporters.

Inevitably, the extra traffic caused long tailbacks on the A453 and delays at the turnstiles, with many Reds fans not being admitted until at least half-time. Similar problems affected the Swindon fans on the approach to Birmingham from Stratford-upon-Avon. Villa officials estimated that some 10,000 supporters remained outside, with many more (including more than 30 of those Forest coaches) being turned back before they had even reached the ground. The chaotic scenes would be debated for weeks afterwards, with many pointing the finger at poor organisation on Villa's part but, to be fair, Forest and Swindon had agreed not to make the match all-ticket, seemingly against the advice of their hosts.

As for the game itself, Forest pressed hard, especially in a relentless first 20 minutes, but Swindon again defended with spirit and determination and the first half finished goalless. The Robins were more adventurous after the interval and Forest's disjointed performance again belied the gap of two divisions between the teams.

It was only in the last half an hour that Forest really made their class tell. Shortly after McKinlay had cleared off the line, the deadlock was finally broken. Moore's shot was blocked on the line and when the ball was eventually cleared it was won back by Winfield, whose raking diagonal cross caught the Swindon defence out of position, allowing Lyons to hit a cross-shot into the roof of the net. Swindon fought back, but ten minutes later Wignall's back-header put Baker through to fire home and make the tie safe. For the remainder of the game Swindon could only try to keep the score down. With six minutes left Moore's shot glanced off the bar, and the third goal finally came in injury time with Barnwell finishing emphatically from the edge of the area.

Five wins in 11 days

The protracted FA Cup tie had already congested Forest's fixture list but the following weekend's busy Easter programme required them to play three games in four days. It was becoming an expensive season for the Reds' travelling fans, but the following Saturday yet another huge following of around 8,000 made the short trip to Hillsborough. Their loyalty was rewarded when Forest finally managed to score twice in a league game again.

Midway through the first half Newton set up Moore to score from the edge of the penalty area. A similarly composed finish from Wignall doubled the lead just before half-time. Wednesday's attempts to get back into the game after the break were frustrated by Grummitt's consistency and their own poor finishing. Overall, though, Forest controlled the match, were worth the 2-0 win and, especially in the first half, looked sharper than of late.

With Liverpool and Manchester United drawing 0-0, the victory moved Forest to within three points of leaders United.

At Hillsborough Wignall had been injured and he would miss the next three games, starting with the home leg of a double-header against Burnley. Newton had also been injured, bringing to an end a run of 152 consecutive league appearances.

In a team nominally containing four wingers, Moore and Lyons lined up on either side of Baker, with the restored Mike Kear and Alan Hinton outside them on the wings. In front of another 40,000-plus crowd on Trentside, Kear made the most of what was now for him a rare first-team opportunity, assisted by Baker in opening the scoring in the first minute and adding a second five minutes before the interval after Baker had got on the end of Moore's cross.

Baker himself took centre stage in the second half. First he received a pass out of defence from McKinlay and burst through the middle to make the score 3-0. He then doubled his tally with a memorable goal. From Hinton's cross, Baker acrobatically sent a perfect overhead kick into the roof of the net. The goal is still talked about to this day by those who witnessed it, including Moore:

> 'Joe's goal against Burnley was a great goal. He had the gift, that I like to see in a striker, of being able to make something out of nothing. It makes me laugh when nowadays a team pays a lot of money for a striker and people say that no one's creating any chances for him. Well, go and create one for yourself!'

Although Burnley pulled a goal back, the final 4-1 scoreline matched Forest's biggest win of the season, the demolition of Manchester United.

With United drawing at Fulham and Liverpool being held to a goalless draw by Arsenal at Anfield, Forest were now just two points off the top with eight games still to play. They had now racked up 18 wins, setting their new record tally in the top tier. The *Nottingham Evening Post* felt they had shown 'the spirit and flair of which champions are made'. While their rise up the league had regularly demonstrated those qualities, Forest's progress owed as much to dogged resilience and determination. They were certainly forced to call upon these attributes when the same 11 players took to the field at Turf Moor in the return game the very next day.

In contrast to Forest's free-flowing football in the first match, this was a tough and rather niggly affair, epitomised when

McKinlay felt the full force of a Burnley boot in his face. Referee Pat Partridge at first allowed play to continue before letting McKinlay be treated and checked for concussion and shock. He was eventually substituted and spent the night in hospital in Burnley.

The Reds took the lead halfway through the first half, Baker powering a header home from Hinton's corner. Without their most experienced defender, Forest dug in to maintain their grip on the game, with Moore and Lyons helping out the defence when required. Six minutes from time Baker made the result safe with his fourth goal in two days.

Including the second replay against Swindon, Forest had now played – and won – five times in 11 days, despite suffering what was becoming a worrying number of injuries. With Liverpool drawing at Highbury, the Reds moved above them into second place, two points behind Manchester United. If not for a last-minute goal from veteran defender Bill Foulkes – a man who would feature prominently later in Moore's career – which gave United a 2-1 win over Fulham, the gap would have been a solitary point.

Despite his bloodied nose, McKinlay was fit to take his usual place four days later for the visit of Southampton, for whom Terry Paine was making his 500th appearance. Kear gave Forest the lead, neatly heading a Barnwell free kick just inside the post for his third goal in two successive home games. After some rough treatment of Moore and Baker, much of which went unpunished, the latter limped off to be replaced by Bill Brindley with half an hour to go. Brindley duly doubled the Reds' lead with the only goal of his Forest career, cleverly converting Winfield's cross with his first touch of the ball.

A few minutes later Kear was fouled inside the box but Hennessey's penalty was easily saved. Shortly afterwards, however, Forest were awarded a second spot kick. Hennessey stood to one side and Moore stepped up to convert. After the game the skipper acknowledged that this indeed marked the end of his career as a penalty taker. Despite a late consolation goal for the Saints, the final score was a comfortable 3-1 win for the Reds.

Everton manager Harry Catterick was a spectator at the match ahead of the teams' FA Cup quarter-final the following weekend, but he was unlikely to have learned much, as a below-strength and under-par Forest were not really tested by relegation-threatened Southampton.

Knocking out the cup holders

While Forest had taken three attempts to beat Third Division Swindon, Everton had secured their place in the sixth round by beating Merseyside neighbours Liverpool at the first time of asking in front of almost 65,000 at Goodison Park.

The quarter-final was played on Saturday, 8 April. Many among the capacity crowd of 47,500 at the City Ground had queued overnight to secure their tickets, with excitement at fever pitch as Forest mounted a genuine challenge for the First Division and FA Cup Double. With Everton selling out their allocation of 11,500, there was a huge demand for tickets, even at increased prices of up to 6s to stand and up to 15s for seats. The rises were somewhat controversial, with Forest officials having to defend them in the face of accusations of profiteering. As usual, tickets got into the hands of touts, with seats changing hands for as much as £5. The packed ground included Sir Alf Ramsey, once again, FIFA president Sir Stanley Rous, Moore's parents and his fiancée, Carol, who had thrown a 'sickie' from her job as a manageress at the GEM supermarket on Loughborough Road.

Goalkeeper Gordon West was out with a broken bone in his hand, replaced by Andy Rankin, but otherwise Everton were at full strength. Forest welcomed back Newton and Wignall, who had both missed the previous three matches. To protect a broken toe, Newton wore an oversized boot he had borrowed from apprentice Steve Pegram.

With the game only two minutes old Baker was badly injured when he was caught by a flying challenge from Brian Labone. Most observers believed this was a premeditated 'reducer' designed to restrict the lively forward's influence on the game. Moore recollects the incident:

> 'Whether it was intentional or not, I don't know. Certainly it was a reckless tackle. The next day Joe's leg was jet black all the way from his hip to his toes. His injury was a massive loss to us.'

Soon afterwards, Hennessey also received a kick on the leg, which troubled him for the rest of the match. Baker gamely tried to play on but his thigh injury left him no more than a 'passenger'. With Forest unsettled by Baker's injury and his immobility giving them fewer options when breaking out of defence, Everton took a grip on the game in the early stages. Just after the half-hour mark Forest finally brought Hinton on to replace Baker, who would play no further part in Forest's quest for honours, though nobody knew his season was over at the time. The versatile Moore took up Baker's central role, with Hinton playing in his customary place on the left wing.

On 36 minutes Everton took advantage of Forest's regrouping to take the lead, Alan Ball sending Jimmy Husband through to fire past Grummitt. Remarkably, this was the first goal Forest had conceded before half-time in four months.

At the break the news filtered through to the crowd of the shock result in that afternoon's Grand National, which was won by 100/1 rank outsider Foinavon. They hoped Forest would be able to achieve an equally sensational result in the 45 minutes ahead.

Indeed, as eventful as the first half had been, it was only a taste of what was to come in the second, with the tension ratcheting up as the action swung from end to end. Husband almost extended Everton's lead, his point-blank header forcing a tremendous reaction save from Grummitt. At the other end Forest pressed hard for the equaliser and it came after 66 minutes when Wignall shot from just outside the box and Rankin fumbled the ball into the path of Moore, who slotted home from eight yards. Galvanised by the goal, Forest came forward again and Rankin had to be alert when Hinton fired in a powerful cross-shot from the left. The Everton keeper tried to start a counter-attack but his hurried throw was intercepted by Barnwell, who sent it back into the danger area. Rankin lost the ball under pressure from Wignall and Moore tucked it home, but Wignall was rightly penalised for a foul on the relieved Rankin.

The momentum was with Forest now and they soon went in front for the first time. Again it was Wignall who set up Moore to shoot left-footed across Rankin from the edge of the area. BBC TV commentator Kenneth Wolstenholme was by now predicting that Moore would no doubt be 'crowned Sheriff of Nottingham tomorrow, I should think!' But Moore hadn't finished his work for the day.

Nor had Everton, though, and with ten minutes left Ball spread a pass wide to Sandy Brown. He flicked the ball past Hennessey, who had committed himself to a challenge, and played it across for Husband to steer in his second goal of the game. Neither team was settling for the draw and they slugged it out like weary heavyweights at the end of a big fight. McKinlay's bullet header from a Lyons corner beat Rankin but was headed off the line by Colin Harvey, then Ball fed Johnny Morrissey, who could scarcely believe it when he saw Grummitt acrobatically tip over his thunderous drive from the edge of the area. With two minutes left, Morrissey's corner was headed on and John Hurst nodded the ball into the side-netting.

With time running out and a replay looking inevitable, this incredible game had one final dramatic twist. Winfield fired in a typical diagonal cross from just inside the Everton half and Wignall once again was first to the ball. He nodded it sideways to Moore, whose volley was blocked by Hurst. Reacting first, Moore shot again and this time the ball hit Rankin's legs and bounced back to him six yards out. As the keeper got to his feet Moore headed the ball past him, only this time – unbelievably – it came back off the crossbar. Finally, at the fourth attempt, Moore nodded it over the goal line from two yards.

Wolstenholme's commentary breathlessly tried to keep up with the drama of those few seconds, 'He's … No, he's not … Yes! He has!' To 1960s Forest supporters, at least, those words will have been almost as memorable as his more famous 'They think it's all over … It is now!' from the previous summer. Wolstenholme then summed up the scene neatly when he observed, 'The crowd have gone completely and utterly bonkers!' The atmosphere had been red-hot throughout, but that goal and the final whistle a matter of seconds later were greeted by an eruption of noise and excitement. Fans spilled on to the pitch as the players tried to leave it, those in red as elated as those in blue were deflated. Despite the early loss of the talismanic Baker, Forest had knocked the holders out of the cup after the most amazing of matches, one which would never be forgotten by those who witnessed it and which would become a familiar part of the club's folklore for those who didn't.

An incredible game was best summed up by the *Sunday Mirror*'s Ken Montgomery, 'Ian Storey-Moore, the Forest left-winger with the build of a boxer and raw courage to match, made himself the hat-trick hero of this colossal FA Cup quarter-final. But I say: Strike 23 medals and hand them to every man who made this the most titanic soccer tug-o'-war of this or any season. It reduced even the greatest of Hitchcock thrillers to fairy-tale tameness. This should have been the cup final.'

Moore's hat-trick clincher was one that is still often referred to as 'that goal', though he was to score another equally memorable goal in very different circumstances a few years later. His memories of the game include the atmosphere – 'electric, absolutely incredible' – and the fact that his mother Lily found the tension was too much for her, fainted and had to be helped from her seat in the stand.

That evening, while Sandie Shaw was winning the Eurovision Song Contest with 'Puppet on a String', the Forest players celebrated at the Parkside Club. This combined the decor of a Victorian brothel and a Mayfair gentlemen's club and offered wining, dining and gambling until 2am. Moore admits to having 'a few more drinks than usual' over the course of the evening.

Understandably, Moore has been asked about the first hat-trick of his professional career on countless occasions over the years and his answers consistently make the same point, namely that Wignall should be considered the real hero. This was arguably the former Evertonian's best game in a Forest shirt – and he didn't even score.

As Moore recalls:

> 'I got the goals and the accolades, but certainly in my opinion Frank Wignall was man of the match. He caused them havoc in the second half. Frank won all the headers and I fed off him and got all the scraps. He was immense that day, especially after Joe went off.'

As a final postscript to this most memorable of matches, in a survey of Reds supporters' all-time favourite games in connection with the publication in 1998 of *The Official History of Nottingham Forest*, this tie received more votes than any other in the club's long history. Despite the passing of over three decades and the unimaginable successes Forest enjoyed during the Clough and Taylor era, this was the match that made the biggest impression on the supporters.

Closing the gap

After the euphoria of the cup, a short trip to Skegness for training and golf beckoned, then it was back to the league and the visit of Aston Villa to the City Ground. With Baker's season ended by

Labone's challenge, Moore remained in the centre of the attack, and Hinton was on the left wing. Lyons gave Forest an early lead with a superb individual goal, beating four defenders before scoring in front of a delighted Trent End.

But Forest lost their way after a bright first half an hour and relegation-threatened Villa fought hard and had much of the play. When Forest made the points safe it was against the run of play. Wignall headed beyond Villa's goalkeeper, leaving Moore to tap the ball into an empty net. The same combination struck again near the end to make it 3-0; Kear crossed and Wignall again won the ball in the air, heading down for Moore to finish. Moore had scored five times in two games – all of them set up by the selfless Wignall – bringing his tally to an impressive 20 goals in 34 league appearances.

Despite being somewhat out of form, for a second time Forest had put together a run of six successive league wins. In so doing they had moved clear of Liverpool and reduced Manchester United's lead to just one point with five matches left to play.

	First Division table (extract), 15 April 1967							
		P	**W**	**D**	**L**	**F**	**A**	**Pts**
1	Manchester United	37	21	10	6	72	43	52
2	**Nottingham Forest**	**37**	**21**	**9**	**7**	**57**	**35**	**51**
3	Liverpool	37	18	12	7	61	41	48
4	Tottenham Hotspur	37	20	7	10	65	48	47
5	Leeds United	36	18	10	8	53	37	46

With an FA Cup semi-final against Tottenham Hotspur to come, Forest were very much 'up for the Double'.

8

The 'Nearly Men'

'We're better than United and we're louder than the Kop. We're second in the league and we should be at the top!'

Forest fans' chant

League form slips

The downside of Forest maintaining their challenge for two trophies was that their matches were coming thick and fast, while Manchester United's schedule was less busy, having been knocked out of the FA Cup back in February. Injuries were starting to have an effect on Forest's small squad at this crucial stage of the season, with Joe Baker already sidelined for the rest of the campaign and plenty of 'wear and tear' affecting other players.

Forest next visited Sunderland, Moore's boyhood favourites. The Rokermen had a lot to play for – they were only three points clear of the relegation zone – so Forest knew they would be in for a tough match. Barnwell failed a fitness test, with Lyons taking his number eight shirt and Kear returning on the right wing.

In what was to prove a frustrating game for Kear and a bitterly disappointing one for Forest, Sunderland took an early lead through future Red John O'Hare. Forest failed to take advantage of the strong wind behind them in the first half, though they rallied after the break, with Moore, Lyons and Kear a constant threat.

The unfortunate Kear saw a shot cleared off the line and was later brought down by keeper Montgomery for what the *Nottingham Evening Post* described as 'the clearest penalty of their season', but the referee was unmoved. After the match, Moore told the *Post*, 'I was positive it was a penalty. I was stepping up to get ready for the kick when I saw the referee had not given it.' Kear's wretched day was complete when he limped off with a thigh injury, Chapman yet again the substitute. Despite more Forest pressure there was no further scoring.

Manchester United had beaten Southampton 3-0 the previous day and their lead was now three points with games running out for the chasing Reds. O'Hare's goal had all but put Forest's best chance of silverware since the 1959 FA Cup win out of reach. Just over a decade later he would, of course, make amends by earning the penalty from which John Robertson scored to win the League Cup against Liverpool.

If Forest were to stay in the hunt for the title they would have to improve on their poor record at Highbury, where they had only won once in nine games since the war. Missing Baker's pace and skill, Forest struggled to impose themselves and their task was made harder when Arsenal took a deserved lead just before half-time.

Just after the break Newton saw his lob beat the keeper but bounce off the top of the bar, but shortly afterwards Forest equalised. Moore had been kept quiet until then but produced a moment of quality, turning sharply to put a half-chance away from a narrow angle after Forest had built from the back in a neat move involving full-backs Winfield and Hindley. The goal saw Moore draw level with Tommy Wilson as Forest's leading First Division scorer in the postwar years. Forest were now having much the better of the play but were unable to add to Moore's goal. The defence was as solid as ever, however, and the game finished in a 1-1 draw. With Forest's chances of clinching the league title more or less gone, the lacklustre first-half performance suggested some players' minds might already have been on the following week's FA Cup action.

Semi-final heartbreak

On Saturday, 29 April Forest made the short journey to Hillsborough, the scene of their semi-final victory over Aston Villa eight years previously. Just as for the Everton tie, cup fever was again very much in evidence as the club's allocation of just 17,000 tickets went on sale the Sunday before the game. Some 25,000 hopeful fans queued, many of them overnight, and as the numbers grew some people were injured in the crush. Others fainted and there were unpleasant skirmishes. The police had to step in to restore order and the start of ticket sales was brought forward to 7.30am, prompting the surreal scene of police officers going round the city waking up ticket office staff so they could make an earlier start. Thousands of fans ended up queueing for hours in vain as the tickets sold out by 10am. Despite the supposedly strict limit of one ticket per applicant, some youths were brazenly showing off multiple tickets and touts were soon openly asking £3 or more for 6s terrace tickets.

Come matchday, traffic was nose to tail as the Forest supporters headed north to Sheffield. Those going by car were joined by dozens of coaches, while British Rail laid on five 'football special' trains to take some 3,000 fans from Nottingham Midland to Wadsley Bridge. Between the club's allocation and tickets acquired from other sources, it was estimated that 20,000 Reds fans took their places in the 55,000 crowd. Outside Hillsborough, touts were once again active, charging up to eight times face value.

Forest would be wearing for the first time their new, supposedly unshrinkable 'Aztec' shirts, which had been presented to the club by local sports outfitters Redmayne and Todd. The majority of their support was on the large Kop terrace, while the players had been allocated the home dressing room, considered by some to be a lucky omen.

In the weeks since Baker's injury against Everton, there had been intermittent suggestions that he might recover in time to play in the semi-final and the team line-ups in the programme included him. There was a certain lightness of touch in the pen portraits, which referred to Bob McKinlay as 'getting on a little' and Moore as 'a quiet and unassuming lad, but obviously one with a great future'.

Baker wasn't remotely fit to play so Forest fielded the same 11 players who had finished the Everton game, with the 'unassuming lad' again taking his place in the centre and Hinton on the left wing. Tottenham were more fortunate, fielding a full-strength line-up, with Jimmy Greaves returning after missing two games with an ankle injury. Ominously for Forest, that starting XI had beaten Birmingham City 6-0 in the replay of their sixth-round tie.

Forest's cause was not helped by an early injury to Frank Wignall after a challenge from Dave Mackay, the forward gamely playing on with one arm clutched across his chest. Even so they dominated the early exchanges and for half an hour looked much the likelier scorers. A cross from Lyons caused panic in the Tottenham defence until Mackay headed the ball out for a corner, then Wignall had a header blocked on the line. Tottenham were limited to isolated attacks on the break as Forest continued to press. Mackay almost scored an own goal in trying to keep out Hennessey's shot, then Moore headed just wide.

Against the run of play, Tottenham took an undeserved lead. Greaves continued his great scoring record against Forest, firing a half-volley in off the post from just outside the box after McKinlay and Alan Gilzean had challenged for a long ball. Moore remembers it vividly, 'We were all over them for the first half hour. Jimmy Greaves never had a kick and then the next thing you see is his arm in the air and he's scored.'

Greaves's precise strike left observers wondering whether it was 'flukey or fantastic' in the words of the *Sunday Mirror*. Greaves himself would later tell his biographer, Norman Giller, that it was a purely instinctive shot from a much longer range than he was used to:

> 'We had been second best for much of the match against an excellent Forest team and my shot out of the blue broke their hearts and made me very popular with my team-mates and our fans. I don't think I scored many more satisfying goals in my whole career. But I can't in all honesty claim that I planned it. In fact, I can recall apologising to that fine goalkeeper Peter Grummitt for a shot that could have been classed as desperate.'

For half an hour Forest had been comfortably the better and more composed team, but the Londoners grew in confidence after the goal and the second half was more even. Grummitt made a double save from Frank Saul and Gilzean, then Greaves and Gilzean both failed to convert Alan Mullery's cross. Forest kept trying to force an equaliser but, with Moore having a relatively quiet game due to the effective attentions of England midfielder Mullery, they relied too much on high balls that Spurs coped with easily enough.

Eventually a rare mistake from the otherwise flawless Hennessey allowed Saul to burst through the inside-left position to fire the decisive second goal high past Grummitt. Saul would later clash aggressively with Hennessey and was the fortunate beneficiary of referee Frank Cowen's leniency after aiming a kick at the Forest skipper.

The remainder of the game saw Forest pour forward incessantly with Tottenham countering at every opportunity. The Reds finally got back into the game with seven minutes left when Hennessey's powerful header from a Lyons corner hit the underside of the bar and was judged to have crossed the line. England then cleared off the line from Lyons, but for all their pressure Forest were unable to find the equaliser and were defeated for the seventh time in nine FA Cup semi-finals. Some of the defeated Forest players left the field in tears, but they could be proud of their efforts. Their injury-hit team had more than matched Tottenham over the 90 minutes and the *Daily Telegraph*'s correspondent felt they had 'produced football worthy of an appearance at Wembley'.

The same Tottenham line-up would go on to lift the cup, beating Chelsea 2-1 in the Wembley showpiece. While Forest's FA Cup run was ending, Manchester United were rubbing salt into their wounds by beating Aston Villa 3-1 at Old Trafford. United's superior goal average meant that to win the league title Forest would need to win their last three games and rely on United losing their last two. In effect, Forest's brave, unexpected challenge for the Double had been definitively defeated on both fronts on the same day.

McKinlay, the sole survivor from the 1959 FA Cup-winning team, said the semi-final defeat was 'the greatest disappointment of my life'. At the club's 'celebration' dinner, which had been arranged at a Sheffield hotel regardless of the result, his chairman, manager and captain were in more bullish mood. Tony Wood was sure that 'we shall go back again next year and go one better', Johnny Carey agreed that the club's day would come, while Hennessey professed himself to be 'proud to be captain of a great bunch of lads'.

Championship beyond reach

Forest had little time to lick their wounds; the following Tuesday they had to take on Manchester City at the City Ground. The match was McKinlay's 600th appearance for the club and some of the stalwart defender's characteristics were apparent in the tribute paid in the match programme to the team's efforts over the course of the season, 'Our reputation for playing good clean attractive match-winning football without resorting to doubtful tactics or to dull defensive play is without peer.'

The 33,000 crowd took Forest's aggregate home league attendance for the season to almost 657,000, just beating the previous highest total set in 1957/58. They were celebrating shortly before the break when Moore crossed for Lyons to score. Lyons later doubled his tally, volleying home after a free kick while the City defenders appealed in vain for offside. With the home crowd in full voice with their chant of 'Give it to Moore', their idol would have added to his 24-goal haul but for two great saves by City's keeper, Harry Dowd.

The later stages of Forest's 2-0 win were an unedifying spectacle. The booking of a City player for a foul on Kear prompted an angry young fan to come on to the field and assault referee Don Payne. The 14-year-old was apprehended by Hennessey and later fined £20 and ordered to apologise to both Payne and Hennessey. As City allowed their frustration to get the better of them, half-back Mike Doyle was dismissed three minutes from time for a bad foul on Lyons. Their assistant manager, Malcolm Allison, had to be restrained by the police from going on to the pitch as City players angrily surrounded the referee. A more conciliatory note was struck by the generous praise for Forest after the game from City manager Joe Mercer, whose father – also Joe – had served with distinction in the middle of the Reds' back line for five years from 1910.

Forest were now three points adrift with two games to play and their slender chance of catching Manchester United was hanging by a thread when they visited The Dell. Like Sunderland a few weeks earlier, Southampton were desperate to win the game, being just one point clear of Aston Villa, who occupied the second relegation spot.

Injury misfortune struck Forest once again, Newton taking a heavy knock on his ankle and having to be replaced by Bill Brindley. Future Tottenham star Martin Chivers gave Southampton the lead, but Forest equalised when Moore's cross led to a scramble and Barnwell scored from the edge of the box.

The result hinged on two controversial refereeing decisions. First, a blatant handball in the home team's penalty area by a Southampton defender was ignored, then at the other end a penalty was surprisingly awarded against Hennessey when Jimmy Melia simply lost his footing. Melia was seen to laugh at the decision and Terry Paine won the game for Southampton, side-footing the spot kick beyond Grummitt's dive. Despite the refereeing, Forest had lacked inspiration up front and the home side had been the more dangerous.

The 2-1 defeat ensured that Southampton would remain in the top flight and it was the first occasion Forest had conceded twice in a league game since the 4-0 thumping at Liverpool in November. Going six months without conceding more than once was quite a feat in a relatively high-scoring era. This highlights the immense contribution to Forest's success of what proved to be the meanest defence in the division, with no team conceding fewer than their tally of 41 over the season.

While the Reds were losing at The Dell, Manchester United were taking full advantage, winning 6-1 at West Ham to clinch the title. The popular yardstick for success in a league is to win at home and draw away and, remarkably, until that emphatic win at Upton Park, United's results had not deviated at all from that pattern in their 16 matches since the turn of the year. Forest's consolation was that the lowest they could now finish was fourth, meaning they would match or better their previous highest league finish and a place in the following season's Inter-Cities Fairs Cup was all but guaranteed.

Even though their hopes of winning the Double had been dashed and their recent away form had seen them gain a single point from three games, there was still plenty to play for when Forest closed the season with a visit to Fulham. They were looking to finish with a win to see off the challenges of Tottenham and Leeds and hold on to second place. The importance of this to the club was evident in the selection of Hindley, Wignall and Moore, all of whom were carrying injuries.

In Baker's absence, Chapman was finally getting a few starts and he gave Forest the lead after eight minutes with a header from

Lyons' cross. Allan Clarke soon equalised, but before half an hour had been played Forest were back in front through Barnwell.

Fulham pressed strongly for a second equaliser, with Grummitt kept busy and, when he was beaten, Hindley cleared off the line. After the Cottagers finally drew level Forest came back into the game and the Lyons–Chapman combination worked again for what proved to be the winning goal, the young forward's header from Lyons' free kick leaving the keeper flat-footed.

That 3-2 win ensured Forest would indeed finish in a club-high of second place. They were fractionally ahead of Tottenham on goal average, though the teams' positions would have been reversed if goal difference, which was introduced in 1975/76, had been used. Both Forest and Tottenham had scored 23 more goals than they had conceded, but Spurs would have prevailed on goals scored (71 to 64).

	First Division table (extract), final positions							
		P	W	D	L	F	A	Pts
1	Manchester United	42	24	12	6	84	45	60
2	**Nottingham Forest**	**42**	**23**	**10**	**9**	**64**	**41**	**56**
3	Tottenham Hotspur	42	24	8	10	71	48	56
4	Leeds United	42	22	11	9	62	42	55
5	Liverpool	42	19	13	10	64	47	51

The defeat to a late goal in that February 'four-pointer' at Old Trafford ultimately proved decisive, as Manchester United finished four points clear. A win in that game and perhaps a point or two more from their indifferent start to the season might have been the difference between the championship and second place for Forest. In truth, though, such was United's form in the second half of the season that it would have taken something really special for a small and increasingly injury-prone squad to overhaul them. United were, in the end, worthy winners, and a measure of Forest's achievement in chasing them so hard for the title is that the bulk of the United side went on to become the first English team to win the European Cup the following season.

Although disappointed at having narrowly lost out in the league and the cup, the overwhelming feeling among Moore and his team-mates was one of great satisfaction at having had such a tremendous season.

Summing up Forest's campaign, the *Nottingham Evening Post* wrote, 'Their prestige has never been higher and they have made this city soccer-conscious as never before.' That second-placed finish would remain Forest's highest until the incredible championship season of 1977/78 under the management of Brian Clough and Peter Taylor.

After 51 competitive games, the players might have been ready for a well-earned rest, but Moore and his team-mates embarked on a post-season trip to Spain for friendly matches against Barcelona (a 2-1 win in front of a crowd of 45,000) and Valencia (a single-goal defeat to their friends from the Fairs Cup encounter five years previously). As they reflected on a long, gruelling, but unexpectedly successful season, Forest could look forward to further European adventures in the months to come.

For his own part, Moore could take pride in a season in which he had well and truly made the 'big time', scoring 21 goals in 39 league appearances, mercifully missing just three games through injury. He had made national headlines with his match-winning goals and FA Cup exploits and performed brilliantly in front of the watching Sir Alf Ramsey, thus earning an international call-up.

9

Sir Alf comes calling

'Ramsey's coming to the game tomorrow.'

Manager Johnny Carey gives his
Forest team the 'heads up'

Stars of the Sixties

Fans of provincial football clubs, Nottingham Forest included, have always suspected their star players would have earned more international caps had they been playing for so-called 'bigger, more fashionable' clubs. Just consider FA Cup-winning centre-half Bob McKinlay: over 600 appearances for Forest – including that incredible run of 265 consecutive games between 1959 and 1965 – yet never selected to play for Scotland. Not even once.

Of course, for every rule there is an exception and in the 1960s that came in the form of McKinlay's fellow centre-back, the cultured Terry Hennessey, who won 39 caps for Wales while playing for Birmingham City, Forest and later Derby County.

As for England, it would be difficult to argue with a setup that won the World Cup. Nonetheless, many of Forest's great players of the decade flirted with having England careers without ever quite establishing themselves. In fact, pretty much Forest's entire forward line, Ian Storey-Moore aside, had played for England at some point in the years leading up to the World Cup triumph but none would make the 1966 squad.

First and foremost, though rather bizarrely, was Joe Baker, someone who could hardly have been more Scottish. Baker was born in Liverpool in 1940. With the city a prime target for German bombing raids, his family moved to the relative safety of Motherwell when he was just six weeks old.

Baker's birthplace meant he could only play for England, somewhat to his distaste, 'It was a hard thing to take because I was a Scot as far as I was concerned.' His England debut against Northern Ireland in November 1959 had been notable for three reasons. He replaced a certain Brian Clough in the starting line-up, as a Hibernian man he became the first player to be capped by England without having played in the English Football League, and, naturally, he scored in a 2-1 win. Four more caps for the 19-year-old followed in 1960. In November that year he also played in a Young England versus Young Italy match. The 1-1 draw was enlivened somewhat when Baker shoulder-charged the Italian goalkeeper into the net; the Belgian referee allowed the goal and was immediately surrounded by the entire Italian team. 'Baker scores and starts a riot' read one newspaper headline the following day.

Before joining Forest, forward Chris Crowe had made his England under-23 debut in November 1959 against France; both he and Joe Baker scored in a 2-0 win. Three more under-23 appearances in 1960 and 1961 were followed by a solitary full international cap – a 1-1 draw, again against France – in October 1962.

Making his debut for England alongside Crowe was Wolverhampton Wanderers winger Alan Hinton. His first international game following his transfer to Forest saw his left-wing cross deflected in by a defender for England's second equaliser in a 2-2 draw with Belgium in October 1964.

In the same month Frank Wignall played for an English Football League representative team in a 4-0 win over the Irish Football League. Although not a full international side as such, the Football League team was considered to be a 'shadow' England side and was managed by the England manager, Alf Ramsey. Wignall scored a hat-trick but, incredibly, Fleet Street gave him mixed reviews, such as the *Daily Mirror*'s headline, 'Wignall hammers a hat-trick – but he fails to shine as an England leader'. Fortunately, Ramsey was somewhat more impressed and three weeks later gave Wignall his first full cap.

The British Home Championship match against Wales in November 1964 saw Wignall make his England debut. Hinton, on his third and last international appearance, set up two headed goals for his Forest team-mate in a 2-1 win. Quite possibly this is the only England match in which Forest players have scored all the goals and made all the assists.

The following month, Wignall won his second cap in a friendly at the Olympic Stadium in Amsterdam to celebrate the 75th anniversary of the Dutch FA. It was not a happy occasion. The *Mirror*'s Frank McGhee was scathing about England's performance in the 1-1 draw, 'When a nation as small as Holland can come so close to victory against the highly paid, supposedly world-class stars of England, it is bad enough. When they do it with a team of part-timers who finished fitter, fresher and faster, it is worse.'

Unlucky break for Wignall

Heading into 1965, Wignall had realistic expectations of making England's World Cup squad the following year. However, his hopes were cruelly shattered by those repeated broken legs in the run-up to 1966 And All That.

The first occasion came in, of all things, the end-of-season Nottinghamshire FA County Cup Final against Mansfield Town in May 1965. Then, having recovered in time for the start of the 1965/66 season and scored five goals in 13 league games, Wignall broke his leg at Anfield at the end of October. The final straw came in January 1966, at the City Ground against Newcastle, when he picked up what was initially thought to be nothing more than an ankle injury. But when an X-ray subsequently revealed he had fractured his leg in the same place as against Liverpool, that was the end of his season and of his dream of leading the attack for England at Wembley that glorious summer.

Alf Ramsey had to start looking at options other than Wignall to partner the prolific Jimmy Greaves, eventually settling on Geoff Hurst. To be fair to Hurst, when they met up many years later the World Cup Final hat-trick hero was magnanimous in telling Wignall, 'If you'd been playing instead of me, we'd still have won.'

After Wignall's injury against Liverpool, Sir Alf's search for a striker had initially led to Joe Baker, then an Arsenal player, earning a recall to the England side after a five-year absence. In November 1965 he scored in a 2-1 win against Northern Ireland and again in a 2-0 triumph over Spain the following month. As a reminder of Baker's heritage north of the border, one match report for the game in the Santiago Bernabéu Stadium in Madrid stated that Baker spoke with such a strong Scottish accent that many of his England team-mates could not understand what he was saying.

What turned out to be Baker's last cap was in a 1-1 draw against Poland in January 1966. In February he signed for Forest and in April he was included in Ramsey's provisional list of 40 for the World Cup. To his tremendous disappointment, he didn't make the cut for the 28 who were asked to report for pre-tournament training at Lilleshall and from which the final, immortal 22 were selected.

Despite his fine form in a Forest shirt over the next couple of seasons producing chants of 'Joe, Joe, Mexico', there was to be no Third Coming on the England scene for a striker forever worshipped in Nottingham as 'The King'.

Of other Forest players of the 1960s, Dick 'Flip' Le Flem earned one under-23 cap in November 1961 in a 5-2 win against the Netherlands in Rotterdam. Playing alongside Le Flem against the Dutch was the superb shot-stopper Peter Grummitt. Despite his outstanding form for Forest throughout the decade, Grummitt was never able to convert his three under-23 caps (the other two coming in November 1963) into full international appearances. The main reason for this can be summed up in two words: Gordon Banks.

Full-back Peter Hindley – 'as tough as old boots, as strong as an ox, no one messed with him', Moore fondly recalls – made his England under-23 debut in a 0-0 draw with Greece in Athens in May 1967, his only international appearance.

Box-to-box midfielder Henry Newton won four caps for England's under-23s between November 1964 and June 1967, scoring one goal. For years he was on the verge of a call-up, but despite being in several England squads, a full international cap eluded him.

Under-23 call-up

Moore had watched the 1966 World Cup Final alone in his digs on Loughborough Road, a short walk from the City Ground. But in the 1966/67 season, as football basked in the euphoria of that golden afternoon, it would be his turn to try to make his mark on the international scene.

Moore's excellent form after breaking into Forest's first team had attracted the attention of Alf Ramsey. Famously averse to wide players – so much so that his World Cup-winning team were dubbed the 'Wingless Wonders' – England's manager was no doubt intrigued by Moore's ability to play on the left, right or in the centre, and by his goalscoring ability.

Like every youngster, it had been Moore's dream to play for his country, and his opportunity came on what he described as one of the proudest moments of his career. On Saturday, 18 February 1967 Sir Alf was among 46,000 at the City Ground to see Forest's 3-0 FA Cup fourth round win over Newcastle United. In a dazzling display of wing play, Moore set up all three goals. A few days later Forest's manager, Johnny Carey, called Moore into his office to tell him the England manager had selected him to play for the under-23s against Scotland. Under-23 internationals were seen as an important stepping stone to a full international cap: half the final World Cup squad of 22 had played for the under-23s.

Moore knew Sir Alf had been watching a few games because Carey would tell the team, 'Ramsey's coming to the game tomorrow.' Moore would have preferred not to know because it just added to the pressure, not that it had seemed to matter in that cup tie.

Moore was allowed to use a telephone in the club's offices to phone his father, at work in the council offices in Scunthorpe, and give him the wonderful news. Naturally Vic, who for as long as Moore could remember had never missed an opportunity to get a ball and have a kick-about with him, was delighted.

On 1 March 1967 the England under-23 starting line-up – the first picked by Sir Alf since he was knighted – included goalkeeper Jim Montgomery (Sunderland) who would, of course, go on to achieve FA Cup immortality with his miraculous double save against Leeds in 1973 before collecting a European Cup winners' medal as a member of Forest's squad seven years later. The rest of the team comprised: Paul Reaney (Leeds United), Cyril Knowles (Tottenham Hotspur), John Hollins (Chelsea), Chris Lawler (Liverpool), Tommy Smith (Liverpool), Bryan Robson (Newcastle United), David Ford (Sheffield Wednesday), David Sadler (Manchester United), Colin Harvey (Everton), and Ian Storey-Moore (Nottingham Forest). Although fierce rivals every Saturday afternoon in the First Division, Moore recalls that all the players got on well with each other, remarking that even Liverpool hard man Smith 'was a really nice guy – he used to kick lumps off me on the field but off the pitch he was a really lovely lad'.

The match itself turned out to be something of a let-down for the near-22,000 spectators and, of course, the England side. It was played on a bumpy pitch at Newcastle United's St James'

Park and, with high winds making the ball unplayable at times, Scotland won 3-1. Smith scored England's only goal, a penalty. One of Scotland's scorers was future Forest star Peter Cormack. Moore recalls with characteristic understatement, 'It was a bit of a disappointing start. It was a horrible cold north-east night. I can't say I really enjoyed it.'

Sir Alf was the model of diplomacy in defeat, 'Naturally I'm disappointed. But Scotland were by far the better team and thoroughly deserved their success.' The English newspapers, on the other hand, felt no need to sugar-coat matters, the *Daily Mirror* proclaiming, 'England flop – no excuses please!'

Despite the inauspicious circumstances of Moore's under-23 debut, Sir Alf kept a close eye on the young winger. Just five weeks after that miserable night in Newcastle he witnessed Moore's astonishing hat-trick in the FA Cup quarter-final against Everton. Moore, fortunately, was completely unaware Sir Alf was in the stands that day, so that knowledge did not add to the inevitable pre-match nerves against the holders. Moore's deadly finishing was soon rewarded with a second under-23 call-up, this time against Austria.

The day itself – 10 May 1967 – was a momentous one for the country. Rolling Stones stars Mick Jagger and Keith Richards appeared in court after drugs had been found during a police raid. And just to show that this really was another time and place, in the evening the House of Commons voted overwhelmingly (by 488 votes to 62) to apply to join the Common Market.

Just over 20,000 turned up at Boothferry Park in Hull, including Moore's parents who had travelled over from nearby Scunthorpe. England won convincingly, 3-0, but for Moore the night was another bitter disappointment; after 36 minutes he was substituted after being injured by a bad tackle. Ironically, he was replaced by Jimmy Husband, scorer of Everton's two goals in that FA Cup quarter-final. It was scant consolation to Moore that the resultant free kick led to England's first goal. He was rushed to hospital for an X-ray but, on this occasion at least, no serious damage was revealed. That said, Moore was a long way off being 100 per cent fit when he turned out for Forest three days later in their final league match of the season, the 3-2 win at Fulham that secured the runners-up spot for the Reds.

Forest played the two post-season games in Spain and then, with their team-mates taking some well-earned rest, Moore, Hindley and Newton flew back to go on the England under-23 tour of Turkey, Greece and Bulgaria. On 31 May Hindley earned his only under-23 cap in the goalless draw against Greece. Three days later Newton scored in a 1-1 draw against Bulgaria in Sofia and he also played in the 3-0 win against Turkey in Ankara on 7 June.

Unfortunately, Moore had caught a debilitating virus in Spain and was too ill to join the tour. It wouldn't be his last dose of bad luck on the international front.

10

Stagnation

'What's he doing playing?
He shouldn't be playing!'

Moore's surgeon to manager Matt Gillies on the player's premature return from injury for the relegation battle at Coventry City in April 1969

European campaign starts

In August 1967, players and fans alike were in optimistic mood following the unexpected challenge for the Double. Hopes were high that Forest could show that their highest ever league finish was not a flash in the pan. That no new signings had been made was seen as a demonstration of faith in the team that had achieved so much. With hindsight that was a little naive, especially given the spate of injuries that had affected the club's chances of winning at least one trophy.

The 1967/68 season began with three wins and a draw, taking Forest to second in the early running. Moore scored in the three games he played in, which included a 3-3 draw with Coventry City at the City Ground. This drew a crowd of almost 45,000, which remains Forest's record attendance for the first home game of a season. Moore went off injured and missed the following match but then played in every fixture until the end of October. He soon embarked on a scoring streak, netting four times in five games, including a 4-0 thrashing of Newcastle United – a performance perhaps inspired by the players being shown a film of the Everton cup tie as part of their preparations – and a hard-fought single-goal victory in the League Cup on his home turf at Scunthorpe United.

Off the pitch, the boisterous nature of Forest's support was troubling some of the letter writers to the *Football Post*, with frequent complaints about the language emanating from the Trent End. These were countered by replies suggesting the problem was no worse at the City Ground than anywhere else.

Forest's reward for finishing runners-up in 1966/67 was to participate in the Inter-Cities Fairs Cup for the first time since 1961/62. They were drawn against Eintracht Frankfurt, who had finished fourth in the West German Bundesliga. At the first leg in Germany, Forest were received with great hospitality, with a buffet laid on and individual mementoes given to the travelling party. The attendance was only around 4,500 because of persistent heavy rain on an uncovered stadium but included a soaked but noisy away support estimated to be a few hundred, a decent following in the days before continental travel became more affordable.

With neither Henry Newton nor John Barnwell available, Moore wore the number eight shirt and played in midfield, while Alan Hinton, in his final game for the club, was on the left wing. Joe Baker, now recovered from that injury against Everton, scored the only goal in one of his best performances for the Reds. Keeper Peter Grummitt also starred in a tremendous Forest display, but the shine was taken off a deserved win by the inexplicable 65th-minute sending-off of Wignall for an innocuous push. It was Forest's first dismissal in a competitive match since 1939.

By the time the teams met for the return leg in Nottingham on 17 October, Forest were without a win in four games and had surprisingly lost 3-0 at Burnley in the League Cup. But with Barnwell showcasing his ability to pick a pass and start counter-attacks, they were back to their best, easing to a 4-0 win with the irrepressible Baker scoring twice. The Germans were under-strength and the aggregate score could well have been more than 5-0; Moore headed against the bar and John Winfield hit a post, while Moore and Baker both had headed goals disallowed.

After a rare free weekend, Forest almost ended Tottenham's long unbeaten home run, leading through another Baker goal until Jimmy Greaves equalised with 12 minutes left, scoring once more against what must have been his favourite opposition.

Record City Ground attendance

The following Saturday, 28 October, saw the eagerly anticipated visit of Manchester United, who were setting out on what would become a historic European Cup-winning campaign.

The game drew the record attendance for a sporting event in Nottingham, attracting 49,946 spectators. Club secretary Ken Smales later wrote of having been tempted to go out into the surrounding streets to find another 54 people to bring through the gates to nudge the final figure to the 50,000 mark. The sheer density of the crowds on the terraces suggested that more than that were actually in the ground, with one explanation being the fabled 'over the turnstile' admission of youngsters by sympathetic turnstile operators.

Whatever the true number of spectators – and their number once again included England manager Sir Alf Ramsey – they were rewarded with another memorable match and a sparkling performance from Forest. Baker scored twice and Wignall added a third to give Forest an unassailable lead. With Grummitt and his defence in top form, United could only manage a single George Best goal and Forest were good value for the 3-1 win – United's first defeat since the opening day of the season.

Having seen off Eintracht, Forest were drawn against FC Zürich with the first leg at home. The Swiss part-timers were not to be underestimated, having knocked Barcelona out in the first round. Ironically, given what was to happen in the second leg, they showed precious little inclination to try for a valuable away goal and Forest were frustrated by their insistence on putting ten men behind the ball whenever threatened. Karl Grob was kept busy in the visitors' goal and he brilliantly saved a Moore header to keep the game goalless at half-time. After the break Forest finally took the lead when the flight of Newton's shot from more than 25 yards deceived Grob. Against the run of play, Zürich equalised with a freak goal. Newton's attempted pass to Barnwell bounced off the referee's legs and centre-forward Fritz Künzli was put through to score.

Shortly afterwards, the game was marred by a loss of discipline on and off the field. The Zürich players reacted angrily to Wignall's challenge on Grob and the centre-forward later said that at least four of them had spat at him. Coins were thrown on to the pitch and the flames were fanned when the Swiss threw them back into the crowd.

When play resumed, Forest took a deserved first-leg lead in the 79th minute when Moore converted a penalty awarded for a handling offence. He then had another goal disallowed, leaving Forest with just a single-goal lead to take into the second leg.

Forest's chairman Tony Wood was an advocate of playing European ties in a single match, in the hope of preventing the kind of dull defensive football Zürich had successfully deployed. Supporters had been charged higher than normal prices for the tie and Wood publicly apologised for the lack of entertainment. He promised that tickets would revert to normal prices if Forest reached the third round.

The final four of Forest's 15 competitive matches in September and October 1967 had seen them take on two European opponents, along with the FA Cup holders and the league champions, and prove themselves well worthy of the company they were now keeping. They went into November in seventh place in the First Division table and hoping to make further progress in Europe, but their season was to take an unexpected turn.

Calamitous oversight

The return leg against Zürich was played on 14 November and FIFA president Sir Stanley Rous was among the crowd of just over 15,000. Moore, out with an ankle injury, followed the game on the radio back in Nottingham. Forest – again backed by an enthusiastic away following – knew they were facing a tough challenge. Despite Zürich showing more attacking intent than a fortnight earlier, Grob's form was the main reason the scores were still level at half-time. After the break Forest defended their single-goal advantage well, but with 20 minutes remaining a half-cleared cross fell to Christian Winiger who beat Grummitt with a firm, low shot. Forest played out the rest of the 90 minutes with renewed urgency but were unable to make a breakthrough.

The Forest players and officials turned their thoughts to the imminent demands of extra time but, to their surprise, the final whistle was greeted by celebrations among the Zürich players, staff and supporters. Forest had assumed that the away goals rule would only apply after extra time and therefore believed they had a further 30 minutes to score a winning goal. However, the laws of the competition, as their hosts clearly knew, actually applied the rule at the end of normal time.

It is hard to imagine that the Forest players were not aware of this and, equally, that nobody at the club had thought to check what would happen if the scores were level after 90 minutes. Evidently the issue had not come up in the Forest party's dealings with officialdom in the run-up to or at the match.

So, with the aggregate score 2-2, Forest were out of Europe because of Zürich's fluke away goal in Nottingham and, it has to be said, their own unprofessional ignorance of the competition's rules. Listening to the drama unfold over the airwaves, Moore wasn't to know, but he would never again get the chance to test himself on the European stage.

That bizarre exit from Europe heralded a sharp downturn in Forest's league form and they lost their next three games without scoring. Moore was back for the 2-0 defeat at Fulham on 18 November but was injured in a challenge with George Cohen, who was making his 400th appearance for the Cottagers. This meant he missed a defeat by the same score against Leeds United, in which the gentlemanly McKinlay was booked for the first time in his 16 years as a professional.

At the start of December Moore returned in the 1-0 defeat at Everton, in which Forest's rotten luck with injuries continued. Barnwell was stretchered off just before half-time and Moore was later injured when keeper Gordon West dived at his feet. Rather than leave his team a man short he came back on to the pitch a few minutes later, limping badly. He would not play again for another two months.

Arrival of 'Slim Jim'

With Moore unavailable and Barnwell out for months with an injured heel, Forest were in the market for reinforcements. Chairman Wood had said the club would buy the first £100,000 player who became available – hardly an astute approach to moulding a team. That player was Jim Baxter and Forest broke their transfer record to secure the services of the maverick Scottish international midfielder from Sunderland. This was certainly a gamble, with all the previous six-figure fees in British football having been paid for forwards, but Johnny Carey was confident, asserting that Baxter 'will make a tremendous difference to the club'.

Sadly, Baxter was starting to show the effects of his heavy drinking. On his day – such as when he tormented England in Scotland's famous 3-2 win at Wembley in April 1967 – he could still be a creative and influential figure, but as Moore wryly recalls:

> 'There weren't many days like that, were there? Jim had a great left foot, was very talented and showed flashes of brilliance. In two or three games he was probably man of

the match, absolutely brilliant, but he couldn't sustain it for long periods, he just wasn't fit enough.'

Moore was never much of a drinker himself and didn't particularly like beer – 'the lads used to laugh at me: they'd be drinking pints and I would be on some stupid little drink' – but he soon became good friends with Baxter:

> 'I really liked him as a person – he was a real character, a real jack the lad. In fact, all the players loved him. To be more precise, when Jim was sober, you'd love him. But when he was drunk he was a bloody nightmare!'

Although the term had yet to be coined, Moore was often the 'designated driver' when Baxter and West Indian cricketing legend Garry Sobers hit the town. Baxter would always start the evening off with a treble Bacardi. The following day he would be vomiting into a hedge before training while, across the road at Trent Bridge, Sobers would score a fifty or take wickets with ease.

Moore and Baxter had a shared love of horseracing. Not long after Moore's injury at Everton, and with his leg in plaster, a friend drove the two of them up to York races:

> 'We were just going for the day but he won so much money – over £5,500 – that he wouldn't go home and wanted to stay another day. He was due at training at Forest the next day.
>
> 'So, we booked some rooms for the night at the Chase Hotel right outside the racecourse. We had no toothpaste, no change of clothes for any overnight stay, nothing at all. It wasn't long before Jim was throwing fivers out of the bedroom window saying, "It's just Monopoly money, Monopoly money!"
>
> 'The next day it poured with rain, Jim lost all his money – and more – and we left mid-afternoon, wending our way

back to Nottingham. Carol and Jim's wife, Jean, weren't best pleased, to say the least.'

Back at the City Ground, Baxter made a feeble excuse as to why he had missed training. His attitude was hardly in keeping with a top-flight professional, as Moore reflects, 'Jim was Jim – he wasn't going to change his lifestyle just because he was at Nottingham Forest.' He remembers one incident in the dressing room after Forest had suffered an abject home defeat:

> 'None of us had played particularly well. When you hadn't played well you tried not to catch the manager's eye because he was sure to pick on somebody. So, you kept your head down, took your boots off, and as we were doing that, Matt Gillies, who was the manager at that time, said to Jim, "That's the worst performance I've seen from a professional footballer in my life."
>
> 'So, Jim got up, tapped him on the head and said, "Don't worry about that, gaffer, there's a lot more where that came from!" Of course, that brought the dressing room down.'

There were occasional glimpses of the old Baxter, though. He opened his account for Forest in style against Stoke City, returning with interest Gordon Banks's clearance from 35 yards, and he scored against Southampton with another memorable strike, controlling a clearance with one foot and smashing a 20-yard volley home with the other. But for such a big fee his signing was undoubtedly an expensive gamble that didn't pay off.

Battle of Elland Road

In early January 1968 Forest's injury jinx struck again with Peter Grummitt replaced in goal at Manchester City by Frank Wignall, who kept a clean sheet for the remainder of the 3-0 defeat. The following Saturday reserve keeper Brian Williamson broke a bone in his hand on his First Division debut against Newcastle United.

Sandwiched in between these misfortunes was an altogether happier occasion when Moore married his long-time girlfriend, Carol Ann Griffiths, at Christ Church in Chilwell, Nottingham. Fortunately, Moore had had his leg removed from plaster the week before. The Forest team attended the ceremony along with Tommy Cavanagh, reserve team trainer Frank Knight, and physio Bob Davies. A splendid buffet reception was held at the popular Nottingham Knight pub but there was no time for a honeymoon – the next day the groom was down at the City Ground working on regaining his fitness.

In early February Moore finally returned to action in a 1-0 defeat at Chelsea, and he was soon back on the scoresheet when he added to Baxter's wonder goal in a 2-2 draw with Southampton.

After beating Bolton Wanderers 4-2 in the FA Cup third round, Forest got the toughest draw possible – away to favourites Leeds United. In only the second minute, home keeper Gary Sprake went down hurt after saving at Wignall's feet. Norman Hunter went in goal while Sprake's injury was assessed and Forest took advantage when Baker delighted the 13,000 Forest supporters among the crowd of almost 52,000 by scoring from Lyons' cross. After Sprake returned the home side soon equalised through Mick Jones before a moment of madness from Baxter gifted them the lead shortly before half-time.

Grummitt claimed the ball from Jimmy Greenhoff's challenge and was set to clear it when Baxter, apparently trying to protect his keeper, clearly pushed Greenhoff for what TV commentator Kenneth Wolstenholme called 'the stupidest penalty of all time'. Johnny Giles's spot kick went in off the post with Grummitt rooted to the goal line. Forest rallied in the second half, despite yet another injury all but ending Wignall's career with them, but there was no further scoring and they were out of the cup.

After a game characterised by reckless tackling and ill-tempered scuffles, the *Nottingham Evening Post*'s correspondent didn't mince his words in his criticism of the referee's leniency and Baxter's stupidity, saying Forest 'had gone down in a kicking match, torpedoed by their own failings at vital moments more than by the legendary power of United'.

Grummitt had actually broken his left arm in the 25th minute, hence his lack of movement for the penalty. Like Sprake, who had torn ligaments in his knee, he had played on after treatment. To the modern observer, the two keepers' determination to keep playing and help their teams despite serious injuries looks as reckless as it does heroic. However, substitutions had only first been allowed in 1965 and, with just one replacement available, the ethos was still very much one of patching players up and sending them back into the fray. Moore was himself a victim of this cavalier attitude on several occasions in his career:

> 'At the time you never gave it a thought other than, "Well, they've asked me to play, so I should play." You never thought about not playing. In fact, a big part of my career was about playing when I shouldn't have done.'

Their last chance of a trophy gone, Forest's form dipped again, just as it had after the Zürich defeat, and they only won three of their remaining 14 league games, finishing 14th on 41 points – 15 fewer than the year before. Despite the disappointing end to the season, a measure of how Carey's team had captured the imagination of the Nottingham public is that 1967/68 saw Forest again set a new record aggregate attendance for home league games, the total of 692,000 beating the record set the previous season by over 35,000.

Moore had missed several of the late-season games with a knee ligament injury. When he did play he wore three different shirts – nine, ten, and 11. This was testament to his ability to play across the front line, which saw him appear at inside-left and centre-forward as well as in his usual place on the left wing.

It also reflected the much-depleted state of Forest's forward line. Alan Hinton had been allowed to join Brian Clough's and Peter Taylor's Derby County – at the time a Second Division outfit – for just £30,000 in September 1967, and in early March 1968 Frank Wignall signed for relegation-threatened Wolverhampton Wanderers for £50,000. Inevitably, four weeks later Wignall scored twice against the Reds in a 6-1 win for his new team at Molineux.

Moore ended an injury-disrupted season with 13 goals from 35 games, a reasonable return in the circumstances. If he could only steer clear of injuries, as a winger with the goalscoring rate of a striker, a fit Moore would be an asset for club and country.

Catastrophe

Forest's bad luck with injuries continued early in the 1968/69 season, with Grummitt, Baker and Baxter all injured in consecutive games. However, they were soon rocked by much more serious misfortune.

On 24 August 1968 Forest, winless in their first four matches, were giving their best performance to date as half-time approached in an exciting game against much-fancied Leeds United at the City Ground. The visitors took the lead after 35 minutes but Forest hit back almost immediately, Dave Hilley heading home Moore's cross. A few minutes later Moore headed against the bar but, as the half came to an end, wisps of smoke began to emerge from under the seating in the middle of the Main Stand.

The smoke thickened and it soon became apparent that a serious fire had broken out in or near the dressing rooms. The fans in the stand abandoned their seats, many of them wisely ignoring the warning in the programme to 'please keep off the pitch at all times' and clambered over the front wall and on to the turf. There they watched as the flames, fanned by draughts under the seating, quickly spread. Moore's wife Carol was helped on to the pitch by future Forest chairman Fred Reacher. The players, realising what was happening, also hurried to get away from the stand, skipper Terry Hennessey and some team-mates breaking a door down to facilitate their escape, with some of them joining the fans on the pitch.

Moore recalls:

> 'We wanted to go and get our clothes but weren't allowed in. One or two of the players tried but they wouldn't let them in. Initially we were kept on the pitch and then we walked round the side of the stand and ended up sitting in the car park in our football kit waiting to see what was going to happen.'

The game was abandoned and soon the flames were tearing through the wooden seating. Fire crews from across the city and county raced to the scene, their final approach hampered by the thousands making their way from the ground. Fans helped man the hoses on the pitch side of the stand, as the fire crews fought to get the blaze under control.

The game was being filmed for ATV's Sunday afternoon *Star Soccer* programme and the broadcaster's three cameras up on the TV gantry were destroyed, their operators having managed to scramble down to safety.

Mercifully, given the rapid spread of the fire, there were no fatalities and only a few minor injuries. But nothing could be done to prevent the almost total destruction of the stand, which had only been refurbished three years earlier. All that remained was the steel framework.

The players, match officials, journalists and some supporters then crowded into the nearby Bridgford Hotel. With the visitors' team bus hemmed in the City Ground car park by fire engines, Don Revie ordered a fleet of taxis to take his players, still in their all-white strip, back to Leeds.

The players' clothes and valuables were lost in the blaze, including Jack Charlton's commemorative World Cup watch, though John Barnwell's monogrammed gold cufflinks were found in the debris by trainer Tommy Cavanagh the next day. All of Forest's club records were also destroyed, including the players' contracts, along with trophies and awards and all the playing kit other than what the players were wearing.

The loss of the stand was a disaster for Forest and undoubtedly had an effect on the club's fortunes in the years that followed. However, as was to become tragically apparent at Bradford City's stadium 17 years later, it could have been so much worse.

As an ironic footnote, the preview of the game in the football magazine *Goal* had been headlined 'Leeds United ready to set fire to Forest', while the number one single in the previous week's pop charts had been 'Fire' by The Crazy World of Arthur Brown.

Purple patch

The show must go on, of course, and the problem of where to play home games was soon solved. Neighbours Notts County were quick to offer the use of their Meadow Lane ground while the debris was cleared and the stand rebuilt. It was agreed that both clubs' reserve teams would play on the City Ground pitch while the two first teams shared Meadow Lane. Forest were helped further by Nottinghamshire County Cricket Club offering the use of their facilities, including dressing rooms.

Four days after the fire, Moore's late penalty earned Forest a well-deserved point at Newcastle United. This marked the start of the most prolific scoring streak of his career – 13 goals in as many games. Two of those strikes came as Forest finally claimed their first victory of the season, winning 5-2 at West Bromwich Albion on 7 September.

It proved to be a false dawn, though, as they then went 13 matches without a win, including all six games played at their temporary 'home' across the river.

During this dispiriting run, Forest set what must surely be a record in professional football by fielding four different goalkeepers in as many first-team matches. Unsettled reserve keeper Brian Williamson had been between the posts since Grummitt injured his thumb but missed the game against Stoke City on 5 October with a neck injury. Grummitt made a less-than-assured return in a 3-3 draw – Moore twice netting with headers – and needed treatment for a knock to his hand in the second half.

Grummitt was unfit to play against Newcastle and, with Williamson seeking a transfer, Brian Sherratt was hastily loaned from Oxford United. However, a 4-2 home defeat convinced manager Carey that the jump in standard had been too much for him. After the game, Carey negotiated a deal with his opposite number, Joe Harvey, for Newcastle's experienced reserve stopper Gordon Marshall, who became the fourth in an unlikely succession of goalkeepers in another defeat at Sunderland a few days later.

As the team around him struggled, Moore continued to impress. By the time he had scored in Forest's comeback from three goals down to draw at reigning champions Manchester City, he had struck in six successive games.

Carey out, Gillies in

Forest finally returned to the City Ground in mid-November, with the Main Stand closed, but it was not a happy homecoming as Arsenal ran out 2-0 winners. After further defeats against Queens Park Rangers and Liverpool, Johnny Carey was sacked at the start of December, a sorry end for the man who had brought several star players to the City Ground, nurtured young talents like Moore and Henry Newton, and steered the club to one of the most successful seasons in its 103-year history.

With assistant manager Bill Anderson in caretaker charge, Forest's long winless run was finally ended with narrow victories against Sunderland and at Ipswich Town, Moore scoring in both games. He also scored in the next match at Stoke City before a second-half collapse saw Forest make an early exit from the FA Cup after a 3-0 defeat at Second Division Preston North End.

On 19 January 1969 it was announced that former Leicester City manager Matt Gillies would take over as Carey's successor. The previous day, Forest's miserable luck had gone from bad to worse when Moore suffered the most serious injury of his career to date in a goalless draw against Gillies' previous employers. He heard a faint click after a challenge from behind shortly before half-time and was unable to put weight on his left leg. It was later confirmed that he had fractured the fibula and was expected to be out for eight to ten weeks. Naturally, this was hugely frustrating for Moore:

> 'I had scored 16 goals by December and I was determined to be the top goalscorer in the league. In his newspaper column Malcolm Allison had said there would only be four or five players who would get 20 goals in the First Division that season and that I would be one of them. I thought I'd give it a real go.'

It would in fact be more than three months before Moore played again. In the intervening period, two Barry Lyons goals gave Gillies his first win in an unexpected 2-0 victory in the snow at Liverpool on 15 February 1969 – still, remarkably, Forest's most recent success at Anfield at the time of writing – and new signing Alan Hill became the team's fifth goalkeeper of the season. When Moore made his return at fellow strugglers Coventry City, Forest were five points ahead of next-to-bottom Leicester, but the Foxes had three games in hand.

Moore gave Forest an early lead, scoring one of his greatest goals by brilliantly beating three players before blasting the ball home. But, far from match fit, he was on the receiving end of some rough treatment and was replaced at half-time. Looking back, he feels he was rushed back too soon in an attempt to secure Forest's First Division future:

> 'There were numerous times when I shouldn't have played, particularly when we were away at Coventry and we needed a point to stay up. They begged me to play. They had pumped a load of cortisone into me – all it does is mask the pain. I scored the goal – it was a good goal, actually – and at half-time I took my boot off. Honestly, my ankle was jet black. The surgeon who had operated on me was in the dressing room and said, "What's he doing playing? He shouldn't be playing!" I was in agony, but we got the point and we stayed up.
>
> 'I did them a service with my goal, but I shouldn't have played. It cannot have done my ankle any good and I guess I had an inherent weakness from then on. But in those days you didn't really have a choice. I had numerous injections in my ankle to play in games.'

With Leicester losing, Moore's goal in the 1-1 draw as good as guaranteed their survival. He missed the last two games but Forest's safety was confirmed with a 1-0 win against Everton before the season ended with an all too familiar sight – promising Northern Irish central defender Liam O'Kane being carried off injured on his debut in a 1-0 defeat at Leeds United.

Forest finished 18th, another great disappointment just two years after coming second. Their survival was probably helped by playing ten of the last 15 games at home, half of which they won. They lost their star player for two-fifths of the season and the fire was an unexpected and traumatic complication. But Forest had yet to win before the Main Stand went up in smoke and they were already struggling at the wrong end of the table by the time of Moore's injury. As well as Moore, Grummitt, Barnwell, Baker and the erratic Baxter all missed large chunks of the season.

They say that luck evens itself out sooner or later. If that is the case, Forest would have been hoping for an improved showing in the league next time round and Moore would have been looking forward to an injury-free season and the chance to make a case for a place on the flight to the 1970 World Cup in Mexico.

On target – and targeted

As the 1969/70 season dawned, Forest were relying more than ever on Moore's goals. Baker, whose best days were now behind him, had left for Sunderland in the summer and the unreliable Baxter had been released, returning to Scotland for a brief spell back at Glasgow Rangers before retiring from the game in 1970. With Forest once again not having strengthened the team, in the opening games manager Gillies gave youngsters Colin Hall and Paul Richardson, a midfielder, starts in the number nine shirt, but neither found the net.

Unsurprisingly, Forest again made a slow start, with two goalless draws followed by a 4-1 home defeat to Leeds on 16 August 1969. Don Revie's talented team showed why they could be admired and despised in equal measure. The win took them past Burnley's record of 30 unbeaten games but their cynical side was on show too, with two players booked for crude challenges on Moore in the opening half hour. Such targeting was something skilful players like Moore were having to get used to. With referees sparing in their issuing of cautions, he could be on the receiving end of multiple foul challenges before getting any protection whatsoever.

Looking to open his account for the season, Moore was mortified to see his penalty saved by Gordon Banks in a 1-1 draw at Stoke, but he finally got off the mark in a 2-1 defeat at Arsenal. Barnwell played a short free kick to Moore, who slammed the ball past Bob Wilson and into the roof of the net from 25 yards. Wilson and Moore would have an even more memorable encounter a couple of years later. Moore also scored the only goal of the game against West Bromwich Albion to finally earn Forest their first win at the sixth attempt.

His next goal came on 3 September in the League Cup at Barrow, an injury-time winner in a bruising game in which the

Third Division side took an early lead, Barnwell levelled and both teams were reduced to ten men as early as the 18th minute, with Sammy Chapman being sent off for Forest.

Moore was being troubled by a knee strain and missed a thrilling 3-3 draw at Wolverhampton Wanderers. He came back with both goals in a 2-1 win against Southampton but then didn't score for five games. By the time he found the net again, in a 2-2 draw against Manchester City in mid-October, Forest had begun a winless run in the league that would stretch to a dozen matches. Their League Cup campaign came to an end with a dismal 1-0 home defeat to Oxford United.

But there were some bright moments too, as Forest came back from difficult-looking away fixtures at Liverpool and Manchester United with a point each time. Indeed, they should have won at Old Trafford. Leading after Moore's first-half penalty sent Alex Stepney the wrong way, they were pegged back by a fine solo goal by George Best just after the break, but should have had another spot kick when Moore rounded Stepney, who brought him down two yards inside the penalty area. For some reason the referee awarded a free kick just outside the box, which Moore flashed inches over the bar.

Forest's away form soon reverted to type with a 6-1 hiding at Elland Road, the first of a run of three defeats on their travels. They were unable to make amends at home where they drew five successive games, Moore scoring as they shared four goals with Tottenham.

Forest's first away win came on 29 November and was worth the wait. In front of the *Match of the Day* cameras and an all-ticket crowd of more than 38,000 crammed into the Baseball Ground, they beat neighbours Derby County 2-0. Forest were allocated just 20 seat tickets, but their fans on the terraces celebrated as goals from Moore and Lyons gave the Reds the East Midlands bragging rights.

That morale-boosting victory sparked a run of four consecutive league wins for the first time in three seasons, with Moore scoring as Forest completed the double over Southampton and beat Wolverhampton Wanderers 4-2. The effects of Christmas on crowds at this time were clear to see. Fewer than 16,000 attended the Wolves game on the Saturday before Christmas – the peak seasonal shopping day in those days long before the internet – but the 1-1 draw against Arsenal on Boxing Day drew almost 39,000 to the City Ground. Moore scored as Forest ended the year with another 1-1 draw at West Ham. Little did he know it would be his last goal of the season.

11

Road to Mexico

'I'd had all my medicals and had even been measured for my sunglasses.'

Ian Storey-Moore

A linesman's flag

Sir Alf Ramsey had been at the City Ground on 11 October 1969 to see Forest take on Manchester City. Moore scored in the 36th minute with a diving header before, a quarter of an hour into the second half, laying on the assist for Barry Lyons to make it 2-0. Sir Alf was impressed by the form of Moore and also the visitors' Francis Lee, who popped up to score two goals in six minutes to leave the result a 2-2 draw.

At the start of December Moore and Henry Newton were included in Sir Alf's squad of 30 for pre-World Cup training, medicals and England's match against Portugal. Forest's manager, Matt Gillies, reflected the pride of the club in saying, 'We're delighted. They have really earned it, both of them. Their selection has given a large measure of satisfaction to everyone down here.' No one was getting carried away, though.

Moore, quoted at the time, said, 'Getting selected for this squad has set me thinking about Mexico for the first time. But I'm not really looking ahead at the moment. I'm just pleased to have got into the 30.'

Newton, who had been in England's training squad of 22 for Frank Wignall's debut all the way back in 1964, was suitably cautious, 'Mexico? That's still a long way off. Getting into this 30 is one thing, getting in the World Cup is another. But at least this is a big step forward. If I hadn't got in this time, I think that would have been it. I was always hoping, but now I've been picked I'm a bit surprised ... There are so many of my type about that it's harder for the likes of me to be recognised than it is for most. You can pick from at least half a dozen in my position.' Prescient words from Newton, unfortunately.

Neither Moore nor Newton made the team or subs' bench that night, watching a 1-0 England victory at Wembley from the stands. However, they did not have to wait long for their next opportunity when both were selected for the squad to face the Netherlands at Wembley on 14 January 1970.

From their time working together for the under-23s, Moore had got on well with Ramsey:

> 'Sir Alf was a very articulate man, a very nice man, a quiet man. He made his point quickly, concisely and that was about it. He didn't get into any lengthy discussions with the team. He wouldn't castigate you for shooting rather than passing, he wasn't that type of manager. He knew what he wanted and how he wanted his team to perform, the formation, tactics, etc. Sir Alf was actually a bit like Brian Clough in that he wasn't concerned about the opposition. He would say, "Do what you can do, play to your strengths, don't worry about them."'

On the Sunday before the match Moore and Newton travelled by train to meet up with the other England players at Lilleshall. When he had first joined up with the England squad for the Portugal match, Moore had been somewhat in awe:

> 'There were people like Bobby Moore and Bobby Charlton who you knew and had played against, but you had never been in their company for a lengthy period of time. It was exciting, coupled with some trepidation and nerves, to start mixing with those icons of British football.'

Moore developed a great affection for his namesake in particular:

> 'Bobby was a really nice man – I thought the world of him. If he was sat here now you wouldn't think he was 100 times capped for England and a World Cup winner. A really nice man, a wonderful guy.'

Another England team-mate he took a shine to was Lee, who was quite a character. On one occasion, Moore complimented him on the new leather coat he was wearing. 'I'll get you one, if you like,' said Lee. Sure enough, the next time Forest played Manchester City, Lee knocked on the dressing room door and gave Moore an identical, brand-new leather coat.

On the Monday the squad trained and there was just a light session the next morning. It was on the Tuesday that Sir Alf told Moore he was in the starting line-up. Newton was to be a substitute. Ramsey advised Moore to 'just play your own game, play how you want, have a wander about like you do for Forest'. The manager appreciated that Moore was not an out-and-out winger as such. 'In that respect, he didn't tie you down, he was fairly flexible in his tactics, so you couldn't blame Alf if you had a bad game,' Moore reflects.

When Moore travelled away with Forest and, later, Manchester United, he would always share a room with a team-mate. With the England squad, on the other hand, each player had a room to himself. So, Moore was left to his own thoughts as he went to bed that evening:

> 'When you know you're playing the next day – playing for England for the first time, which was a massive thing – you don't get a lot of sleep! You think, "Don't let yourself down."'

On the day of the Netherlands match, the squad had breakfast and then did some exercise; nothing more than a warm-up, just a gentle jog to get a feel for the day. A spot of lunch was followed by a couple of hours' sleep in bed, then around five o'clock, a bit of tea and toast.

So, to the match itself, and the incredible array of talent on display that night as Moore made his debut. England's starting line-up included World Cup winners Gordon Banks (Stoke City), Martin Peters (West Ham United), Jack Charlton (Leeds United) and Bobby Charlton (Manchester United), with Geoff Hurst (West Ham United) one of the substitutes. The rest of the team comprised Keith Newton (Everton), Terry Cooper (Leeds United), Norman Hunter (Leeds United), Francis Lee (Manchester City), Colin Bell (Manchester City), Mick Jones (Leeds United) and Ian Storey-Moore (Nottingham Forest).

Despite fielding such illustrious names, an excuse of sorts for what turned out to be a disjointed England performance was that they were considered to be fielding an 'experimental' team. Nonetheless, all but Moore and Jones would make the final squad of 22 for the Mexico World Cup.

Actually it was the Netherlands who – having failed to qualify for any World Cup since 1938 – were now undertaking their own experiment, one that would see them progress from semi-professional obscurity to the invention of Total Football and two successive World Cup finals. Indeed, four of the Dutch team that night – Rudi Krol, Wim Jansen, Wim van Hanegem and Johan Cruyff – would play in the team defeated 2-1 by West Germany in the 1974 final, with two others – Rinus Israël and Piet Keizer – being unused substitutes in Munich.

All the home fans and pundits expected an easy victory. Indeed, the attitude of the press towards the merits or otherwise of the Dutch team had changed little since Frank Wignall had played against them just over five years earlier. Unfortunately, Moore's parents were unable to be at Wembley because of his father's poor health at the time.

The extremely cold but dry weather at the turn of the year had given way to mild, wet conditions which made the Wembley pitch heavy going. England made a blistering start. In a seven-minute spell early in the first half, Moore had no fewer than four attempts on goal: one saved at point-blank range, two cleared off the line and a headed goal after 26 minutes that was ruled out – controversially and, almost certainly, incorrectly – for offside. Bobby Charlton crossed from the right to the far side of the penalty area where Mick Jones ran in to beat two defenders and head back across the six-yard box. Showing a poacher's instinct worthy of Jimmy Greaves, Moore ghosted in past the static defence to nod the ball into the net. It looked to be a perfectly good goal but to everyone's surprise, including the Dutch, the linesman flagged Moore offside, denying him a dream debut goal.

In time Moore reconciled himself to having been just offside, but the Pathé newsreel available on the internet tells a different story. Freezing the video footage at the crucial moment and imagining a VAR-type line drawn across the playing surface shows Moore to be a good yard onside.

So what should have been a goal on his first start for England – and what, on another day, could well have been a hat-trick – was not to be. As the match progressed, Cruyff and his team-mates took control of midfield, keeping possession for long periods. Ultimately, the Dutch created more chances but the match ended goalless. 'I give Holland every credit for their display. All of them played very well,' Ramsey acknowledged afterwards.

Interviewed at the time, a rather self-deprecating Moore said, 'I wish it had been a better game for my debut, but on the whole

I was quite satisfied with my first game.' Certainly, when he dreamed of playing for England for all those years he could hardly have imagined that the Wembley crowd of 75,000 would end up singing 'What a load of rubbish'. Not that their dissatisfaction had been directed against Moore, one of the few players who came through the disappointing draw with their reputations enhanced.

In fact, he received unanimous acclaim from the press.

'Ian Moore's performance must have given Sir Alf much satisfaction … [and he was] desperately unlucky not to have scored,' reported the *Daily Sketch*. Meanwhile, the *Daily Telegraph* said, 'No England player looked more dangerous than Moore… [who made] a most satisfactory debut.' That sentiment was backed up by the *Daily Express*'s verdict, 'Only three men impressed and looked fit enough to wear the label "Wanted in Mexico": Gordon Banks and Jackie Charlton, the two veterans, with newcomer Ian Moore.'

Two of the all-time great sports writers agreed. 'Ian Moore began his entry into international football with some strong running, intelligent positioning, good accurate passing but it was his determination and his attacking flair that has surely earned him further opportunities in this company,' wrote Brian James in the *Daily Mail*. 'Alone, Ian Moore emerged from this shambles with his reputation enhanced,' added Hugh McIlvanney in the *Sunday Observer*. And from the legendary Tom Finney, writing in the *News of the World*:

> 'Ian Moore must have slept happy Wednesday night for, from what I saw, he was deserving of his place in England's next international. He is Britain's most improved winger and – with Peter Thompson – I would rate him as the finest winger in the game today.'

Interviewed in the *Nottingham Evening Post*, Forest manager Matt Gillies gave a typically analytical assessment of what he considered had been a good start to Moore's international career:

> 'Ian was one of the few successes of the evening. With a bit of luck he might have had three goals. Throughout the game he was having to make bricks without straw, but he did show the kind of things that Sir Alf Ramsey must be looking for with a view to Mexico. He showed that he has close control, ability to shield the ball, and although he did not do as well in the air as I thought he might, his shooting was good. I can remember him losing the ball only once when a Dutch defender did not fall for his double body swerve. And he was twice heavily brought down when he was going strongly. He also took his goal very well even though it was rubbed out by a hairline offside decision.'

But it was the opinion of Sir Alf that mattered most, of course. 'I know I would have played in the next game,' remembers Moore, 'because Ramsey said to me afterwards, "You did enough to be in the next squad."'

Henry Newton was an unused substitute against the Netherlands. Halfway through the second half, with the match goalless and the crowd growing restless, Newton was told to get warmed up. But just as Sir Alf was about to bring him on, Francis Lee pulled up injured and the manager changed his mind and, instead, brought on defensive midfielder Alan Mullery. When, five minutes later, Hurst was substituted for Jones, it became the first time England had made two substitutions in a match. Unfortunately, Newton was not one of them and was left on the bench. Despite Sir Alf telling him, 'There'll be other times, Henry,' he would never play for his country.

History repeats itself

Both Moore and Newton were widely tipped to be heading for the World Cup in Mexico. During the 1969/70 season, Forest supporters had high hopes that these two fan favourites would indeed spend the following summer helping England defend the Jules Rimet Trophy in Mexico. To the tune of a certain song from Disney's *Snow White* they would sing, 'Heigh ho, heigh ho, It's off to Mexico, With Ian Moore and Hen-er-y, Heigh ho, heigh ho.' Fans' expectations were heightened when both players featured in the highly prized World Cup Coin Collection, available if you happened to buy your petrol from Esso garages in 1970.

Moore reflects, 'I'd had all the medical stuff to go to Mexico and then Arthur Mann sort of ruined it for me.' Almost four years to the day that Frank Wignall suffered the injury that ruled him out of the 1966 World Cup squad, Moore was to meet the same fate.

On 7 February, three weeks after the Netherlands game, Forest were playing a league match away at Manchester City. City included Ian Bowyer and Stan Bowles, who would both go on to win trophies with Forest, but it was a future Notts County player who literally made his mark on the game. After just five minutes, Moore was watching City's goalkeeper, Ken Mulhearn, tip his shot past the post when full-back Arthur Mann, playing his first game for ten months, slid in shockingly late and ruptured Moore's ankle ligaments. Moore recalls:

> 'I was standing there watching the ball go past the post and suddenly he hit me. I don't think he meant to cripple me but it was a very late tackle. I had never had such pain in my life. I was in agony and they had to give me morphine. I was sick on the team coach on the way back to Nottingham.'

Moore's injured ankle had been X-rayed at Maine Road and he brought the images back with him. On the Sunday Forest's club doctor came to Moore's home, looked at the X-rays and assured him that he would be playing again in ten days. Nonetheless, the following morning Moore went to hospital where a stress X-ray was carried out to determine whether there was any ligament damage. The prognosis from Mr Jackson, the consultant, was clear, 'Sorry, sir, we're going to have to operate this afternoon, you've severed your ligaments. I'm going to do my best to try and stitch them together,' which he proceeded to do. 'Mr Jackson was brilliant, a great man. He sorted that problem out straight away,' Moore recalls gratefully.

With his leg in plaster after the operation, Moore did body work in the gym every day. He assumed that as soon as the plaster came off he would be able to start playing again almost immediately.

In the meantime Sir Alf kept in touch with Forest to monitor Moore's progress. He told Matt Gillies that if Moore could get fit he would be going to Mexico. In anticipation of this, Moore had the necessary blood tests and inoculations and was even measured for sunglasses.

In the second week of March the plaster was taken off. Moore went down to the City Ground and put his kit on, 'I couldn't believe it – I could hardly put my foot down. I thought, "Oh no, it's going to take longer than I had reckoned," and I didn't play again that season.'

Neither the injured Moore nor Newton would make the provisional 28-man squad for Mexico that was announced on 25 March.

Interviewed for *Shoot!* magazine just before the Mexico World Cup, Moore declared:

> 'The life of a professional footballer is not all glamour. There is pain and … heartache. Early in February … I had a dream shattered … [when] my hopes of going to Mexico with England's World Cup squad were blasted sky-high. Forest were playing against Manchester City … and, with the match barely five minutes old, I went down in a tackle and they carried me off. My leg hurt like mad, but I still thought it was only something like a jarred nerve.

'The club specialist told me that the ligaments were badly damaged and I would have to keep the leg in plaster for five weeks. I didn't give up hope [and] kept doing body exercises so that I would be ready to play almost as soon as the plaster was taken off. [But] time was not on my side and when Sir Alf announced the men to go to Mexico I wasn't among them. I am in no way bitter at being left behind. Sir Alf … could not afford to risk taking along anyone who wasn't 100 per cent fit.

'I felt I was almost on the plane when that tackle came. That's football. You have to take the knocks no matter what happens.'

Moore now reflects:

'I watched the 1970 World Cup thinking to myself, "Maybe I would have got on the pitch." It's all hypothetical, of course, but just to have been in the squad and to have been there would have been an absolute dream. Hopefully, if I had been fit enough I would have been in the squad of 22 – Sir Alf said I would have been, so I'll take him at his word.'

Dreaming of West Germany

Despite having been cruelly denied an opportunity to play at the World Cup in Mexico, Moore had good reason to think that the next World Cup in West Germany was a realistic target. He told *Shoot!*:

'This summer I will join most of you by watching England's progress by permission of a satellite and television. And instead of brooding over what I might have missed, I will start dreaming of a World Cup spot all over again. You see, I am 25. When the World Cup is played in Munich in 1974 I will only be 29. I don't think that's too old.'

Moore did indeed remain in the England manager's thoughts. In the first competitive match managed by Sir Alf since England's shattering 3-2 quarter-final defeat against West Germany in Mexico three months earlier, on 23 September 1970 Moore played for the English Football League against the Irish Football League at Norwich City's Carrow Road.

Unfortunately, as with his under-23 appearance against Austria, Moore did not last until half-time, being substituted midway through the first half after injuring his left ankle in crossing the ball into the penalty area. The headline in the *Nottingham Evening Post* the following day referred, perhaps inevitably, to Moore's 'injury jinx'.

On 20 February 1971 Sir Alf was at the City Ground to see Moore score the only goal against Burnley, tucking home a poacher's finish from six yards out. This was enough for Ramsey to include Moore in his 'shadow' England side when, on 17 March, the Football League beat the Scottish Football League 1-0 at Hampden Park in Glasgow.

This time Moore was able to make a vital contribution to the outcome. After just six minutes he started the move that led to the only goal, crossing from the left for Burnley's Ralph Coates to eventually score. Despite the sparse crowd of less than 18,000 dotted around Hampden's vast terracing, the match was a predictably feisty affair. So often on the receiving end, after 26 minutes Moore was lectured by the referee for retaliating after Motherwell's Tom Forsyth had brought him down with a bad tackle.

For the first half the Football League played 4-2-4 with Moore and Coates on the left and right wings respectively. In the second half Coates was withdrawn to midfield in a 4-3-3 formation. The change in shape led to a disjointed performance and the Football League were somewhat fortunate to eke out an uninspiring 1-0 win. 'Ramsey bandits rob the Scots' claimed one newspaper – and that was south of the border.

That would be Moore's last match for an England representative team.

Coveted by Clough and Taylor

Of the various Forest players of the 1960s who earned under-23 or full international honours, Terry Hennessey, Alan Hinton, Frank Wignall, Peter Grummitt and Henry Newton had something else in common: they would all at some stage be signed by Messrs Brian Clough and Peter Taylor. Soon, the dynamic duo would set their sights on Ian Storey-Moore.

12

Big fish in a small pond

'I was afraid I'd miss the big time.'

Ian Storey-Moore

1969/70 season peters out

Following Moore's catastrophic injury at Manchester City, Forest failed to win any of the next 11 games, the first a 5-0 drubbing at Burnley. This was John Barnwell's last competitive match for the club and, with Peter Grummitt and Terry Hennessey having both made their final appearance earlier in the season, there were ever fewer survivors from the tremendous team of 1966/67. Inspired signings such as Frank Wignall, Hennessey and Joe Baker, together with the emergence of the likes of Moore and Henry Newton, had laid the foundations of that team, but since then Forest's recruitment had been more miss than hit and the youngsters promoted from the reserves had rarely grasped their opportunities to hold down a first-team place.

Just to show that it never rains but it pours, in Forest's second game without Moore, who was watching from the stand, keeper Alan Hill sustained a badly broken arm against Everton. Typical of Forest's misfortunes, this came just a month after the out-of-favour Grummitt had reluctantly left for Sheffield Wednesday. Hill would never play again. Awarded a testimonial by the club, he combined working as a publican with roles at Forest as coach, assistant manager and chief scout. He would become a familiar presence on the touchline as Forest collected silverware in the Brian Clough era.

Yet another goalkeeper arrived – the team's sixth in two seasons – when Dave Hollins was signed on loan from Mansfield Town. Forest finally won again on the last day of the campaign, when a rare Alex Ingram goal was enough to beat Ipswich Town. By the time they retained the Nottinghamshire FA County Cup with a 2-0 victory against Notts County, reserve keeper Eric Hulme had become yet another player to don the green jersey.

Forest finished 15th, a mid-season purple patch the main reason they were spared a battle against relegation. Their reliance on Moore was clear – they earned twice as many points with him in the team as without him. But he would spend the World Cup summer watching the games on television and fighting to be fit when the new season started in August.

One hundred goals

As the 1970/71 campaign began, Moore was hoping to finally put his injury troubles behind him and play a full season for the first time in four years. He played in all three tour games in Sweden, bagging a hat-trick in a 4-2 win against Landskrona. But by the time of Forest's one home pre-season friendly against Hamburg, he had picked up a leg strain in training and wasn't risked.

To take some of the responsibility for goalscoring away from Moore, manager Matt Gillies deployed Peter Cormack as a second striker. The versatile Scot, who could also play in midfield, had been signed in March for £70,000 from Hibernian. He responded to being played up front with three goals in those four pre-season games. At the other end, Forest hoped to have solved their goalkeeping woes with the signing of Jim Barron from Oxford United.

Moore was fit to play in the First Division opener at home to Coventry City and scored with a diving header in a 2-0 win. Forest made a steady start to the season, drawing their next three games, Moore scoring again at Newcastle. He also converted a penalty as they ended August with a 4-1 win against Wolverhampton Wanderers to rub shoulders with the more fancied teams at the top of the early league table.

Unfortunately, Forest had developed a habit of going on long winless runs and after the Wolves game they only managed one more league victory before the end of the calendar year, failing to so much as score in the next six league games. Meanwhile, having both scored in a 2-2 draw with Airdrieonians in the Texaco Cup, Cormack and Moore repeated the feat to beat Huddersfield Town in a League Cup replay, Moore getting an assist for Cormack's headed opener before scoring with a header of his own to make the game safe.

Moore had been left limping after a challenge in the Huddersfield game and just two days later his hopes of an injury-free season were dashed. The ankle injury picked up playing for the Football League meant it would be more than two months before he played again and Forest would win only one of the ten games he missed.

In that time Forest had their first experience of a penalty shoot-out, losing from 12 yards after the second leg of the Texaco Cup tie at Airdrie also finished 2-2. They finally won again in the league, beating Blackpool 3-1 on 10 October 1970 in what was Henry Newton's last game for the club and, as a substitute for Paul Richardson, John Robertson's first. Newton was the latest big-name departure from the 1966/67 team, joining Everton in a deal that saw Northern Ireland international midfielder Tommy Jackson switch to the Reds in part-exchange.

Forest then went ten more league games without winning, failing to score in the first four of them. Moore made a goalscoring return at Burnley and added further goals in a humiliating 4-2 defeat at home to Derby County – in which he missed a penalty – and a 1-1 draw against Chelsea.

On 2 January 1971 Forest had a chance to end their barren run in a home FA Cup tie against Second Division Luton Town but could only manage a 1-1 draw. In a bizarre incident, the game was held up for 14 minutes when one of the goalposts snapped after John Winfield got tangled in the netting after hurrying back to try and keep out Malcolm Macdonald's goalbound effort. Luton were convinced that the ball had already crossed the goal line just inside the post before Winfield uprooted it, but the referee presumably felt that as there was no clear proof either way he was unable to award the goal.

Having scored the only goal when Forest at last won again in the league, at West Bromwich Albion, Moore missed the 4-3 win in the cup replay at Kenilworth Road two days later, when Macdonald found himself on the losing side despite scoring a hat-trick. Two Moore goals earned another valuable win against Newcastle United before the visit of Orient in the fourth round of the FA Cup saw another oddity.

When the team in red ran out before the start the home fans duly cheered them – until they realised they didn't recognise the players, whereupon Forest took the field wearing, for some reason, an all-white kit. The match programme actually indicated that the teams would be wearing these colours but without offering an explanation. Again Forest struggled to overcome lower-division opponents, Moore scoring a penalty in another disappointing 1-1 draw. The replay two days later at Brisbane Road was abandoned at half-time because of a waterlogged pitch. Sammy Chapman told reporters that he kicked the ball three times with all his strength, only to see it travel no more than two yards through the mud. Waggish spectators claimed it was the only match ever abandoned because the players were at risk of drowning. But Forest eventually won the rearranged replay thanks to a goal from one of Graham Collier's rare starts.

Moore then scored three times in four games, helping his team to welcome home wins against Southampton and Burnley, though his penalty at Tottenham Hotspur on 13 February wasn't enough to keep Forest in the cup as they lost by the odd goal in three.

At this stage Forest were just two places above the relegation zone but a run of seven wins in ten games went a long way to ensuring their safety. Unusually for Forest, three of those wins came in away games, a surprise single-goal victory at Tottenham, a hugely satisfying 2-1 defeat of Derby (with Moore heading in the decisive second goal) and a 3-1 win at Manchester City, in which a promising youngster by the name of Duncan McKenzie scored twice.

That run of improved form included Moore's first league hat-trick in a 3-1 win at home against Crystal Palace on 27 March. The match programme had included a feature on Moore having completed a century of first-team goals for the club and mentioned that Palace were the only First Division team that he had yet to score against. He completed his season's scoring with goals in wins against West Ham United and at Blackpool, after which Forest's season petered out as they failed to score in the last three matches.

Incredibly, and in stark contrast to the injury problems of recent years, Forest had been able to play the same back five – Barron, Hindley, Winfield, Chapman, O'Kane – in all 58 of their friendly and competitive matches. Despite a few heavy defeats, this gave Forest a certain degree of defensive solidity, which was ultimately enough to keep them away from the relegation dogfight at the end of the season. The main reason they could finish no higher than 16th was their over-reliance on Moore (22 league and cup goals) and Cormack (13) to find the target, the next-highest scorer managing just four. They were the outstanding players in a very ordinary team and within a year Forest would find themselves needing to replace them both.

Beginning of the end

Optimism was in short supply among the Forest fans at the start of the 1971/72 season. It had become increasingly apparent that the Double-chasing team had been the exception and not the rule – Forest were now viewed among the clubs expected to face a battle to avoid relegation. Once again there were no new faces, but one familiar figure no longer on the City Ground scene was Tommy Cavanagh, who had been summarily dismissed: 'I would not have left Forest as my heart has always been in the club, but there has been a clash of personalities and I suppose I have trodden on a few toes.' It wouldn't be long, however, before Moore renewed acquaintances with the highly respected coach.

Bob McKinlay took over as first-team coach. He had called time on his playing career the previous autumn having made 682 appearances, a club record that surely will never be broken. Enabling him to extend his time on Trentside was a fine gesture towards an outstanding servant, but there were concerns about his lack of coaching experience and whether his quiet and undemonstrative nature was suited to getting the best out of players.

There was mixed news concerning Moore. Fans were relieved and delighted that he had signed a new four-year contract, despite his growing misgivings at the direction the club was taking, but he was sent off for the only time in his career half an hour into a pre-season friendly at Kaiserslautern. Manager Gillies stood by his player, describing Moore's dismissal as 'a diabolical decision', but Moore freely admits to retaliating after being on the receiving end of some rough treatment:

> 'This great big German just kicked me, so I turned round and belted him and got sent off – in a friendly! Quite out of character, really. You wouldn't believe it but I had to go to an FA inquiry in London, just for being sent off in a friendly game. All that way with Gillies and [club secretary] Ken Smales. Anyhow, I got off and didn't get suspended.'

Moore's good disciplinary record having stood him in good stead, he took his place in the team for the remaining friendlies and the first league game, a tough trip to Anfield. Liverpool fielded a young signing from Moore's home town of Scunthorpe by the name of Kevin Keegan, in whom Forest had been interested before deciding he was perhaps not quite good enough. Needless to say, Keegan scored 12 minutes into his debut. Liverpool proved too strong for a spirited Forest side and won 3-1, Moore scoring from the penalty spot after Neil Martin was brought down by Ray Clemence, another former Scunthorpe player.

Moore scored another penalty to give his team their first points of the season, against West Ham United in their third match, but, in a sign of things to come, Forest's only win in the next 12 was against Fourth Division Aldershot in the League Cup. Not for the first time, Moore's form was better than the team's and by mid-October he had already racked up ten goals, including two in the return with Liverpool, a 3-2 defeat that left Forest rock-bottom with just seven points from 13 games.

Defeats were becoming increasingly the norm for Forest. Low points included a 6-1 thrashing at Tottenham, surrendering the East Midlands bragging rights in a 2-0 defeat to Derby County – Moore having a penalty saved at 0-0 – and the sending-off, at a time when this was still a relatively noteworthy occurrence, of Sammy Chapman against Leeds United.

During a miserable, goalless run from mid-February to mid-March Moore finally prepared to say goodbye to the club he had served with such distinction for a decade:

> 'I thought, "I'm 27 now, I've got to try and finish off at a bigger club if I possibly can." Nothing against the club, nothing against the fans, who had always been fantastic with me. It was just a question of trying to enhance my prospects of an England career at a bigger club. There was always this sense that if you were at a smaller club you had less of a chance of getting back into the England team than if you were in London or Manchester. It was a

> tremendous feat for someone at Forest just to get into the England side.'

Good days were few and far between but they included a first away win of the season, at Huddersfield Town, and the emergence of a talented young attacking midfielder from Northern Ireland. Martin O'Neill had been plucked from his law studies in Belfast and scored, as did Moore, in a testimonial match for Notts County stalwart Jack Wheeler. O'Neill then marked his competitive debut with a goal after coming on for John Robertson in a welcome 4-1 win against West Bromwich Albion in which Moore also scored. Moore was not surprised to see O'Neill settle so quickly:

> 'I remember the first practice match when he came over from Northern Ireland. Gillies had been eulogising about me to Martin, saying, "We've got one world-class player." Well, Martin picked the ball up in midfield, drifted past about four players and smashed it in the top corner. I said to the manager, "I'm supposed to do that, aren't I!?"'

A close friendship developed, which, like so many from Moore's playing days, endures to this day.

The injury misfortune of recent years had not deserted Forest and, remarkably, on 11 December 1971, for the third time in five years a key player suffered a serious injury in a match against Everton. After Joe Baker and Alan Hill, the next victim was Liam O'Kane, who had successfully swapped positions with Peter Hindley, moving across from centre-half to right-back. With his reading of the game and a great ability to make immaculately timed tackles, O'Kane had developed into a fine international defender.

In a niggly game marred by Everton's spoiling tactics, O'Kane suffered a double fracture to his right leg in a challenge from John Hurst that had the Trent End baying for blood but drew no punishment from the referee. Forest won 1-0 thanks to a fortunate goal from ex-Evertonian Tommy Jackson, who knew precious little about it when Henry Newton's attempted clearance rebounded off his back and into the goal.

O'Kane's season was over. Forest moved quickly to reinforce their defence, their generous wage offer tempting European Cup winner Tommy Gemmell to move from Celtic to take the left-back berth, with O'Kane's place going firstly to the versatile Doug Fraser and later to Hindley.

Gemmell made his debut against Arsenal at the City Ground on 27 December 1971, a match etched into the consciousness of a generation of Forest supporters.

13

That goal

'Storey went one way, Moore went the other, and I was left in the middle.'

Arsenal goalkeeper Bob Wilson

Which one?

Many a player remains known long after their career ends for a special goal, one that stands out from all their other strikes. However prolific their scoring record might have been, there will be one particular goal that ranks above all the others and lives on in supporters' collective folk memory of the player and, by association, team in question. It tends to be referred to simply as '*that* goal', those two words being enough to bring fond memories flooding back to those who witnessed it and to prompt respectful recognition in those who didn't, with no further explanation required.

Like those of any club, Forest supporters are instantly reconnected with a special moment at the mere mention of a player's name. They might be associated with one goal – think of Colin Barrett slaying European champions Liverpool just as their fans and players were boasting that one goal was not enough. But for some players '*that* goal' will elicit the response, 'Which one?' Johnny Metgod's free kicks come to mind here, be it a last-minute chip beating Manchester United or a 30-yard rocket stunning West Ham. Ian Storey-Moore belongs firmly in this latter category.

That extraordinary winner in the dying seconds of the 1967 FA Cup quarter-final against holders Everton ticks all the boxes to justify '*that* goal' status. The timing, its importance to the game and to Forest's season, not to mention the raw courage, dogged determination and sheer persistence that saw Moore force the ball over the line at the fourth attempt with the exhausted Everton defence transfixed and helpless – it all adds up to a goal worthy of being forever evoked by those two little words.

Moore has, of course, always been the first to praise Frank Wignall's role in all three goals. By contrast, Moore's second career-defining '*that* goal' would be very much an individual effort.

Haunted by relegation

Five seasons after that glorious challenge for the Double, the Forest team was much changed, the only survivors from 1966/67 being Moore and defenders Peter Hindley, John Winfield and Sammy Chapman, who had become a first-team regular after dropping back to a central defensive position. Weakened by the sale – and inadequate replacement – of several star players, the Forest of 1971/72 were struggling. By Christmas, they were next to bottom with just four wins in 23 games. On five of the seven occasions they had managed to score more than one goal they had still contrived to lose the match.

Forest's festive home fixture on Monday, 27 December – the Boxing Day bank holiday – was a visit from Arsenal, winners of the Double the previous season; not exactly the opposition you would choose when confidence is low. Moreover, the Gunners travelled to Trentside having just augmented their line-up with the purchase for a British-record £220,000 of Alan Ball from Everton.

For months, Moore had been pursued by a succession of top clubs keen to boost their 'goals for' column. Despite a relatively indifferent run of form – he had not scored for five games –

transfer speculation was growing, with bids of £200,000 or more expected and Ball's record already under threat.

Having shared top billing five years earlier with the likes of Grummitt, Baker, Hennessey and Newton, Moore was now unquestionably the standout performer in the team. With ten league goals he was easily Forest's leading scorer, as he would be in five of his last six seasons at the club. With the Reds sliding ever closer towards an ignominious relegation, it was to Moore that team-mates and supporters alike looked when morale needed lifting, when hope had to be reinvigorated and, most of all, when a goal was required.

All eyes on Alan Ball

In that relegation-haunted season the crowds at the City Ground fluctuated wildly, the number of casual supporters who joined the diehards varying according to the team's form and the attractiveness of the opposition. Some would-be spectators still worked a half or full day on Saturdays, while many more would be playing in Nottingham's thriving amateur football scene, one of the most extensive in the country. But over Christmas there were no such distractions and the holiday games were traditionally watched by bumper attendances. A season's best attendance of 42,750 were in the City Ground eager to see the Double winners and Ball.

Many turned up at the last minute. Club secretary Ken Smales told the *Nottingham Evening Post*:

> 'Our electronic turnstile counter showed that there were only 28,000 people in the ground at 2.45pm and still only 35,600 admitted five minutes before kick-off ... We were a little worried when the police decided to allow people to sit inside the boundary wall on the track around the pitch. There is an FA directive that clubs should not allow people to watch the match from the track because it makes it very

> easy for excited fans to run on the pitch. But the police have the final say in these matters.'

In the days when *Match of the Day* showed the highlights of just two games, a few seconds of footage from another match would be shown in the brief round-up of the day's sport at the end of the evening news bulletins. On this occasion, the news camera was at the City Ground for Ball's debut in an Arsenal shirt, but it was Moore's goal that became the story of the match – and another famous debutant who gave him his chance of glory.

Following Liam O'Kane's broken leg against Everton, Forest had persuaded Celtic's legendary European Cup-winning full-back Tommy Gemmell to swap the banks of the Clyde for those of the Trent. Nobody knew at the time, of course, but he would be the unexpected answer to a future trivia question, technically being the first Forest player to have lifted the European Cup.

Few will remember George Graham tucking home George Armstrong's low cross for Arsenal's equaliser in the 1-1 draw, but nobody present will ever forget Forest's goal, which came after a quarter of an hour. An Arsenal attack at the Trent End broke down and was headed clear by Lisbon Lion Gemmell, a few yards outside the penalty area. Moore, in space, did what came naturally and took the ball quickly forward. Ball tracked his run, but Martin O'Neill was keeping pace alongside Moore and Ball seemed unsure which of them to cover. Ball was wearing his distinctive white boots and to this day Moore recalls seeing them out of the corner of his eye as the Arsenal number eight pursued him almost the length of the pitch. On he went until he reached the penalty area at the Bridgford End. Ball finally decided to commit himself to a challenge, but Moore slipped between him and Peter Simpson, then evaded Bob McNab's desperate lunge. At this point, Moore distinctly remembers thinking, 'Well, I'd better not miss now!' Fortunately, he had enough energy left to slot the ball past Bob Wilson into the corner of the net. The distance he had run with the ball was later measured by Forest officials as 74 yards.

The top football reporters of the time were at the City Ground that day. David Miller of the *Daily Telegraph* called the goal 'magnificent', stating that Moore 'fully deserved the tumult of applause'. The *Daily Mirror*'s Ken Jones wrote that the goal was 'good enough to nourish the prospect that Moore may eventually take over from Ball as Britain's costliest footballer'. But only Norman Giller of the *Daily Express* gave the goal the prominence it deserved, stating that 'Ian Moore unwrapped the goal of a lifetime' and adding, 'Forest could justifiably demand £250,000 for him if his form against Arsenal is a guide to his market value.'

Even half a century later, neither the press nor Forest fans show any sign of tiring of asking Moore about this (or rather, *that*) goal. He is flattered by the attention and grateful that those 11 seconds and 74 yards of skill and tenacity continue to mean so much to so many people. This goal still features regularly in supporters' surveys into Forest's greatest. Arsenal's keeper Wilson, for his part, considered it the best goal he ever conceded and was good-natured enough to recall it with the neat, self-deprecating observation, 'Storey went one way, Moore the other, and I was left in the middle.'

Out-Besting one of the very best

Until the relatively recent re-emergence of that news footage, the goal lived on in the memories of those who were there to see it but could only be imagined by everyone else. There are, though, parallels with a frequently shown, and thus much better-known, goal scored by Manchester United's George Best that same year, netting against Sheffield United after an unstoppable run through the Blades' defence. Not the least of these parallels is the strange reluctance of the defenders to put in any sort of challenge for the ball and, if necessary, 'take one for the team', especially as these were the days when you virtually needed to hospitalise your opponent to get more than a stern talking-to from the referee. But, if anything, Moore's was arguably the better of the two goals, as Best received the ball midway inside the opposition half, whereas Moore had much more to do, dribbling from just outside his own penalty area before finally tucking the ball home.

The similarities don't end with the comparison of those two goals, either. Moore and Best both roved around the pitch more freely than their usual number 11 and number seven shirts would otherwise have dictated, and both were capable of scoring with either foot or their head and from a variety of ranges. They had easily been the most popular players with the female fans at their respective clubs from the 'swinging' part of the 1960s onwards. With his long dark hair, untucked red shirt, the adulation of the crowd and a mesmerising effect on the opposition, it is easy to see why Moore's arrival at Old Trafford a few weeks later was seen by many as a move to ultimately replace the wayward genius. This wasn't the case but with this incredible strike against Arsenal, Moore arguably out-Bested one of *the* very best.

Relegation-bound

Despite Gemmell's unwitting assist for Moore's wonder goal, the experienced Scottish international could do little about Forest's long winless run after the Everton game in mid-December, but towards the end of the season he had an unexpected purple patch in front of goal and scored five times in nine games, including a 35-yard rocket of a shot in a surprise 4-0 thrashing of Coventry City.

Back to the turn of the year and after that draw with Arsenal, Forest were 21st in the table. As the outstanding player in a team that looked doomed – and despite signing that contract extension – Moore was always going to be the subject of interest, particularly as the March transfer deadline drew near. The persistent rumours about his fate didn't help Forest's stability as they desperately tried to make up ground on the teams above them.

After a creditable 2-2 draw at Manchester City on New Year's Day, Forest lost eight games in a row, including what was becoming a traditional FA Cup exit to lower-league opposition – 3-1 at Millwall on this occasion. The first of those eight defeats was by a single goal at home to Crystal Palace, who survived an early Forest onslaught almost entirely orchestrated by Moore. The *South London Press* was sufficiently impressed by Moore – and dismissive of his colleagues – to headline its match report 'Ian Storey-Moore 0 Crystal Palace 1'.

As the defeats racked up and his departure looked inevitable, Moore scored what proved to be his final two goals for Forest in late January against Leicester City and at Southampton. Then the Reds once again contrived to go four games without scoring a single goal, including a 4-0 drubbing at the Baseball Ground on 19 February. Rather ironically, as it would transpire, this was Moore's last game for Forest. Having reluctantly decided his ambitions of winning silverware were unlikely to be achieved, a battle for his signature ensued. Quite what a battle that would be he could never have imagined.

A little over two months later, the club's relegation to the Second Division would be confirmed.

14

'Brian Clough's on the phone'

'The most remarkable transfer deal in the history of the game.'

Vince Wilson, *Sunday Mirror*

Personal terms

Mid-morning, Friday, 3 March 1972: sitting opposite Ian Storey-Moore in the otherwise deserted bar at the Edwalton Hotel, Manchester United's manager was dumbstruck. Moore repeated himself, 'I'm sorry, Mr O'Farrell, I can't accept those terms.' With that, Frank O'Farrell, heir to Matt Busby's Old Trafford empire, stood up, politely shook Moore's hand, and left the room.

Barely a quarter of an hour earlier O'Farrell had arrived at the popular hotel and restaurant on the outskirts of Nottingham fully expecting to complete the signing of Forest's star striker. Time was running out for the man who the previous season had guided Leicester City to promotion from the Second Division before being poached by United. After beating Forest 3-2 in early December to go top of the table, United had gone nine games without a win to slip to seventh. O'Farrell was under pressure but had the backing of the board to spend – and spend big – to turn round United's fortunes.

Having signed future captain Martin Buchan from Aberdeen for a club record fee of £120,000 earlier in the week, O'Farrell hadn't anticipated any difficulty in finalising the deal for Moore. Subject to agreeing personal terms with the man he hoped would reinvigorate United's misfiring forward line, he was authorised to agree a £200,000-plus transfer fee with Forest. This would put Moore in the same league as World Cup winners Martin Peters and Alan Ball.

On his way out of the hotel a visibly upset O'Farrell, a decent and honourable man, spoke briefly with the assembled Forest hierarchy who were waiting in the dimly lit reception area – manager Matt Gillies, assistant manager Bill Anderson, and club secretary Ken Smales. He got in his car and drove off along Nottingham's ring road towards the motorway and back to Manchester. A wasted journey, he must have thought.

Gillies was somewhat taken aback. Just the day before he had arranged the mid-morning rendezvous between Moore and O'Farrell in anticipation of Forest pocketing a cheque for the best part of a quarter of a million pounds as they sought to sell the relegation-threatened club's most valuable asset. With their 1966/67 'nearly' season now a fading memory, and the ill-fated signing of Jim Baxter aside, the Reds had well and truly become a selling club.

At the start of the 1967/68 season, Alan Hinton had been sold to Brian Clough's Derby County for £30,000. In February 1970 Clough persuaded his chairman, Sam Longson, to part with £110,000 to take Terry Hennessey to the Baseball Ground. In a curious twist of fate, Longson had appointed Clough, one of Moore's boyhood heroes, on the recommendation of another, Len Shackleton. Indeed, it was Shackleton who had helped Clough get his start in management by putting in a good word for him at Hartlepools United back in 1965.

Five months later Everton, the 'Merseyside Millionaires', paid £120,000 for Henry Newton. Again Clough had been interested but Forest had made it clear that they wouldn't sell the midfield dynamo to their fierce local rivals. Three years later Everton did sell Newton to Derby and he went on to make over 100 appearances for the Rams, winning the First Division championship with them in 1974/75.

In early 1972 Forest were eager to cash in on Moore's star quality and, in so doing, become the first club to sell three players for six-figure sums.

Lies, damn lies and rumours

Neither Gillies nor, before him, Johnny Carey would discuss possible transfers with Moore, who reflects, 'It was a case of "make your own way in life". There was no question of being given advice on this, that or the other. Nobody mollycoddled you – it was up to you whether you made the grade.'

Right from the start of the 1971/72 season transfer rumours surrounding Moore had been rife despite him agreeing to a new contract with much-improved terms. '*That* goal' simply fuelled speculation that Moore's transfer was on the cards. He knew it, his team-mates knew it and so did the supporters.

On the pitch, Moore was as committed as ever. Mercifully injury-free, he had played the full 90 minutes in all of Forest's 38 league, cup and friendly games up to and including the traumatic 4-0 loss at the Baseball Ground on 19 February 1972, a feat matched only by central defender Sammy Chapman.

Off the pitch, on the other hand, Moore did little to dispel the transfer rumours. After all, Forest's top goalscorer was entering his peak playing years and, despite his deep affection for the club, he didn't want to be spending any time in the Second Division; that would hardly help his ambition to get back into the England reckoning.

It was around this time that Moore was approached by a well-known, somewhat controversial, public relations 'consultant', Kenneth 'Splashy' Johnstone, the moniker reflecting his uncanny ability to get sensational stories 'splashed' across the front and back pages of the national newspapers. Johnstone's clients included high-profile players such as Ray Clemence, Pat Jennings, Colin Todd and Charlie George, and somewhat against his better judgement Moore engaged Splashy to, in effect, place stories in the newspapers to advertise the fact that he was disillusioned with Forest and 'open to offers'. To Moore's lasting regret, however, many of these stories included alleged quotes from him – all completely fabricated by Johnstone – that denigrated Forest, their fans and the city.

For instance, from the *Daily Mirror*'s 'The Saturday Star' feature:

> 'I've had many disappointments and apart from one year when we did well in the league and reached the semi-final of the cup, the club has not known much success. Who knows, I might have been a better player in a better team, but really there's not a lot of enthusiasm for the game in Nottingham. The fans soon lose their loyalty. I don't think the public are very interested in football. It's a bit of a depressed area now.'

The article did at least conclude by stating that 'more than anything Moore wants Forest to be a success', but that did little to help his relationship with the club's chairman and committee. Matt Gillies, known as 'the nice guy of football', would never call Moore into his office to ask him to explain comments that had appeared in the press – he knew it was just paper talk. Articles allegedly quoting Moore continued to appear in the press, however, such as, following that woeful FA Cup defeat at Millwall:

> 'Everything seems dead for me now. I appreciate Forest's position, but in three years' time I'll be 30 and past the point where clubs would be willing to pay a big fee for me. I wish I'd never signed a four-year contract at the start of the season.'

At the time Moore denied the words but not the sentiment.

Press talk or not, Gillies finally acknowledged publicly that the speculation had had an unsettling effect on the team. At Moore's request, on 20 January he held a 45-minute 'clear the air' meeting with the player. Speaking to journalists afterwards, Gillies said, 'We have discussed the situation thoroughly and Ian has agreed to go out and play hard for the club. We need him to play his part in our fight against relegation.' Moore confirmed, 'Yes, I'm staying to help Forest.'

The following Saturday Moore scored what would be his last City Ground goal, beating Leicester's Peter Shilton after half an hour. Unfortunately, it was to no avail as a 'fluke' goal – by Leicester forward Keith Weller's own admission – and a last-minute own goal by Peter Hindley condemned luckless Forest to a 2-1 defeat. At Southampton a week later Moore again gave Forest the lead but this turned out to be a mere consolation as they lost 4-1.

Within a couple of weeks, pretty much all the top First Division clubs had expressed an interest in signing Moore, the Reds having by now made it clear that they wouldn't stand in his way if the right offer – claimed in some quarters to be as much as £260,000 – was received.

The early favourites to get Moore's signature were Manchester City. Their flamboyant but astute manager, Malcolm Allison, believed Moore was the only player potentially available who could enhance what was already a formidable set of attacking options comprising full internationals Francis Lee, Colin Bell, Mike Summerbee and Wyn Davies. Allison declared, 'He can score goals. I think he would score goals for us.'

Chelsea were reportedly willing to pay £220,000 for Moore's services. Wolverhampton Wanderers had gone further and actually offered that amount but apparently Gillies wanted a player in part-exchange to help with the relegation fight and Wolves were unable to agree to that.

Moore knew from his friend Henry Newton that Everton were interested, as were Double winners Arsenal and Bill Shankly's Liverpool. The following year, after having played against Liverpool, Moore was being interviewed by a radio reporter in the players' tunnel. The man who would become one of Shankly's successors, first-team coach Joe Fagan, came up to him and said, 'Ian, you went to the wrong club!'

Two clubs in particular had been assiduous in tapping up Moore. Derby County's assistant manager Peter Taylor would regularly telephone Moore to let him know that he and Brian Clough were interested, insisting 'Ian, don't sign for anyone else.'

Moore knew Clough and Taylor well, having played charity cricket matches with them, been their guest at the races, and occasionally bumping into Taylor, Nottingham born and bred, in and around the city. He enjoyed their company and particularly liked Clough's sense of humour and his witticisms. He had always got on well with the two men he had admired ever since he and his father used to watch them turn out for Middlesbrough at Ayresome Park all those years earlier. He had often wondered what it would be like to play for the dynamic duo.

Frank O'Farrell, on the other hand, used a less direct approach, enlisting the help of a friendly journalist to see if Moore would be interested in joining the squad he was in the process of rebuilding at Old Trafford. In a series of telephone conversations O'Farrell's intermediary promised Moore £200 a week – double what he was on at Forest – and a £10,000 signing-on fee. At the time the average weekly wage in the country was around £30.

Despite all this, Moore was surprised when, on Thursday, 2 March, a week before transfer deadline day, Matt Gillies called him into his office after training and told him, 'Can you get to the Edwalton Hotel tomorrow morning? I want you to talk to Manchester United first. And if you can't agree terms I'll get hold of Brian Clough for you.' With just 12 games of the season left and Forest now firmly in bottom place still with just four wins, it seemed the club really were intent on selling their leading scorer; Moore had 13 league goals, as many as Peter Cormack, Duncan McKenzie and Neil Martin combined.

And so to the Edwalton Hotel. For whatever reason, United's manager had been unable to confirm the promised signing-on fee. Moore felt misled: the perils of being tapped up. 'What about what we talked about over the phone?' asked Moore. 'I don't know anything about that,' replied O'Farrell.

Which was all a bit strange, bearing in mind that O'Farrell had himself been put in a similar position when negotiating his own salary to take over the reins at United. Busby had offered O'Farrell a salary of £12,000 plus bonuses. When O'Farrell demurred, chairman Louis Edwards interjected, 'Oh no, Matt, that's wrong, it's £15,000 plus bonuses.' O'Farrell's sense that Busby had tried to short-change him damaged his trust in his illustrious predecessor.

After O'Farrell's abrupt departure, Gillies and his entourage waited for Moore to show his face. 'Well, Ian, what happened?' Gillies enquired when Moore, having regained his composure, eventually appeared. 'We couldn't agree personal terms, Mr Gillies.' Gillies immediately put Plan B into action.

All alone at the Edwalton Hotel

Seemingly unruffled by the turn of events, Forest's manager went into the phone booth in the hotel's reception, dialled the number and said, 'Hello, Brian, I've got Ian Storey-Moore on the phone for you.' Gillies handed Moore the Bakelite receiver and Moore swapped places with him in the booth.

Their conversation was short but sweet:

'I can't agree terms with Manchester United, Brian.'
'Don't worry, son, we'll be right over. Where are you?'
'The Edwalton Hotel, just outside Nottingham.'
'We'll be there in half an hour. Don't go anywhere.'

Moore put the phone down, turned round and walked over to where Gillies, Anderson and Smales were waiting, slightly conspiratorially, in a dark corner of the oak-panelled foyer. To his astonishment, as soon as he told them that Clough and Taylor were on their way, like bats out of hell the three Forest officials made a hasty exit and drove off. Moore couldn't believe they were going to leave him on his own to await the arrival of the men from Derby County.

Moore walked back to the bar area, sat down and waited:

> 'I may have been 27 years old but I was as nervous as a kitten. Not to put too fine a point on it, I was shitting myself, thinking, "How do I deal with these two?" They were both strong characters and, as a double act, quite formidable. My mind was spinning. "How do I get out of this now if I don't want to go to Derby? Even if I do go, where are they going to play me? They've got Hinton, Hector and O'Hare." Instead of Hinton? Probably not: Alan was playing well. Hector, the main goalscorer, well, you couldn't leave him out. John O'Hare, a good centre-forward, great with his back to goal. I really didn't know.'

Clough and Taylor arrived at the same time in separate cars. They made quite an entrance and were directed to where Moore was waiting. He stood up and shook their hands.

Pleasantries exchanged, they got down to brass tacks. Or, rather, Clough did – Taylor sat to one side, a silent, somewhat intimidating presence. First the soft sell, 'Come on then, Ian, let's start talking. We need you. We want you. I'll get you back in the England team. But we've got to ask you a few questions about your personal life. Right, are you a boozer?'

'Not really, Mr Clough. I drink with the players but only a glass of wine or half a pint.'

'Are you a womaniser?'

'No, I'm married now, Mr Clough. When I was younger, absolutely, I was chasing the girls like anyone else.'

'Are you a gambler?'

'No, not really, the odd flutter now and again but I wouldn't say I'm a gambler.'

'Do you smoke?'

'No, I've never smoked, Mr Clough.'

Clough turned to Taylor, 'Peter, we can't fucking sign him, he's a fucking liar!'

Then Clough looked back at Moore, 'Right, come on then, son, how much do you want?'

Moore was on his own, no agent, no advisers: he had to think on his feet. He decided to see if Clough would match the terms O'Farrell, through his journalist friend, had 'offered' but reneged upon.

'£200 a week, Mr Clough.'

'£200 a week? Roy McFarland's not on that.'

'I know that, Mr Clough, but I can guarantee you 20 goals a season.'

'Listen son, if I want a fucking guarantee, I'll buy a fucking washing machine.' And after a pause, 'Don't worry, son, I'm only kidding!'

Clough agreed to everything Moore had asked for, including the signing-on fee. Moore trusted Clough implicitly as a man of his word and when a blank contract – the details to be filled in later – was placed in front of him, he signed without hesitation. He also signed the transfer form that, once countersigned by Smales and his counterpart at Derby, Stuart Webb, would allow the Football League to recognise the transfer. As requested, Moore post-dated his signature for the following day, Saturday, 4 March.

Formalities over, Clough said to Taylor, 'Right, Peter, you take him back to the Midland Hotel.' Derby were due to play Wolverhampton Wanderers at the Baseball Ground on the Saturday and the Midland, about a mile away from the stadium, was where the Derby players would spend the night before a home game.

Clough stood up, 'I'll get down to the Forest ground, sort them out and get the thing done and dusted.'

In light of the events that followed, Clough would later remark, 'We had signed 23 players before that and the other clubs' secretaries' signatures had been no more than a rubber stamp. Can anyone blame us for expecting this to be the same?'

Moore agreed with Taylor that, rather than going with him straight to Derby, he would drive home, let Carol know what was going on, pack an overnight bag with a change of clothes, and make his own way to the hotel. Back at home in Bingham he explained to Carol that he had signed for Derby rather than, as they had expected when he left home earlier that day, Manchester United. At least they wouldn't have to move house.

On parade

Around eight o'clock on the Friday evening, Moore was having dinner with his new team-mates-to-be. He was already on good terms with several of the Derby players. Moore's former Forest colleague, Alan Hinton, was there. Moore had great respect for him. Surely he wouldn't be taking his place on the left wing? He had played with Roy McFarland for the English Football League representative team a year earlier and got on well with him.

Dinner was interrupted as Clough walked in. 'We're all sorted. They even offered me the job there!' Everybody toasted the club's new signing and the rest of the evening passed pleasantly, the only slightly discordant note being Archie Gemmill's annoyance at being denied his habitual early night.

Waking up on Saturday morning in his hotel room, Moore switched on the radio by the side of his bed. He had expected the headlines on BBC Radio 2's nine o'clock news bulletin to be about some country or other testing a hydrogen bomb or a trade union calling a strike. Instead, it was that 'the Ian Storey-Moore deal' had fallen through.

Wondering what on earth was going on, Moore hurried downstairs to where everyone was having breakfast. Clough reassured him, 'Don't worry, son, it's all done.'

After breakfast Clough told Ron Webster, Derby's right-back, to take Moore to Sinfin Lane where the Rams' youth team were due to play. He would join them later. When Clough arrived at the ground, he and Moore had a stroll around the pitch. 'Don't worry, it's all sorted,' Clough insisted.

Then it was back to the Midland Hotel for the pre-match meal and on to the Baseball Ground for the Wolves game. By now press photographers had gathered outside the ground and Clough proudly posed with his new signing. When asked by journalists about reports that the transfer might not go through, Clough said, 'He's a Derby player and was a Derby player at approximately seven o'clock last night.' Moore added, 'I don't know anything about that. All I know is that I've joined a great club.' Later, Clough was reported as saying:

> 'As far as I am concerned, there is no problem. We are giving Forest the forms to sign, and that will complete the deal. As far as we are concerned, we have signed Ian and I am not really concerned what any other party might feel. Ian will be in our team on Wednesday.'

Peter Taylor added, 'I am surprised there seems to be some difference of opinion about this deal. We have Ian Moore's signature and we feel this makes him our player, which is what he wants.'

Inside the ground, Moore was invited into the dressing room before the match. At Forest, managers Johnny Carey and Matt Gillies would come in wearing a suit, collar and tie, say a few words and that was that. Clough, by contrast, was sitting on a bench with his shoes and socks off, sleeves rolled up, a drink in hand, totally relaxed. His team talk consisted of instructions such as, 'Roy, put Dougan on his arse in the first ten minutes.' Moore had never seen a manager like that, describing him as 'a complete one-off'.

Moore watched the match in the stands sitting next to Clough. At half-time he was paraded on the pitch by Taylor and Webb. Over the loudspeaker the announcer declared that Moore had been signed for a British record fee. Moore was excited to be there; Derby had an excellent team and were challenging strongly for the league title. He waved to the crowd and received a rapturous welcome. It wouldn't last.

Derby won 2-1. Afterwards Clough arranged for one of his friends to take Moore and his wife out for a meal on the Saturday evening. Carol, having driven over to Derby in her car, stayed the night at the Midland Hotel.

An uneventful Sunday morning was followed by a visit to Clough's home for a cup of tea and a chat. Clough's charming wife, Barbara, was naturally very welcoming, and impromptu entertainment was provided by their children Simon, aged seven, five-year-old Nigel, and Elizabeth, who was four. After a convivial afternoon, Carol dropped Moore off back at the Midland and returned to Bingham. She had left their pet Alsatian, Laska, with Moore's sister, Anne, and didn't want to impose on her unduly.

Meanwhile, at the City Ground an emergency meeting of the nine-man committee that ran the club was taking place, the second in two days. Committee members were angered at the way Clough and Taylor had paraded Moore as their new signing even though Forest had not formally agreed to the transfer. Ken Smales later described this as 'a gimmick which had blown up in Mr Clough's face'. Feelings were running high, with two members of the committee threatening to resign if the transfer went through. In the end, long-standing animosity towards their local rivals and distaste for Clough's showmanship led the committee to decide they couldn't possibly let Forest's star player join Derby. Smales wryly observed that his own signature had never been in such demand since, in his days as an off-spin bowler for Nottinghamshire CCC, he had taken all ten wickets against Gloucestershire in 1956. The all-important transfer form would remain unsigned.

Tony Wood, Forest's former chairman and now vice-chairman – apparently well known for his anti-Derby County sentiments – was tasked with relaying the committee's decision. Late on Sunday evening, after informing Sam Longson, Derby's chairman, Wood telephoned Moore's wife, stating, 'Listen, Carol, there's no way we're going to let Ian sign for Derby County, we're simply not going to let him go there. You might as well get him to come home.'

Taken aback by this bolt from the blue, Carol rang the Midland Hotel. On being put through to her husband, Carol passed on Wood's message – or, more precisely, instruction. Moore said he would return in the morning.

Parting of the ways

First thing on Monday Moore had packed his bag and was in the process of checking out of the Midland when Clough entered the hotel. Derby's manager knew by now that the transfer was off. To give him the benefit of the doubt, quite possibly his chairman hadn't told him the full story about how Forest's committee had vetoed the deal at the last minute. After all, Clough and Longson's relationship was famously fractious.

Clough's demeanour had changed completely and much for the worse. Implying that Moore had been playing Derby off against United in order to extract better terms, he threw the contract at Moore, declaring, 'There's no more – that's all you fucking well get!'

Startled, Moore replied, 'I don't want any more – it's not a question of that. You must know as well as I do that Forest aren't going to let me come, Brian.' But to no avail: uttering a further profanity in the direction of Moore, Clough stormed off.

Later that day Clough told reporters, 'I am sorry Moore has changed his mind, and I am sorry for him that he has missed out in not joining a fantastic bunch of players. All the same, I sincerely wish him well with United. That is my last word on the whole affair.' Except, of course, it wasn't.

A few months later Clough made his lingering grievance against Moore clear when he gave his side of the story to the *Sunday Express*:

> 'I still have immense regret that Ian Moore joined Manchester United six months ago … because he would have been the final, vital link. As an old goalscorer, I like to see them go in the net. And Moore was the man we decided was the right one to help us get goals … I told Ian that by joining Derby he was completing a fine team. By joining United, however, he was merely the beginning of a rebuilding operation. At his age, that had to be important to him.
>
> 'Ian was so positive that he even signed the forms blank – he trusted me that much about his terms that he left me to fill everything in later … But as the world now knows, Forest suddenly went cold on the deal. With Moore's signature, with Moore's assurance that he was delighted to be a Derby player, I was baffled. And I still am baffled today by it.'

Sadly, Moore's friendship with his boyhood hero – the two men brought together by a love of cricket and horseracing – would be permanently shattered by the embarrassing episode of the transfer that never was.

The situation had not been helped by the machinations of Splashy Johnstone. Throughout the transfer saga he had continued to provide false statements to the press, such as these quotes attributed to Carol, 'The position is very upsetting. I am disgusted at the way Forest have treated Ian over the transfer,' and, 'I asked Ian to come home so that we could talk about this. I wanted him to have the chance of reconsidering about going to Derby.' Such reports led Clough to believe that Carol had played a large part in his failure to sign Moore.

Rather too late in the day, the slow-to-anger Moore had had enough and dispensed with Johnstone's 'services'. He has apologised to the club, its supporters and the good people of Nottingham many times for his part in enabling those derogatory stories to be published and continues to do so. He regrets his naivety and the offence caused.

But the damage was done. Apart from one occasion a few weeks later – when Clough phoned asking Moore to be sympathetic to Derby's perspective when giving evidence to the resultant Football League inquiry into the whole affair, over which the Rams were fined £5,000 – Clough would not speak to the forward again for more than two decades.

Unlike their manager, Derby's players never bore any kind of grudge against Moore, and he became good friends with Roy McFarland and Colin Todd in particular.

Despite Clough treating him as *persona non grata*, Moore retains huge respect for Old Big 'Ead's remarkable achievements at both Derby and Forest.

It was only when they bumped into each other at a social event a couple of years before Clough's 2004 death that a reconciliation of sorts took place, with Clough remarking to Moore, 'They tell me you're not as big a shithouse as you used to be!'

O'Farrell returns

Monday morning, 6 March 1972: members of the press gathered at both the Baseball Ground and City Ground to see which team Moore would turn up to train with. His failure to show up at either sparked one of the biggest manhunts since the Great Train Robbery.

Moore took his time making his way back home from Derby. Rather than the main road, the A52, he took the slow, scenic route of B-roads through the ancient, peaceful villages of south Nottinghamshire. He felt as though he had been caught up in a whirlwind over the preceding 72 hours and needed time and space to clear his head and work out what was going on.

He couldn't understand why Forest would arrange for him to meet Clough and Taylor – and on his own at that – if they never had any intention of letting him go to Derby. Perhaps Matt Gillies, knowing of Derby's keen interest in signing Moore and acting with Forest's best interests at heart, had failed to consult properly with chairman Jack Levey and vice-chairman Tony Wood before inviting Clough to the party. That rather charitable interpretation of events did little to assuage Moore's embarrassment at the turn of events.

While Moore meandered home, Levey stirred the pot a little, issuing a statement that read, 'We started negotiations with Manchester United, who were first in the field. Somehow Derby came into it. We want to conduct this transfer on a correct basis and to be fair to everyone. As far as we are concerned, Moore is still a registered player with Forest.'

Journalists doorstepped Moore's sister, Anne, to see if she could reveal where her brother was. She knew but didn't let on. They even contacted distant relatives in the north-east hoping they might know.

Eventually Moore arrived home. Soon he received a call from Gillies, 'Manchester United still want you, they're coming over.' Upon hearing this, Moore and Carol decided to drive back out into the countryside to talk things over. Parked in his Ford Capri in a country lane, they tried to make sense of the events that had engulfed them that weekend.

How could he have allowed himself to be paraded in front of over 30,000 fans at the Baseball Ground before the transfer had been signed, sealed and delivered? Had he been naive to accept the assurances Clough had given him? And if Manchester United really were still interested, surely that was a pretty good alternative, wasn't it?

They returned to Bingham and waited. Around five o'clock O'Farrell arrived, this time with the legendary Sir Matt Busby. As he parked his gold-coloured Mercedes in front of Moore's house, the man who had managed United to European Cup glory four years earlier caused quite a stir. The whole street came out to see him.

Over a cup of tea, Busby took the lead in explaining what United's plans were. The team was in transition: great players like Charlton and Law were coming to the end of their careers and Best had started to lose his way. Moore, along with other first-class signings such as Martin Buchan, would play a vital role in ensuring the club's future success.

'Would you be happy if I went to United?' Moore asked Carol. She replied, 'I want you to do what you think best.' With that, Moore shook hands with Busby and O'Farrell and the deal was done.

While Moore went upstairs to pack fresh clothes and some training kit into his holdall, Carol prepared to give an exclusive interview to a BBC TV crew. She admitted the last few days had been an emotional roller coaster, 'I would have been just as happy if he had said to me, "I will sign for Derby." But this is the biggest decision of his life. All I want to do now is have a good cry. The tension has been terrific. I'm so glad it's all over.'

Soon the Mercedes departed as Busby drove O'Farrell and Moore to the City Ground to sign the transfer forms. Moore was the first to sign; it was a bittersweet moment. He was sad to leave Forest, who had placed their faith in him as a skinny 16-year-old schoolboy from Scunthorpe.

This time the club secretary's signature was immediately forthcoming. Moore looked at the clock in Smales's office. It showed the time was a quarter to seven – three days earlier he had been driving to the Midland Hotel for dinner with the Derby team.

United's manager, former manager and their new signing started their journey to Manchester. En route they stopped at Woodall service station on the M1 near Sheffield. Finding a quiet corner, they completed and signed Moore's contract. Overnight Moore stayed at a small hotel in Manchester, feeling understandably drained but, at the same time, excited at the prospect of what lay ahead.

On the Tuesday morning Moore met the United team. Before a light training session a press photographer came to take a picture of Moore with his new team-mates. Denis Law helped break the ice, saying, 'You'll have to hurry – he's only here for a couple of days, he's going to Everton at the weekend!'

15

From Reds to Red Devils

'United fans, who have hailed so many great players in their time, loved him.'

Ronald Crowther,
Daily Mail sports reporter

A bigger pond

So, after finding himself the reluctant subject of a tug-of-war played out on the nation's front pages, Moore was now a Manchester United player. He was relieved that the saga of his transfer was finally over, though more than a little embarrassed by the events that had led him to Old Trafford. He still regrets that he had no chance to thank the supporters, who had been so good to him for so many years, and to say his goodbyes to his Forest team-mates:

> 'I didn't have time to speak to any of the players. They knew it was going to happen and I was going to leave, but until it actually happened I didn't really have the time to speak to any of them. That weekend was like a whirlwind. I spoke to Sammy Chapman on the phone while I was at the Midland Hotel in Derby, to tell him what a mess it was and what was happening there, and that I wasn't going to be able to sign for Derby County. Whether he told the rest

> of the lads, I don't know, but anyway by Monday it had all been in the press.'

The team he so nearly joined would go on to win the league title for the first time, albeit by the narrowest of margins, finishing a single point ahead of their three nearest challengers. But there was no more glamorous club in the country than Manchester United and Moore now felt he had hit the big time.

In his later years at Forest, it had become increasingly the case that if the opposition could keep Moore quiet their chances of a win would be considerably enhanced. With the likes of George Best, Denis Law and Bobby Charlton still plying their trade at Old Trafford, Moore was no longer that big fish in a small pond.

He recalls his arrival at Old Trafford:

> 'When I first went there, I was quite nervous, thinking, "Cor blimey, I'm going to be in the same dressing room as Best, Law and Charlton." A young lad from a council estate in Scunthorpe sitting in the same dressing room with those three icons. It was quite a nervy occasion.'

But despite several of their European Cup winners still featuring regularly, United were by now a declining force. They had finished runners-up to neighbours Manchester City in the league a fortnight before beating Benfica at Wembley in May 1968, but in the following three seasons had ended up 11th, eighth and eighth again. Although they had started the 1971/72 season in fine form and topped the table as recently as early January, they had not won a league match since beating Forest by the odd goal in five on 4 December and had once again drifted out of contention for the title.

Law and Charlton were starting to show their age and Best was causing concern with his headline-grabbing lifestyle off the field and his growing inconsistency on it. It was becoming

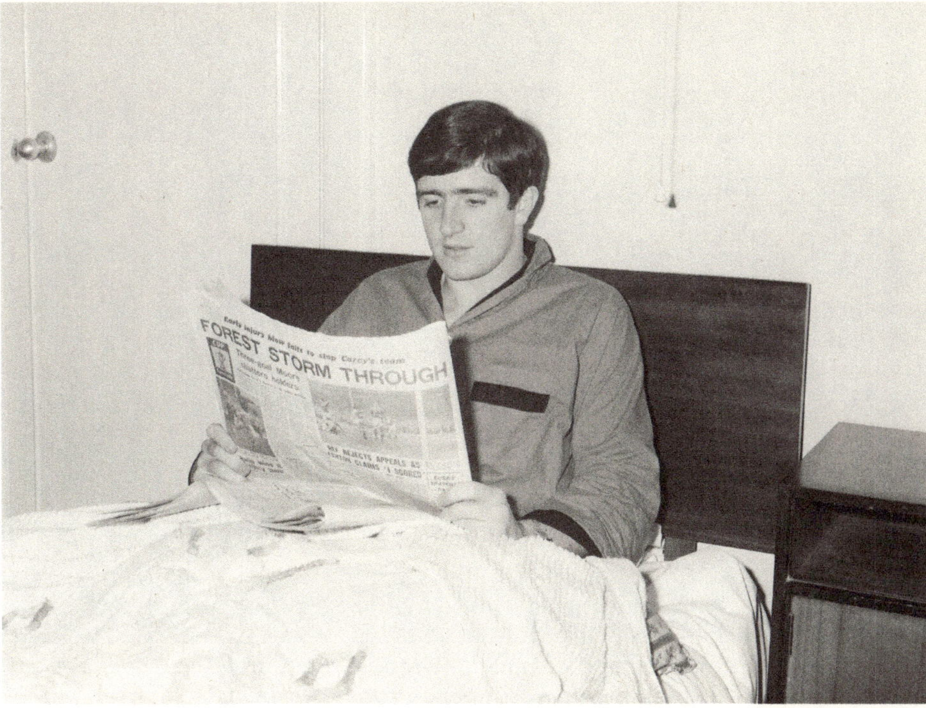

Read all about it! *Reading the report on the Everton match in Monday morning's paper at the team's hotel, Skegness, 10 April 1967*

FA Cup semi-final draw: *Later that day, listening to the draw for the FA Cup semi-final with Alan Hinton, Peter Grummitt and Terry Hennessey*

Guard of honour: *The wedding of Ian Storey-Moore and Carol Ann Griffiths at Christ Church, Chilwell, Nottingham, 8 January 1968. The newly-married couple are joined by (from left): Frank Wignall, Tommy Cavanagh (coach), Peter Hindley, Frank Knight (reserve team trainer), Bill Brindley, Peter Grummitt, Bob Davies (physio), John Winfield, Jeff Whitefoot, Barry Lyons, Johnny Quigley, Henry Newton, Alan Hinton, Sammy Chapman, Colin Hall*

Mexico beckons: *Henry Newton and Moore receive their call-up papers after being selected by Sir Alf Ramsey for the squad of 30 for pre-World Cup training, medicals and the match against Portugal at Wembley, December 1969*

The cap fits: *Carol and Ian sporting his England Under-23 and full international debut caps*

Beating Clough and Taylor's Derby County: *Shooting in a 2-0 win at the Baseball Ground, 29 November 1969, as John McGovern (far left) looks on*

Iconic: *Left: Moore sports Forest's iconic 1960s and early 1970s all-white away kit at Crystal Palace, 17 January 1970. Right: Moore in the Garibaldi Red in August 1971, the start of his final season with Forest*

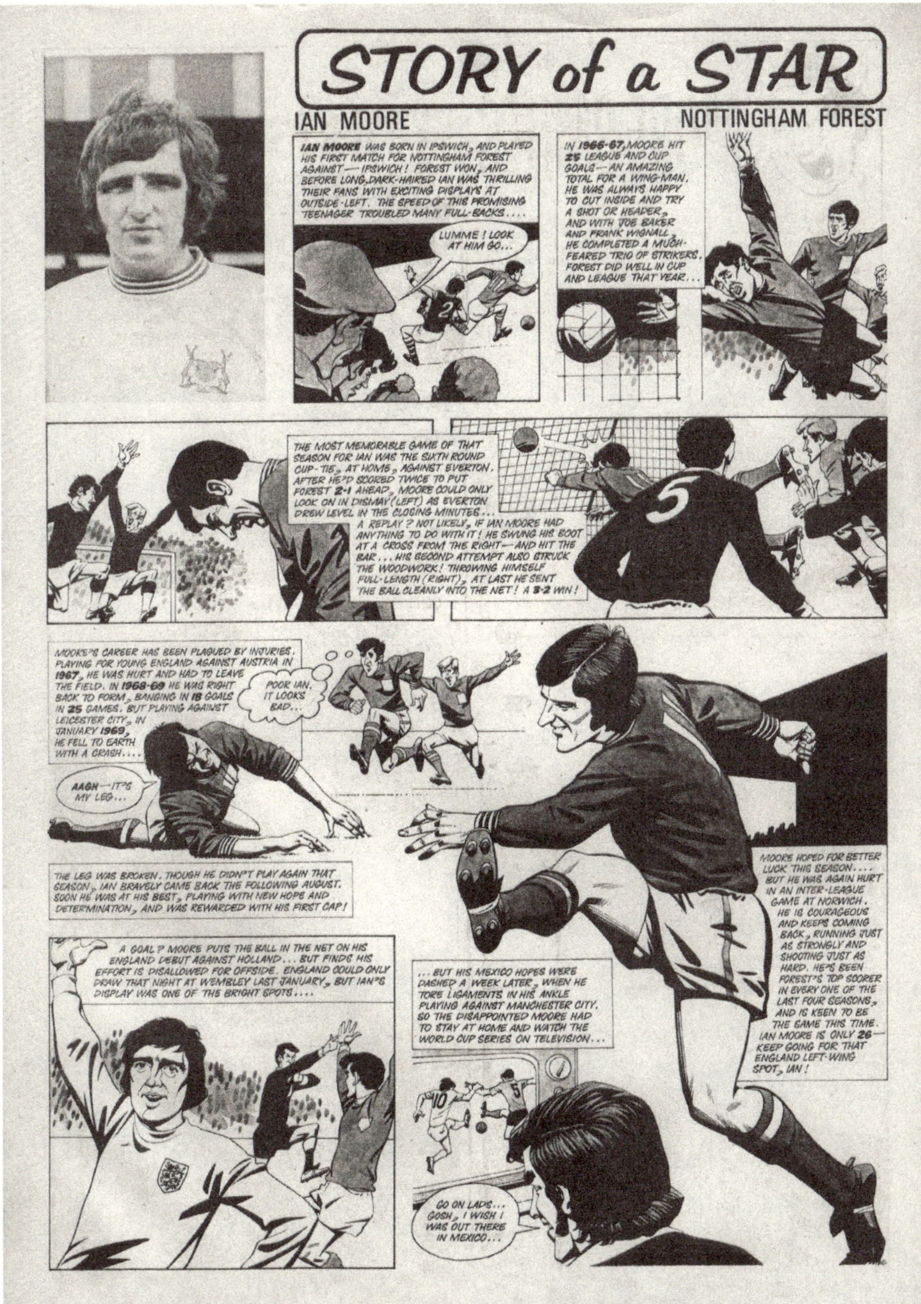

Nottingham Forest's own 'Roy of the Rovers': *Storey-Moore's career with Forest up to and including missing the 1970 Mexico World Cup through injury, as depicted in Tiger comic*

Nottingham Forest vs Arsenal, 27 December 1971, City Ground: *After running 74 yards and dribbling past three defenders, Moore slots the ball home past Bob Wilson to net one of the greatest goals ever scored by a Forest player*

Late in the second half, Moore leaves Arsenal debutant Alan Ball still chasing shadows. Note the overflowing crowd by the touchline

Occupational hazard: *With fan club members at the Nottingham Forest Supporters' Club*

Final goal at the City Ground: *Moore scores against Leicester City, 22 January 1972*

'Don't worry, it's all sorted!': *Brian Clough introduces Moore to the press as Derby County's new signing outside the Baseball Ground, Saturday, 4 March 1972*

Moore is paraded on the pitch by Peter Taylor

apparent that United were in need of new blood. Manager Frank O'Farrell needed to shore up the team's defences, boost their goalscoring prowess and, importantly, give the fans something to be positive about.

The first of these needs was met shortly before Moore signed with Martin Buchan joining from Aberdeen, the centre-back having been targeted by O'Farrell for his leadership potential as well as his defensive abilities. It was hoped that Moore would meet the second need by both creating and scoring goals. With the positivity of the fans perhaps in mind, the boss declared that he was prepared to make further additions if the right player became available.

By the time Huddersfield Town visited Old Trafford on 11 March 1972, United had gone 11 league games without a win, scoring just six goals in the process – an almost unimaginable run for a team of their stature with such a renowned forward line. Coincidentally, Huddersfield were also winless in 11 matches and only the wretched form of the Forest team Moore had left was keeping the Terriers off the bottom of the table. More than 53,000 turned out to see Moore make his debut – Law was the man dropped to accommodate him – and Buchan his first home appearance.

In his programme notes, O'Farrell made clear his opinion of the controversial transfer saga:

> 'It is not for me to criticise the methods of Derby County and Brian Clough in their determination to buy Moore, except to say that I have my principles in these matters and that no player should be subjected to undue pressure but should have complete freedom of choice.
>
> 'That is what Manchester United gave Ian Moore and if we lose a player through following our principles then my conscience is clear and I'm sure that in the long term it is the right policy.'

Finally free to get on with the business of playing football, Moore put in a fine performance and his presence also seemed to help one of his new team-mates. Best had not scored a league goal in three months, but the Northern Irish superstar opened the scoring in the first half and the two immediately showed signs of forming a good partnership. Moore twice drew saves from Huddersfield's goalkeeper and, shortly after the hour mark, his efforts were rewarded with a debut goal. He set up Best for a shot which the keeper saved and Moore reacted quickest to head home the rebound.

The events of the previous week had taken their toll on Moore and he was relieved that his debut was deemed to have gone well:

> 'I felt absolutely drained that Saturday, I wasn't anywhere near 100 per cent. I think it was nervous tension with what had happened and I didn't feel my sparkling self that game at all. I was glad to get it out of the way. I was absolutely shattered after the game. It was pleasing to get off the mark with a win and I got a decent press that day, so that was nice.'

The 2-0 win saw United move back up the table to sixth place. Meanwhile, back at the City Ground fewer than 10,000 – a boycott producing the lowest league attendance since 1955 – saw Moore's beleaguered former team-mates slump to a 2-0 defeat to Ipswich Town, an eighth straight defeat. When the stadium announcer declared, rather too gleefully for most tastes, that Moore had scored on his debut for Manchester United, he was, by popular account, 'sacked in the morning'. At the end of the match, dog handlers and mounted police had to break up a chanting mob that was attempting to storm the boardroom. The mood had turned nasty, replacing the gallows humour on display during the match itself when the Trent End had sung, 'We've sold the best team in the land'.

United were next in FA Cup action, drawing at home to Stoke City in the sixth round and losing the replay. Moore was cup-tied for these games, having played for Forest in their third-round defeat at Millwall, so he had to wait a fortnight for his second United appearance. When it came, he put in a man-of-the-match performance against Crystal Palace. He crossed for Alan Gowling to bundle in United's second goal in a comfortable 4-0 win and scored the third with a fierce right-footed shot into the roof of the net from the edge of the penalty area after his free kick had been blocked by the Palace wall.

In the next game, a 3-2 win at Coventry City, Moore went one better with a goal and two assists. His headed pass set up Best to open the scoring and he played an indirect free kick for Charlton to score the third. In between, he accelerated clear of two defenders and scored with a precise low shot from 25 yards. He recalls this as being his favourite goal in a United shirt.

United's mini-revival soon came to an end as they took just a single point from their next four games. Having scored in each of his first three appearances, Moore was unable to keep the run going, though he did twice bring the best out of Peter Shilton in a 2-0 defeat at Leicester City. His next goal came in a 3-2 win at home to Southampton, when United came close to losing a three-goal lead.

Return to the City Ground

All eyes were on Moore the following Saturday, 22 April 1972, as he made a return to the City Ground with United. Forest's relegation was all but confirmed and Moore recalls his apprehension at the possibility of being the player to hammer the final nail in his former club's coffin:

> 'I didn't want to play. I wish I had gone up to our manager and said, "Can you say I've got an injury or something?" I just felt strange playing there, playing against my friends, who I'd known for so many years, and they were in a relegation scrap. I remember Bob McKinlay saying to me before the

> game, "Take it easy, Ian, we don't want to get relegated." That put me in an even worse position! I thought, "Oh God, don't score," but also, "If I get an easy chance I've got to put it in or they'll think the game's bent."'

The reluctant Moore played but got his wish not to be the one to relegate his former club, as the game finished goalless:

> 'Throughout the game I was thinking, "Dare I score?" I remember being interviewed, "In a way it's been a sad day for me, having to come here and play against my team-mates, and possibly being responsible for them getting relegated." I didn't want that: I had a lot of good friends I'd grown up with. It was an awful game. I just didn't feel right at all and was glad to get the game over.'

The point Forest earned meant they survived – for a few more days, at least. Whether it was down to Moore's misgivings or the Forest defence showing a solidity that had been all too rare that season, his influence was limited to a couple of blocked shots and he was penalised for handling the ball in an attempt to convert Brian Kidd's cross. In fact, the greater goal threat came from Moore's replacement in the number 11 shirt, Duncan McKenzie, and the player who had taken on the mantle of being the Reds' biggest star after his departure, Peter Cormack.

A 3-1 defeat at home to Wolverhampton Wanderers in their penultimate match three days later all but sealed Forest's fate. The next day Crystal Palace, without a win in their previous ten matches, beat Stoke 2-0 and Forest were down.

United finished their season with the eighth and ninth games of a frantically busy April. Inconsistent to the end, an abject performance in a 3-0 reverse at Arsenal was followed by a win by the same score at home to Stoke, their FA Cup conquerors. Moore was at his best and he scored the second goal, Law playing him in to finish from ten yards after he had instigated a neat exchange of passes.

For the third season in succession United finished in eighth place. Moore had hit the ground running with those goals in his first three games and his total of five goals from 11 appearances meant he was scoring at a similar strike rate to that of his Forest career. Indeed, he was perhaps something of a talisman for United, as their only wins after he joined them had been the five games in which he had scored. That bigger pond clearly held no fears for him.

Life in a northern town

When he first moved to Manchester, Moore lived in a guest house in Salford while he looked for a house with Carol, who had stayed in Bingham but would come up to watch him play. After games they would return to Bingham for the rest of the weekend. On Sunday evening or early on Monday morning, Moore would travel back up to Manchester in time for training. Whichever cross-country route he took, he could reckon on a two-hour drive each way. While he was still living on his own, he would often spend time with George Best. Despite Best's fondness for drinking and his own relative abstemiousness, there was no reprise for Moore of his previous 'designated driver' role and his leisure time was relatively low-key compared with former times in the company of Jim Baxter and Garry Sobers:

> 'We used to go and have a bit of lunch. George's friends had a barber's shop in the centre of Manchester and we used to go down there. His boutique was nearby, so I'd spend a couple of hours there before I went back to the hotel.'

The tiresome weekly commute finally came to an end when the Storey-Moores found a house just outside Wilmslow, on Styal Road. Moore socialised more with his team-mates at lunchtime after training than in the evenings, though he and Carol did go for the odd meal with Best and his girlfriend and occasionally had a night out with other footballers such as Howard Kendall and Alan Ball, whom Moore and Best would also see at Haydock Park races.

Carol loved living near Manchester and took to the friendly people she met there. Among the more colourful acquaintances the Storey-Moores made were members of the so-called 'Quality Street Gang'. To quote one of its leading lights, Jimmy 'The Weed' Donnelly, some of the QSG's members 'were straight businessmen, some were rogues, leaning more in one direction or the other depending on circumstance or opportunity … We could all look after ourselves and some were very hard men indeed.' They moved in the same circles as local celebrities from the worlds of television, sport and music. One of their favourite haunts was an after-hours club called the Showbiz, run by Philomena Lynott, the mother of Phil, lead singer with Thin Lizzy, inspiring him to write songs such as 'The Boys Are Back in Town' and 'Johnny the Fox Meets Jimmy the Weed'.

Moore found the members of the QSG he met good company and recalls them with a chuckle:

> 'A lot of them were club owners and bouncers and this sort of thing and they were decent people, but I think they could look after themselves. We got on really well with them – really funny people. We had a laugh and a joke with them when we were out with them.'

He recalls one memorable night out after a midweek game:

> 'George Best said to me, "Do you fancy going to a nightclub in Moss Side?" Of course, it was the worst area in Manchester, a big area for drugs. I said, "Moss Side? What's there?" "A nightclub called Russian Dave's."' "Are

> you sure, George?" "We'll just go and have a quick drink and that's it." "Oh, all right then."
>
> 'We had only been in there for ten minutes or so when suddenly all the lights came on. It's only been raided, hasn't it! I'm sat with George and a policeman came over and asked me for my name and address. Then he looked at George and said, "Name?" And George looked at the police officer as if to say, "You don't know who I am? Are you winding me up?"
>
> 'That was in the period before Carol moved up. After that I was under lock and key!'

When it came to football, Moore was naturally struck by the enormity of Manchester United in terms of the level of media interest and the fan base. The club's higher profile ensured the national press was always well represented at games, which was not always the case at Forest. In the early 1970s United were challenging Liverpool for the highest average home attendance in the country and were also known for their large away following. Moore was impressed by the size and grandeur of Old Trafford compared with the less-developed City Ground and he found United's other amenities very different too.

At Forest, the plan in the early 1960s to develop a fully equipped training ground, including floodlights and changing rooms, had not been realised. So, on days when they didn't use the pitch at the City Ground the players would get changed there, then carry a bag of footballs along the Trent to train on the pitch at Lady Bay. Then, with no food and drink provided by the club, the players would head to MacKay's, the local cafe next to the ground, for a cheese sandwich and a cup of tea.

United, though, had a separate dedicated training ground, The Cliff. While it was hardly a world-class facility by modern standards, it had a gym and its own cafe, where the players could get a welcome bite to eat and have a chat over a hot drink before going home after training. The banter among the squads was, of course, much the same at both clubs, each having its share of jokers and more reserved individuals.

At United, Denis Law was very much in the 'joker' category, that 'going to Everton' quip on the day Moore met his new teammates helping keep things light-hearted on what could have been a nerve-wracking day for the slightly star-struck newcomer. Likewise, on his first matchday, he was the butt of another of Law's jokes. When Moore turned up in what he considered a smart suit and shirt, Law asked, 'Can you get those shirts in white?' and Moore found himself replying, 'It *is* white!'

Another player Moore remembers as quite gregarious was goalkeeper Alex Stepney, a good friend of Law's and always up for a laugh. Other players he liked included Paddy Crerand – 'a nice guy, a real laugh, a real character – hard as nails, as well' – and fellow newcomer Buchan.

Unsurprisingly for someone who was relatively shy by nature, Moore also got on well with some of the quieter members of the United squad, such as versatile central defender and midfielder David Sadler ('quite unassuming, but a nice guy'), long-serving left-back Tony Dunne ('a really good player but very gentle person') and right-winger Willie Morgan, who liked a chance to go off for a round of golf. One player who largely kept himself to himself was Bobby Charlton. While Moore found him to be affable and approachable, Charlton would come in, train, have a shower and leave. 'He was very professional, kept himself fit, and was a good role model for younger players to follow,' says Moore.

Extroverts and introverts alike, the players made Moore very welcome, his versatility perhaps helping as it was clear he hadn't been signed specifically to replace any one player. As we have seen, there were comparisons to be made between Moore and Best as each came to be seen as their team's brightest star.

But Moore still bridles at any suggestion he was signed to replace Best:

> 'I don't think I particularly took anybody's place. George had so much ability he could play anywhere. I'm not putting myself in the same bracket, but I could play anywhere along the forward line and George was the same. It was such a privilege to play with him. Some stupid people said they bought Ian Storey-Moore to replace George Best. Well, let me tell you that there's no way anybody could replace him. It was a stupid comment – I think he was irreplaceable in terms of ability. No one could match George's natural ability.'

Moore found that training wasn't so different from what he was used to, but much more attention was paid at United to coaching. The enthusiastic Tommy Cavanagh's role at Forest had been largely to get his players fit, a task he undoubtedly applied himself to with relish. In contrast, United's Malcolm Musgrove was more of a coach and took a measured and theoretical approach. Moore did several coaching sessions with him on the 'functional and tactical stuff'. The manager's role was largely motivational and it was felt the players should know what was required of them:

> 'In those days there was very little tactical advice such as, "I want you to do this if we lose the ball there." Basically, we were told, "We paid a lot of money for you – go and do what you need to do. Produce the goods."'

The matchday preparations at the two clubs were very similar, though, right down to the pre-match meal, which, inevitably, was steak and toast, washed down with a cup of tea. Moore recognises with amusement that this was 'the worst thing you could have – they were naive in those days about that sort of thing'. As he would find to his cost, there were other aspects of player care that were surprisingly poor for a top professional club.

Out of the frying pan

United were clearly hoping that the additions of Moore and Buchan would help them make a longer-lasting impression at the top of the league in the 1972/73 season, but, as things turned out, they suffered one of their worst starts to a season.

For the opening game against Ipswich Town, 51,000 packed into Old Trafford, full of the usual early season hope and expectation. Bobby Robson's team would go on to win silverware later in the decade, but in 1972 they were mid-table opposition at best, so it was something of a surprise when the visitors won by the odd goal in three.

The fixture computer had given United a double-header on Merseyside for their first two away games, starting at Anfield on 15 August. Liverpool raced into a two-goal lead within the first 20 minutes and there was no further scoring. United had been unable to get a grip in midfield and thus offered little service to Moore and his fellow forwards. The result was the same four days later at Goodison Park, though United's performance was much improved. They were still not creating many chances and the only time Everton's keeper was beaten was when Moore's header was cleared off the line by his friend and former team-mate, Henry Newton.

United were bottom of the table after three games and were the only team still searching for their first points of the season. A run of three home matches in eight days gave them a good opportunity to kick-start their season. They finally earned their first point against Leicester City, their goal coming from a Best penalty after Moore was fouled. Further points followed from goalless draws against Arsenal – United's best performance of the season to date – and Chelsea.

United had only scored two goals in their six fixtures, but they doubled that tally against West Ham United the following weekend, though the game ended in yet another draw. Moore, who had been substituted against Chelsea, opened his account for the season against the Hammers. He scored from the rebound when a shot from Law was blocked to put United 2-1 up after 77 minutes, but they were unable to hold on for a win.

A fifth successive stalemate followed as the Red Devils were held to a 2-2 draw at Oxford United in the League Cup, Charlton equalising in the 87th minute with a shot from 30 yards. When Coventry City won 1-0 at Old Trafford, the Manchester clubs were in the bottom two places in the table, each with four points from their eight games.

The elusive first win of the season finally came in the replay against Oxford and Moore proved the difference between the teams. Ten minutes before half-time he beat several defenders in a mazy dribble and scored from 16 yards. With the scores level early in the second half Moore earned a penalty which was converted by Best, who then made the game safe at 3-1 after Moore's shot had hit the keeper's chest. There was no sign yet of an improvement in the league, though, and United were somewhat flattered by the scoreline when Wolverhampton Wanderers ran out 2-0 winners at Molineux. Their quest for a win would be no easier in their next match, which saw champions Derby County visit Old Trafford.

The spotlight was firmly on Moore as, for the first time since his sensational transfer, he faced the team he had so nearly joined. Moore felt there was no ill feeling between him and Derby – indeed, Brian Clough had reportedly already made an audacious attempt to buy him from United – but the reaction of the Rams' supporters was predictably hostile. Any nerves Moore felt before the match disappeared when Best set him up to open the scoring with a header just after the half-hour mark. Two goals in the space of ten second-half minutes from striker Wyn Davies – making his debut after joining from neighbours Manchester City – and right-winger Willie Morgan made the game safe. United finally had their first league win at the tenth attempt, but the scoreline was harsh on an aggressive Derby team that had impressed in midfield but been let down up front. Clough refrained from speaking to

Moore that day, even resisting the temptation to offer an opinion or two from the touchline when Moore was playing on the wing in front of him.

Another striker made his debut in the next match, Ted MacDougall's transfer from Bournemouth having taken United's spending on front men to almost half a million pounds in the calendar year. He had little service, though, and United lost to a disputed late penalty at Sheffield United, leaving them bottom of the table with just six points. For Moore, having left a Forest team struggling to stay in the top flight, it seemed like a case of out of the frying pan and into the fire:

> 'After thinking that I'd had all the difficult times at Forest since that good team broke up and thought I was going to a team that was hopefully progressing, it was back to square one again with United, which was disappointing.'

On 3 October United again had trouble against lower-league opposition in the League Cup. Their visit drew more than 33,000 to Eastville, where they needed a goal from Morgan three minutes from time to take Bristol Rovers back to Old Trafford for a replay. They didn't find the Third Division side any easier to deal with at home, however. They were a goal down when Best's penalty from a foul on Moore was easily saved and, although they equalised on 81 minutes through Sammy McIlroy, Rovers scored three minutes later to pull off a famous win.

In between the League Cup matches United had shared four goals at West Bromwich Albion, with Moore central to their comeback after they had trailed 2-0 early on. Best got them back into the game before half-time, converting from the spot after Moore's cross was handled. Within a minute Albion missed a spot kick of their own, which they would regret when Moore headed Best's corner in off the crossbar with 14 minutes left. United were rooted to the foot of the table and after the Bristol Rovers defeat they had won just two of their 16 matches. They finally won again when MacDougall's first goal for the club was enough to beat Birmingham City and lift them up two places.

Moore had an off day in a 2-1 defeat at Newcastle a week later and was replaced by Bobby Charlton, who scored United's goal late on. Charlton kept his place for the visit of Tottenham Hotspur and scored United's consolation in a 4-1 thrashing which saw Martin Peters take full advantage of the Red Devils' defensive frailties by scoring all four goals.

Moore was back in the team that gave a better account of themselves in an entertaining 2-2 draw at Leicester City. He set up United's first goal, feeding Best, who beat Peter Shilton after a mazy run. That week's *Sunday People* gave the United squad's average ratings for the season to date. Best, for all his off-field troubles, was the only one to score more than 7.0, with Moore's 5.8 ranking him in the middle of the 19 players listed.

If that rating was unspectacular, there was a genuine but little-known reason why Moore had not been more effective – he had been unwell since the summer.

United had played a pre-season friendly at Torquay United, where Frank O'Farrell had been manager a few years previously. The game had finished goalless, though Moore had come within inches of scoring on several occasions, but he was unable to play in United's next friendly and it would be several months before he felt properly fit:

> 'We had two pre-season friendlies at Torquay and Bournemouth. I was that ill with either hay fever or a virus that I couldn't play in the second game at Bournemouth. I felt dreadful. It really took it out of me for the start of that season. I didn't feel particularly good at all and I don't know what it was, but I didn't really start playing how I could play until probably about the beginning of October that season, when I got it out of my system.'

By now there was much media discussion of United's struggles, which were variously attributed to the management style of O'Farrell, the continuing influence (some said interference) of former manager Sir Matt Busby – now a director of the club – and splits among the players, with a minority of star players perceived as being given preferential treatment. Moore never felt the latter to be the case, though he does recall the comparisons with Busby:

> 'The dressing room wasn't totally behind Frank, definitely not. I felt sorry for him, really. No disrespect to Sir Matt, who was a wonderful manager, but with him being in the background it was always going to be difficult. From the older players you used to hear comments like "Matt wouldn't have done this" and "Matt wouldn't have done that".'

These concerns would have been forgotten, temporarily at least, when United – still bottom of the table – upset the form book by beating leaders Liverpool 2-0 on 11 November. In a much-improved team performance, Davies scored the first when Ray Clemence half-stopped a shot from MacDougall, who scored the second. United were the better team in a game dominated by the defences, but things might have been different if Moore's old team-mate Peter Cormack hadn't failed to score with only Alex Stepney to beat early on or headed against the bar towards the end.

Unfortunately, the action on the field was not the only story from the meeting of the two north-west giants. In a season in which the problems of football-associated violence appeared to be getting worse, 75 arrests were made at Old Trafford. This was rather unfortunate timing for O'Farrell, whose programme notes had castigated the media for 'manufacturing sensational news' about hooliganism and making 'trouble where there was none'.

Any hopes that United might have turned a corner by beating Liverpool were quickly dashed when they lost 3-0 in the following week's derby at Maine Road. Football seemed to take second place to foul play and score-settling in a physical encounter notable for the lack of control from the referee and self-control from the players. Bobby Charlton, renowned as one of football's gentlemen, described it as 'a disgusting game' and it was a surprise that no player was dismissed and only two were booked. Even the usually mild-mannered Moore got caught up in the ill discipline. Describing the game as 'a virtual free-for-all', the *Sunday Mirror*'s correspondent was moved to observe that 'neither Marsh, Summerbee, nor the normally reserved Moore acted exactly like angels'.

When sporadic spells of football broke out, United were well beaten. Colin Bell scored City's first and third goals, in between which his powerful shot was turned into his own net by the unfortunate Buchan. After the game City's Mike Doyle questioned the attitude of some of the players in what he described as 'the worst United side I have played against'.

The following week against Southampton Moore put in his best home performance of the season, Davies and MacDougall again on target in a 2-1 win. The *Sunday Mirror*'s somewhat restrained reference to his 'honest effort' was high praise compared to its lambasting of an apathetic display from the troubled Best. United then won successive games for the first time thanks to a surprise 2-0 win at Norwich City, which was the Canaries' first home defeat of the season as well as United's first away win. After 13 minutes MacDougall chased down a seemingly overhit long ball from Dunne and crossed for Moore to score. Two minutes from time, Moore returned the favour, running through the Norwich defence and setting MacDougall up for the second.

The confidence boost of achieving consecutive victories was short-lived, though, and the following week fellow strugglers Stoke City won 2-0 at Old Trafford. It would be little consolation to Moore that the press considered him the best of a bad bunch.

United had been without Best, who had been suspended by the club for two weeks. His behaviour was becoming increasingly problematic, with his energetic social life having a detrimental effect on his day job. His team-mates still respected his abilities on the pitch, but it would annoy the likes of Charlton when Best missed training or otherwise acted unprofessionally. The contrast between the two was stark – Charlton the elder statesman of the team, model pro and family man, Best the charismatic single man, living life to the full and enjoying the attention his looks and talent attracted.

Moore feels any talk of a feud between the two United all-time greats is exaggerated. He never witnessed their reported refusal to pass to each other – 'ridiculous!' – and feels it was more a case of them being totally different characters:

> 'On the field they got on well together. I just think it was that Bobby didn't condone the way that George led his life. But George was George, wasn't he? The only place they didn't get on was off the field. I think they both still respected each other as players.'

Neither was in the team when things went from bad to worse in a particularly lacklustre 5-0 defeat at bottom club Crystal Palace. This was United's first defeat by such a margin in nine seasons. Law and Moore were the only outfield players to emerge with any credit from a dreadful performance. Palace winger John Hughes was another opponent to label this United team the worst he had ever seen.

16

End of an era

'I never realised you were such a good player.'

Tommy Docherty, after his first game as Manchester United manager, to Ian Storey-Moore

O'Farrell out, Docherty in

Inevitably, Frank O'Farrell's future as manager was by now in serious doubt. He had reason to feel undermined by the club's board, who had not backed him with a vote of confidence as United's form slumped. The dressing room was not a harmonious place, with some players at odds with both O'Farrell and the board in the light of the George Best saga. The manager now seemed to be faced with the choice of selling Best, reluctantly working with him to try to get United out of trouble or resigning.

Apparently with O'Farrell's knowledge – though not necessarily his approval – chairman Louis Edwards and director Sir Matt Busby had made an awkward attempt to appease the unsettled Best, with youth team coach Paddy Crerand – not O'Farrell – mediating. The end result was the decision not to put Best on the transfer list. O'Farrell declined the offer to attend the ensuing press conference.

There was even an attempt to have Best move in with Crerand, possibly more in hope than expectation that the senior player might help steer him back towards a more professional attitude.

Crerand, a great servant to the club, did his best to put the wayward star back on the straight and narrow. Perhaps inevitably the arrangement was short-lived.

Best was briefly back at Old Trafford on the Monday after the Crystal Palace debacle, though he didn't join his team-mates in training and declined to comment to the press when he left after just half an hour. The United board met the following day, 19 December 1972, and, sensationally, sacked both Best and O'Farrell, along with assistant manager Malcolm Musgrove and coach John Aston. Best promptly declared his intention not to play football any more, though in the itinerant years that followed he would line up, with varying degrees of success, for Fulham, Hibernian and several US teams, before putting in several blink-and-you-missed-it appearances at clubs around the world.

Moore had liked O'Farrell but took a pragmatic view of his fate:

> 'I think it was expected because of the results. Time was running out for Frank, really. He was a really nice guy, a gentleman, and it was sad what happened. He had a difficult task there and I think that it was inevitable that, because of the results, they were going to try and replace him.'

Before long, there was speculation that Scotland manager Tommy Docherty would take over the Old Trafford hot seat, possibly keeping the international job on a part-time basis.

On the Thursday that week the directors held a meeting of all the club's staff, as they were concerned at the effect on the players of the incessant media attention as United lurched from crisis to crisis. Recent acquisition Ted MacDougall had already had to deny reports that he was wanting to move on. Moore, though, had admitted to feeling unsettled. Nine months earlier he had, with mixed feelings, left a Forest team in the midst of a vain battle against relegation. He could not have expected to find himself in another battle against the drop the following season, with the star-studded United team disintegrating and in disarray:

> 'There was general disaffection with the way things were going. There was a lot of unrest there in the club at the time amongst the players and staff, but you had to get on with it. You couldn't really fault any of the players; they took me on board. It was just probably the wrong time to go there, as the club was going through a transitional period. The great players like Bobby, Denis and Paddy were getting to the end of their careers and George was coming and going and not quite sure what he wanted to do in life.'

The meeting the directors instigated was welcomed by club captain Bobby Charlton, who said the players had appreciated it and would pull the club out of trouble. Docherty, newly appointed and having relinquished the Scotland job, identified restoring the United players' confidence as his first task but offered no comment when asked about Best.

His first game in charge was the visit of high-flying Leeds United on 23 December 1972 and the team responded with a much-improved performance in a 1-1 draw. Leeds' equaliser came seconds from the end of added time but the United players took encouragement from having come so close to an unexpected win. Moore had one of his best games for United and had a hand in their goal, threading a pass down the wing to Willie Morgan, who crossed low for MacDougall to score.

Already the downcast mood around Old Trafford had lifted and after the game several players noted the instant effect Docherty's presence was having. Moore commented on the praise the new manager gave his players at half-time, adding – tellingly – that this was a nice change.

Moore was clearly making a good impression on the new manager. Early in his tenure, Docherty told him, 'I never realised you were such a good player,' a great boost to Moore's confidence:

> 'Tommy was a gregarious character. He certainly engendered optimism and confidence within the players, me included. I wanted to play for him. He was very complimentary to me and I got on well with him.'

Docherty soon brought in a familiar face in Tommy Cavanagh, the trainer who had helped make Moore's Nottingham Forest team fitter and tougher. He was the same bubbly, bright taskmaster Moore had known at the City Ground and had different strengths from those of his predecessor at Old Trafford:

> 'Whereas Malcolm Musgrove was a tactical and functional coach, Tommy was a fitness fanatic. We used to do an awful lot of running with him at Forest and that continued at Man United.'

Moore recognises that Cavanagh's style was not to every player's liking and fondly recalls an incident from the new trainer's first day at the club:

> 'Denis passed the ball with the outside of his foot in the first training session and Tommy blew the whistle and said to him, "You don't pass the ball like that!" And Denis looked at me and said, "Is he barmy?" Telling Denis Law how to pass the ball – it was hilarious!'

On Boxing Day 1972 Moore found himself at the Baseball Ground for the first time since that fateful weekend in March. The match drew Derby's biggest crowd of the season to date, with over 35,000 already in the ground when the gates were locked, after which hundreds more – mainly United followers – climbed over the walls to get in. Predictably, Moore got a hostile reception from the home supporters. He didn't let the crowd put him off his game, though, and scored United's goal in a 3-1 defeat.

The Rams had just gone three up when Moore gave United hope with a headed goal from Kidd's cross, then – uncharacteristically, but understandably – he promptly flashed a double V-sign at the barracking fans:

> 'I went and gave them the V-sign, which I'd probably have got fined for these days. I got so much abuse as soon as I walked on the pitch, which I knew I would, but Matt Busby came in after the game and said, "Well done, Ian, well played." I think he knew I was under a lot of pressure and had a decent game, so that was nice because I'd got slaughtered by the crowd.'

After Moore's goal, United rallied but were unable to get back into the game.

Derby's team that day included Moore's former team-mates Terry Hennessey and Alan Hinton as well as future Forest stars John McGovern, Archie Gemmill, John O'Hare and Colin Todd.

Moore's performance impressed Docherty, who felt his performance was 'excellent in view of the stick the crowd were giving him'. But Derby were rampant, making much the better use of a predictably muddy Baseball Ground pitch and exposing United's frailties in midfield and at the back.

Docherty was quick to reinforce those areas, signing right-back Alec Forsyth from Partick Thistle, Arsenal midfielder George Graham, central defender Jim Holton from Shrewsbury Town as well as Celtic forward Lou Macari. Moore would be unable to take the field with them for a couple of months, however, as the bad luck with injuries that had dogged him at vital stages of his career occurred once more.

Injury curse strikes again

United's first match of 1973 saw them go down to a 3-1 defeat at Highbury on 6 January, with Kidd scoring their consolation goal after Moore hit the post. The following week, Moore and his team-mates were going through their paces in a routine training session at The Cliff.

The damage was done in the gym during a simple kick-around. The surface was hard with a loose, gravel-like dressing, which meant it could be slippery and difficult for players to keep their feet. Moore challenged for a ball with David Sadler, United's captain, slipped and landed awkwardly on the same ankle Arthur Mann's horrific tackle had injured three years before. Moore knew straight away that something was badly wrong, but United's medical staff were not so quick to identify the problem. Moore recalls the 'awful' playing surface with a wince and is surprised that there were not more injuries on it. To this day he remains bitterly disappointed at the medical treatment he was subsequently given:

> 'After the injury there was no scan. It was ridiculous what they were trying to do – they pontificated for four months. They didn't really know what it was. They did an X-ray – nothing broken. But they didn't realise the ligament was torn in two. They didn't have a clue what it was until it was too late. Unfortunately, the treatment I got there just wasn't particularly good.'

During the weeks that followed, in training Moore found he could manage no more than 70 to 80 per cent of his normal game. He felt embarrassed and even questioned himself as to whether it was all in his mind.

After repeatedly breaking down while training, however, Moore decided to take matters into his own hands and went to see the consultant, Mr Jackson, who had operated on him after his injury playing for Forest at Manchester City. At his surgery in The Park in Nottingham, Jackson told Moore that he knew what needed to be done but that it would be unethical for him to perform the operation as the player was in the care of the medical staff at United.

Moore was not the only player to suffer in this way. The same club surgeon who eventually operated on him also told Denis Law there was nothing wrong with his knee before a subsequent operation found a loose bit of bone. The facilities and player care at what was arguably the biggest club in the country were clearly a far cry from what they are now.

Without Moore, United lost at Wolverhampton Wanderers in the FA Cup, then won only one of the next five league games. Struggling for consistency in the absence of the player now widely considered to be their most effective forward, United were desperate to get Moore back into the team. By the time he returned, on 3 March, it was for a clash of the bottom two, with visitors West Bromwich Albion three points behind United. Goals from Kidd and Macari gave United a 2-1 win, but Moore was taken off near the end and, to add to their injury worries, keeper Alex Stepney broke two fingers in his left hand.

Moore's last action of the league season came the following week in front of fellow strugglers Birmingham City's biggest crowd for over 20 years. More than 51,000 packed into St Andrew's and most went home happy as the Blues won 3-1. Moore's second attempted comeback from his ankle injury was over at half-time, when he was substituted.

His third and final attempt to retrieve his season came against Bari in the Anglo-Italian Cup at the start of April. He needed treatment early on after going over on his ankle and although he carried on playing and scored United's second goal in a 3-1 win, he finally had to admit defeat and was carried off at half-time and again substituted.

As his repeated, abortive attempts to make his comeback showed, Moore had a certain freedom of movement in his ankle, but not enough to see him through the rigours of competitive football:

> 'Once the swelling had gone down, I got to the stage where I could run in a straight line. It was when I stopped or deviated quickly – which was my game really, with the ball, going past people – it just used to give way. I was really trying to get fit again but I was missing that extra ten or 20 per cent.
>
> 'The injury happened in early January and it wasn't until May that they decided to send me to Harley Street and the specialist knew straight away. He said, "You need an operation." The surgeon at Man United, who had said there was nothing wrong, was the one who operated on it. Usually, when they operate, they come back in the next two to three hours and tell you what they've done. When I finally saw him two or three days later he said, "I've done my best, but it's the main ligament in your ankle. It's frayed so much I couldn't stitch it together."
>
> 'So, consequently, there was always going to be a weakness there. I did try, but I lost the ability to move in and out at pace, which was a key part of my game. It just wasn't the same.'

Moore's curtailed season saw him score six goals in 30 league and domestic cup appearances, a tally matched by the wayward Best and only beaten by Charlton's seven (from nine more starts). Had he managed to play the full season Moore would almost certainly have been United's top scorer. United revived sufficiently under Docherty to finish 18th, three places and a relatively comfortable seven points above the bottom two relegation places, which were occupied by Crystal Palace and West Bromwich Albion. The players celebrated United's survival at a party held by Louis Edwards at a Manchester hotel, though Moore's season had had anything but a happy ending. He would have to set his sights on getting fit over the summer, in the hope that both he and United would enjoy better fortune in Docherty's first full season in charge.

Bowing to the inevitable

For all the usual pre-season optimism, it was clear that there were still major problems at United. Their survival the previous season proved to be no more than a stay of execution. Just six years after they had become the first English club to win the European Cup, United would finish 21st and be relegated. Famously, the *coup de grâce* would be dealt towards the end of the Manchester derby by a back-heeled goal from a sheepish Denis Law, who had moved to the blue side of the city after Docherty had given him a free transfer.

Moore would only wear a United shirt twice that season, though. When he started training he could feel that his ankle was still not right, but in September he made his last attempted comeback, against Leicester City. The Foxes had made an unbeaten start to the season, which they maintained with a deserved 2-1 win. After his long absence from the team, Moore was once again one of the few United players to emerge with any credit from an all too familiar lacklustre performance. United's goal came from a late penalty which, unusually, was tucked away by Alex Stepney. He had scored a spot kick in a close-season game in Spain, but the team's goalkeeper taking a penalty in a league match was hardly a ringing endorsement of the confidence and self-belief of the outfield players.

Three days later United took advantage of Moore's namesake, Bobby, being dropped by West Ham manager Ron Greenwood. Two fierce long-range strikes from Brian Kidd put them in a commanding position and, two minutes after a Billy Bonds penalty had given the visitors hope, Moore restored United's two-goal lead with what would be the last goal of his professional career in

England. As a cross came into the Hammers' penalty area, Martin Buchan's younger brother George deceived the keeper by jumping over it, allowing Moore to hit a scuffed, right-foot shot just inside the post. 'A bit of a mis-hit,' Moore recalls with typical modesty.

Recurring fitness problems caused by his damaged ankle meant that would be Moore's final game for United.

Testimonial

When Moore retired from professional football at the end of 1973, the powers that be at Manchester United generously paid him an ex gratia 'golden goodbye' of £20,000. Although the club had recouped through insurance a substantial portion of the original transfer fee, they had been under no obligation to make such a payment and it reflects great credit on United that they chose to do so.

For his part, Moore said, 'I wouldn't have swapped the chance to play on for United for all this money. I really loved the game and I liked those United fans. There's so much more I wish I could have done for the club.'

Although his all-too-brief time at Old Trafford didn't qualify him for a testimonial match, a testimonial dinner was arranged in Moore's honour at a variety club in Wythenshawe. This was organised by the area manager of a well-known, national chain of betting shops. George Best and Sir Matt Busby attended, among many others.

The souvenir programme for the evening testified to the high regard in which Moore was held in footballing circles. The tributes were led by Tommy Docherty:

> 'Ian Moore has been a tremendous loss to Manchester United ... No one will ever completely fill the gap he left. He was a 20-goals-a-season man ... my type of player.
>
> 'I remember the day he destroyed Leeds as a raiding winger with Willie Morgan doing the same on the right.

The memory of that game … sums up my frustration … The real tragedy [is] a man like George [Best] fully able to play but without the desire, and a man like Ian who would have given up everything to play but is now physically unable to do so.'

Reflecting the continuing affection for Moore at his former club, Nottingham Forest's chairman Jim Willmer wrote:

'Ian came to Forest straight from school and showed us very early on that he had quite outstanding ability. He was always a very conscientious and most popular player, and during his first-team career with us became known as one of the game's great individualists. The tragedy of his enforced retirement from football is that he still had a real future in front of him.

'Now that Ian has returned to settle in the East Midlands we see him regularly at the City Ground. Forest have gained a new and welcome supporter but football has lost a very fine player.'

The directors, management and players of Manchester City took out an advert in the programme sending Moore their best wishes. Manchester United's own advert said, 'It was our pleasure to have signed you, Ian,' while Forest added, 'There'll always be a welcome among old friends, Ian.'

In his contribution entitled 'The man who belonged to the golden era of goalscoring wingers', *Daily Mail* sports reporter Ronald Crowther regretted Moore's lack of opportunity on the international scene:

'Ian Moore bows out of British football as the kind of player that it can least afford to lose. And that is not just a way of acknowledging his gentlemanly manner and his sporting approach. He will be badly missed because he belonged to a vanishing breed of soccer specialists – the goalscoring wingers.

'In an era in which the Ramsey cult caught on and British soccer began to give less scope to forwards who could outflank defences, Ian was a throwback to the golden era of wing play … It is ironical that he should have played in the era of the Garrinchas and Jairzinhos of the world outside but in the wrong age for scoring wingers in his own country.'

Crowther went on to say:

'For me, the most unforgettable thing about his goals will not be so much the impressive tally but the electrifying manner in which he scored them. Ian, in his explosive bursts, had that special brand of hostility that could lift the drabbest of games to exhilarating heights.

'Although he had the finishing power to match the boxing champion's killer punch, no footballer I have met had a more gentle manner off the playing pitch.

'United fans, who have hailed so many great players in their time, loved him and he quickly began to show his warmth of appreciation for them.'

Fellow journalist Derick Allsop continued the theme:

'Ian Moore's too-brief career at Old Trafford cheated Manchester United supporters – a breed schooled in excellence – of one of the most exhilarating sights in football. And yet Moore still gave them glimpses of what might have been; of those rare gifts that would surely have added his name to that post-Munich triumvirate of greats – Charlton, Law, and Best.'

In his written piece, Moore said that he would always look on Manchester as his second home, adding:

> 'Injury dogged me during my brief stay in Manchester. My career never took off as I hoped it would when I joined United. Then, when they needed me most, I had to give up football … I would love to stay in touch with all my friends in Manchester. Once again my sincere thanks to everyone.'

But of all the tributes paid to Moore in that souvenir programme, the most poignant came from Brian Clough. Despite the acrimony of Moore's on-off transfer to Derby still being fresh in the mind, Clough wrote graciously:

> 'Derby County would have won the league championship by three or four more points in 1972 if Ian Moore had joined us instead of Manchester United. That's how highly I rated him. But I wouldn't have used Ian as a winger. He would have been an orthodox striker alongside John O'Hare, and he would have suited our style of play perfectly.
>
> 'I wanted to manage him. I wanted to put him where he should have been … at the very top … He always excited me, and he is a very nice person. He wasn't soured by the profession, not one of the hard people.
>
> 'I wish him the best of luck … from someone who knows what it is like to have a playing career ended prematurely by injury.'

Unfortunately, despite Clough's best wishes, Moore would shortly, once again, be out of luck. The man who organised the event pocketed the money raised that evening, £8,000, and was subsequently taken to court then given a suspended prison sentence. However, Moore never saw a penny and had to make do with a fortnight's holiday at a hotel in Malta courtesy of the individual's employer.

On reflection

Moore looks back on his United years with fondness but, understandably, considerable frustration. He rates Tommy Docherty's first match in charge as the most memorable game of his curtailed spell at Old Trafford:

> 'The Leeds game – how well we'd played, considering the position we were in, against a really good team. And we were winning 1-0 until – with probably the last kick of the game – Leeds equalised. I knew I'd played well in that game and the fans really got behind the new manager. That game sticks in the memory because of the circumstances surrounding it – Tommy's first game, poor old Frank leaving.'

He rates his fine solo effort at Coventry in his third game for United as his favourite goal for the club but regrets not being able to make the kind of prolonged goalscoring impact at Old Trafford that he had at Forest:

> 'I would have loved to have stayed at Manchester United and maybe tried to get 100 league goals there like I did at Forest, which I might have done if I could have had five years there. I'd have loved to have made my mark more at the club, with it being such a massive club, and done better there in terms of performances and goals. But it was a difficult time for me with that injury. I was probably 80 per cent all right. I'd just lost that explosive burst that I had. I couldn't really go past people. I just wasn't the player I was, it was as simple as that. Who knows what might have happened if I hadn't got injured? It put the mockers on my career at 28 years old.'

Moore never completely cut his ties with United. Until recently, he attended former players' dinners with his old friend Jeff Whitefoot, but with Whitefoot no longer able to attend and the hiatus in social events brought about by the Covid pandemic, he has not been for a few years. He still receives a club calendar each year and is grateful to be remembered by Manchester United half a century after he left.

17

Gone for a Burton

'It's not so much a comeback as an attempt at a comeback.'

Ian Storey-Moore upon signing for Burton Albion

On the comeback trail

Throughout his career Moore played in numerous charity football matches. The very first was on 11 April 1962, a week after his reserve team debut, when he turned out for a Nottingham Forest youth team against a Bulwell FC XI captained that day by Jack Burkitt in a match to raise money for the Highbury Hospital League of Friends and the Notts FA Benevolent Fund. The *Nottingham Evening News* wrote enthusiastically about 'the clever inside-forward from Scunthorpe'.

After having been forced to retire from professional football, Moore was still playing the occasional Sunday afternoon charity match with other ex-players. He was beginning to think that his bad ankle was improving and wondered whether the damaged ligaments had knitted together somehow. At one such charity fundraiser in September 1974 Moore played alongside his old Forest team-mate, Frank Wignall. 'Big Frank' had just joined Burton Albion, newly promoted to the Southern League Premier Division, and had been made their captain. He knew that even a less-than-fully fit Moore would be more than a handful for non-league defences and told Moore he would put in a word for him with Burton's manager, Ken Gutteridge, a former Birmingham City and Sheffield United player.

Sure enough, the following day Gutteridge was sitting in the launderette Moore and his wife were running in Bingham, trying to persuade him to join Albion. Moore, who had kept fit by playing squash and coaching a local amateur side, was unsure. He had only recently turned down an offer to play for Tamworth where Terry Hennessey, whose own career had also been cut short by injury, was now the manager. Gutteridge persisted and Moore eventually agreed, saying, 'I'm not sure, Ken, to be honest. I've not trained or played properly for a long time, but if you want me to, I'll give it a go.'

Despite his reticence, Moore was struggling to adjust to life after football. Inevitably he missed the dressing room banter and the thrill of matchday. Interviewed at the time, he admitted, 'I enjoyed going down to the ground in the morning. We moaned about training, of course, but there were a lot of laughs, really. And you get used to looking forward to Saturday.' One thing he didn't miss, though, was the full-backs who would try to kick him into the stands or send him on his way for yet another X-ray or plaster cast.

On 8 October Moore went to watch Burton beat Gresley Rovers 1-0 in an FA Cup second qualifying round replay. The following day he started training with the Brewers for the princely sum of £5 travel expenses.

Newspaper reports of the comeback of the 'quicksilver winger' included the rather melancholic observation that Moore's signing for Burton completed 'one of the saddest riches-to-rags tales in modern soccer history'.

Interviewed at the time, Moore rather wistfully sought to play down expectations:

> 'During the summer I played a lot of squash and a few games on a Sunday, and there hasn't been much reaction from the

ankle. So, when Burton asked me if I would like to join them, I thought it was at least a chance to play football at some kind of level again.

'It will be a thrill just to kick a ball in competition again. I'm fit and the thrill of playing is wonderful. I just hope people don't expect too much from me.

'I think the ankle will stand up to non-league soccer. But even if things go very well there is no chance of my returning to league football again. But I'm on trial during the next few weeks. I'll see how things go. If they don't work out, then I'll hang up my boots for good.

'Football still means a lot to me, so having this chance to play will make Saturdays worth living for again. I realise there won't be thousands watching and the grounds will be half empty. But just playing will be enough to keep me happy.'

That very same week Wignall, who had passed his coaching badges, announced that he would be leaving to take up a three-year contract as manager of the national side of Qatar, an opportunity arranged by the Football Association. His immediate task would be to prepare the Qatari team for the 1976 Gulf Cup. As he packed his bags at his home in Nottingham, Wignall told reporters, 'The money is fantastic and I'll not be sorry to see the back of the weather … We've been promised a nice three-bedroom villa and no expense has been spared … I feel this is a chance to prove myself as a coach … I hope this will lead to bigger things.'

Wignall asked Moore to join him in the Middle East. Although tempted by the climate and prospect of a tax-free salary, Moore decided to stay put to see where the resumption of his playing career would take him.

On 19 October Moore made his debut for Burton against Stafford Rangers at Eton Park in the next round of the FA Cup, renewing his strike partnership with Wignall, who was still waiting for his plane tickets to Qatar to arrive. The pitch was so hard that Moore had to wear training shoes (his favourite yellow ones) rather than studded football boots. The match ended goalless, though the *Derby Evening Telegraph* reported that Moore had shown some of his old form. Burton lost the replay 2-0.

In the Albion team that day, alongside the two former England internationals, was a talented 19-year-old, Peter Ward, who had been signed from local amateurs Borrowash Victoria at the start of the season. His goalscoring feats had already attracted the attention of several league clubs. Apparently, Nottingham Forest had been promised the opportunity to buy Ward should Burton decide to sell him. In the event, a familiar name from Moore's past appeared on the scene.

Peter Taylor was now the manager of Third Division Brighton & Hove Albion, Brian Clough having departed in the summer for his ill-fated 44-day tenure at Leeds United. Back in the summer of 1962 when he helped organise that Inland Revenue charity cricket match, Taylor had just signed as a goalkeeper for Burton. He had gone on to manage them for three years before teaming up with Clough at Hartlepools United for the start of their incredible managerial partnership.

Taylor and Gutteridge started negotiating the transfer of Ward to the south coast club for £4,000. When the news of this broke in the press, Gutteridge resigned in protest at the alleged leaking of the story by Burton's chairman, Tom Bradbury. The following week he teamed up with Taylor, joining Brighton as their player-coach, quite possibly on the understanding that they would in due course sign Ward.

Burton's reserve team trainer (and owner of a local post office and grocer's) Harry Bodle took over as caretaker manager. Bodle had had an eventful footballing career. He was a member of the Birmingham City team that in 1946 lost in an FA Cup semi-final replay to eventual winners Derby County. Later, as manager of Accrington Stanley, he had resigned a month before the club quit the Football League because of financial difficulties.

After a slow start to the season, Burton's league form improved, helped by the prolific Ward and by Moore adjusting to the rigours of non-league football. The FA Cup disappointment was soon forgotten as Albion embarked on a storming run in the FA Trophy. On 30 November, in the third qualifying round, Burton drew 3-3 at Mexborough Town, an injury-time equaliser by Moore forcing the replay. He scored again in the second match, an easy 3-0 win.

Another replay followed in the first round proper, Burton defeating Atherstone Town 4-2 at Eton Park. Home wins against South Bank and Mossley in the following two rounds set up a quarter-final away at Dagenham of the Rothmans Isthmian League. Albion had reached the same stage three years earlier before losing 3-0 to Macclesfield Town.

On 9 March 1975, in pouring rain, Albion took the lead through Ward, only to be pegged back by a 35-yard screamer by Dagenham's Paul Currie, brother of England international Tony. The *Sunday Telegraph* described what followed:

> 'At this point it seemed that Dagenham would crush the Southern League team … but their momentum was destroyed by the elegant Storey-Moore … Moore, who has known more illustrious days with Manchester United and Nottingham Forest, picked his target spot while an arc of three defenders backed off instead of tackling him.'

Ward scored his second goal in the final minute to make the final score 3-1. The *Sunday Mirror* went so far as to describe the match as 'breathtaking'.

Insurance premium

Moore's successful return to competitive football, albeit at non-league level, had not gone unnoticed. At the start of February 1975 there was speculation in the national press that Moore was the subject of interest from some Football League clubs and that he might even make a sensational return to Old Trafford. Indeed, Manchester United manager Tommy Docherty was quoted as saying that he was 'definitely interested in having a fully fit Ian Moore back in my squad'. Having learned his lesson from the Derby County transfer saga three years earlier, Moore declined to comment on the rumours.

In fact, the only substantive enquiry Moore received was from Third Division Peterborough United, but there was a major financial impediment to such a move. When Moore had been forced to retire at the end of 1973, Manchester United had received an insurance payout covering a substantial portion of the £200,000 transfer fee they had paid Forest. The insurers would have to be reimbursed should Moore ever return to the Football League. Therefore, it was too great a financial risk for any club to take a chance on the 30-year-old knowing that his ankle might go again at any time.

Another Wembley dream shattered

Moore had scored four goals and made three assists in Albion's FA Trophy cup run. In the semi-final they faced Matlock Town of the Northern Premier League over two legs. On 28 March 1975 a crowd of over 5,000 at Matlock's Causeway Lane ground saw a keenly fought affair – in every sense of the word.

Albion outclassed their hosts in the first half, Moore being hacked down several times and having to receive treatment off the pitch for an injured ankle. Just before half-time the hosts' player-manager, former Sheffield Wednesday defender Peter Swan, was sent off for punching Albion's centre-forward Doug Hickton. Yet despite playing against ten men for the entire second half, Burton had to wait until the second minute of injury time before Frank Corrigan scored a penalty for a 1-0 win.

The report in the *Burton Daily Mail* exclaimed that 'Burton Albion are through to Wembley!' Albion were certainly confident of completing the job at Eton Park; a local businessman was sounded out about donating £500 to buy blazers so that the players could look smart as they walked out under the twin towers and, on the day of the second leg, the team went to a Berni Inn for a celebratory steak before the match. Unfortunately, they were over-confident.

On 5 April, in front of 5,400 expectant supporters, Burton seemed overawed by the occasion. They weren't helped by having two strong penalty claims turned down, the first after just ten minutes when Moore, who was just about to shoot, was brought down from behind. Halfway through the first half a similar challenge on Ward likewise went unpunished. In fact, nothing went right for Albion, defenders having off days and Moore a rare quiet game. Matlock won 2-0. Afterwards, in the dressing room the players were shattered. Outside the scene was no less desolate – the litter-strewn terraces deserted, the ambition of the club and the town in ruins.

Burton had needed to get to Wembley to balance the books and the semi-final defeat left them in a parlous financial state.

The Brewers regrouped to finish 1974/75 in a creditable fifth place. Shortly after the final whistle blew on the last game of the season, former manager Gutteridge approached Bodle and made an offer for 25-goal Ward. Negotiations for the youngster's transfer to Brighton, for a fee now agreed at £5,000, were concluded within 24 hours, leaving potential suitors such as Forest out in the cold. Five years later the Reds, with Clough and Taylor at the helm, would end up paying £400,000 for him.

In the meantime, Moore had left Eton Park for pastures new.

18

Foreign fields

'The AstroTurf was like concrete.'

Ian Storey-Moore

America calling

One afternoon in February 1975 Moore was unpacking a delivery of washing powder at the back of the launderette he and Carol had bought to provide a retirement income. The telephone rang and Carol answered it. 'It's Bill Foulkes,' she shouted across to her husband.

Foulkes was a Busby Babe who, like Bobby Charlton, had survived the Munich air disaster in 1958 and gone on to win the European Cup ten years later. Indeed, Foulkes had scored the winning goal against Real Madrid to send United through to the Wembley final against Benfica. He had been a tough, uncompromising centre-half who would spend as much time as possible in the gym, lifting weights. Described by Moore, who had played against him in the 1960s, as someone who 'couldn't run but was as strong as an ox', Foulkes had played almost 700 games for United before retiring in 1970.

During Moore's time at Old Trafford, Foulkes had been the youth team coach. Moore had heard that he had recently been appointed manager of Chicago Sting, a new franchise in the North American Soccer League, and was intrigued to get the call. He knew that several high-profile players had been recruited to the NASL. His former England squad colleague Peter Bonetti, by that time Chelsea's reserve team goalkeeper, had recently agreed to play in St Louis, while Mike England, the former Welsh international and Tottenham central defender – and Moore's opponent in that 1967 FA Cup semi-final – had joined Seattle Sounders. Boston Minutemen had even signed Portugal's 'Black Pearl', Eusébio, while New York Cosmos had set their sights on making a marquee signing and were for a time linked with George Best.

'How would you fancy playing over here in Chicago, Ian?' enquired Foulkes. Moore was flattered by the offer, 'I'm grateful you've asked, Bill, but I've got a business to run now.' 'We'll put you and Carol up in a nice apartment, all expenses paid. Why don't you think it through and let me know as soon as you can? The season starts in just over a month's time.' Moore agreed to let Foulkes have his answer by the end of the week.

It didn't take long for the couple to decide to give it a shot. Moore had enjoyed his time in the US during Forest's five-week post-season tour of North America in 1965. Also, the wages would certainly be welcome. Crucially, they knew someone who could manage the launderette for the five months or so that they would be in Chicago – the soccer season ran from April to August. Further, the standard of the NASL was probably not much different from the Southern League Premier Division in which he was playing for Burton Albion, so Moore felt that he could do himself justice in that environment.

By coincidence, the following day, before Moore had had a chance to tell Foulkes he would move to Chicago, he received a second call from the States. This time it was from former Charlton Athletic forward Eddie Firmani, who was now managing Tampa Bay Rowdies in Florida. Like Chicago, Tampa Bay had been newly admitted to the NASL, which was expanding from 16 to 20 teams, with four regional divisions of five teams each.

Firmani made a similar offer to Foulkes except that he was able to offer Moore the opportunity to play on grass for the Rowdies' home matches – the Sting and most of the other teams played on AstroTurf, at the time a relatively new invention. This was tempting because Moore had heard bad reports about the artificial grass surface, but out of loyalty to his former Manchester United colleague he felt obliged to decline Firmani's offer. He immediately phoned Foulkes and accepted his invitation to try life in the Windy City.

Sting in the tail

Moore flew to Chicago in early April, Carol following a few weeks later once she had put all the arrangements in place for the launderette to be managed in their absence.

The Storey-Moores' home from home was an apartment, rented for them by the club, in the Edgewater Beach complex at the northern end of the famous, 15-mile-long Lake Shore Drive. Close to numerous restaurants and bars, overlooking Lake Michigan and surrounded by a park on one side and beach on the other – 'it was like being by the sea' – the luxurious accommodation was a world away from their pleasant, detached house in a cul-de-sac in sleepy Bingham.

Some aspects of life Stateside took a little getting used to. On one occasion, having been given a free meal for two at a Mexican restaurant as the reward for a 'Most Valuable Player' performance, Moore's first taste of the spicy food left his senses reeling. But otherwise they soon settled in, enjoying Chicago and the lively social life it had to offer.

Another feature of life in the US's 'second city' that was far removed from rural Nottinghamshire was the weather. When Moore arrived, the Illinois winter was turning to spring but Lake Michigan was still frozen over. Then, seemingly without warning, in May and June the temperature shot up and every day was roasting hot. The NASL was being held in the summer so as not to clash with the American football season. The unbearable heat and high humidity made it impossible to play football during the day. Instead, the players would assemble on the beach around six o'clock in the evening and do a couple of hours' training.

The Sting's *1975 Media Guide* for newspapers, radio and television channels contained descriptions of each member of the team. Having been signed just before the start of the season, Moore was the only player not to have a photograph accompanying his pen portrait, which read:

> 'Ian Moore, forward, 5 feet 11 inches, 170 pounds, 30 years old. Forced out of big-time soccer by a serious ankle injury when he was rated the best winger in England while playing with Manchester United, Ian Moore has made a remarkable comeback after six months' layoff and a stint with non-league Burton Albion.
>
> 'Manchester United collected a huge insurance payoff, preventing Moore from returning to the First Division team. Moore scored more than 100 league goals for Nottingham Forest and was that team's leading scorer for five seasons before his transfer to Manchester United for $480,000. When he joined United, he made a quick impression with his skills, even though his new team was already blessed with the likes of George Best, Denis Law and Bobby Charlton. Ian's full name is Ian Storey-Moore, but he prefers the simpler version.'

Although Moore's photograph wasn't in the guide, a sketch of him in his trademark number 11 shirt, taking a shot at goal, featured on the front cover. Nine of his team-mates were British and they included another ex-United player, defender Clive Griffiths, and forward Gordon Hill, who was on loan from Millwall. Most of the British players in the NASL were – like Moore – past their prime, but Hill was a notable exception. Aged just 21, he would end the season with 16 goals and seven assists in 21 appearances and was named in the NASL's All Star team. Hill's success with the Sting prompted Manchester United to sign him and he went on to win the FA Cup with them.

Chicago Sting had been established in late 1974 by a local commodities broker, Lee Stern. The team's name was inspired by the popular movie of the time starring Robert Redford and Paul Newman, which was set in Chicago. The club's logo was a cartoon of an angry bee guarding a football. Stern acknowledged that it might take a few years to turn a profit but reckoned that 'soccer' would soon become more popular than American football.

The boldness of that claim – and the scale of the challenge – was evident in the Sting's first home game of the season, against Denver Dynamos on 2 May 1975. Played at Soldier Field, the 55,000-capacity home of NFL franchise Chicago Bears, the match was watched by a mere 4,500 spectators, all seated in a single section down one side of the pitch. That was only half the attendance when, a decade earlier during that end-of-season tour, Forest and German Bundesliga side Hannover 96 had played a friendly at the same venue.

'It was a massive stadium. It felt quite surreal, like playing in a vacuum,' Moore recalls. 'The biggest crowd we got was about 14,000 when we played Poland in a friendly game, because Chicago has a big Polish ethnic population.' The average home attendance during the Sting's inaugural season in the NASL was just 4,300.

Late in the game with Chicago trailing 1-0, Moore, making his debut, had a shot handled on the line. Unfortunately, he missed the resultant penalty and Denver went on to win 2-0. 'A bit of a choke' was Moore's blunt admission to the press after the match.

That loss followed the season-opener, a tempestuous 1-0 defeat at Vancouver Whitecaps in which ex-Notts County defender

Eddie Cliff, on his debut for Chicago, had his leg broken by a crude tackle from behind that was not even penalised by the referee. That incident led Foulkes to complain to the press, 'I'm very worried about the officiating I've seen here … We've brought some very skilful players here from England and I just hope the referees will protect them. If the game is to develop in this country the skilful players must be allowed to play.'

Moore made amends for that penalty miss in the next game, a 3-2 home win against Dallas Tornado. Trailing 2-0 at half-time, Moore's 85th-minute header capped a fine second-half comeback by the Sting.

The next game, at home against Los Angeles Aztecs, saw Chicago record back-to-back wins. Perhaps the most memorable moment of the evening's entertainment, though, was the ceremonial kick-off, a staple of American sport, by *Playboy* magazine's 1975 Playmate of the Year, Marilyn Lange. Evidently, the powers that be at the Sting were so impressed that the following season they actually selected Lange, who played for her college's women's football team in Hawaii, as their fourth draft pick and gave her the number nine shirt. As they say, 'Only in America.'

Such distractions aside, the mixed start to the season for the Sting and for Moore himself continued. On 21 May, in Texas for a match against San Antonio Thunder, the team took the opportunity to visit the Alamo. Moore remembers the game itself clearly:

> 'We played at around ten o'clock at night with the temperature still around 100 degrees Fahrenheit. In the crowd there was this huge guy on the halfway line with a great big drum; every time they attacked he would shout, "Go, Thunder, go!"'

Apparently, Moore had been imbued with some of Davy Crockett's fighting spirit:

'I had an argument with Gordon Hill about him not passing the ball to me. I hit the crossbar with one shot but we managed to win 2-1.'

Two days later, against San Jose Earthquakes at Soldier Field, Moore had a goal disallowed in the second half of overtime. Although he scored his penalty, Chicago lost the shoot-out. The last game in May saw the Sting lose 2-0 at the Portland Timbers, future Forest star Peter Withe scoring one of the goals. So, by the end of May the Sting had won three, lost four.

The month of June started with the Sting playing in front of over 16,000 at the Memorial Stadium in Seattle. Despite Moore rolling back the years to score with a 20-yard shot – again in the 85th minute – it wasn't enough to prevent the Sounders running out 2-1 winners. The Sting's inconsistent form continued with a 1-0 win against Denver Dynamos followed by a defeat by the same scoreline to Peter Bonetti's St Louis Stars.

Having played in nine consecutive league matches since his arrival in the States, Moore's luck ran out. He had found the artificial pitches difficult to play on; running in a straight line was easy enough, but the synthetic surfaces were unsuited to Moore's twisting and turning style of forward play. 'It was so hard, there was no give at all. In one match I broke my big toe when I slid to a stop,' he recalls. On 20 June, in a season-best 6-2 win against the Philadelphia Atoms, he fell awkwardly on Soldier Field's AstroTurf and damaged his ankle. The injury meant he missed the next five NASL games plus the friendly against Poland.

Meanwhile, having failed to lure George Best a couple of months earlier, New York Cosmos astounded the sporting world when they announced the signing of Pelé, tempted out of retirement by a three-year deal worth almost $5m. Incredibly, one of the coaches at Cosmos was none other than the man who had given Moore his apprenticeship at Forest all those years before – Joe Mallett.

Naturally, matches involving Cosmos were always televised live. When they didn't clash with the Sting's fixtures, Moore would watch them avidly but somewhat frustratedly:

> 'I remember watching Pelé's debut. Talk about driving you bonkers – every five minutes the TV commentator would announce, "We're leaving Pelé's return for station identification." Even if he was just about to have a shot at goal, they would stop and cut over to the adverts. It was crazy. So, in the end, I didn't see that much of him!'

During Moore's enforced lay-off unrest was stirring at the Sting. The team's American players felt they were being harshly treated by Foulkes, a tough coach and at times a difficult man to play for. Moore got on well with him because of their time together at Manchester United, but the local players were fed up with him, held a team meeting and tried to get him sacked. They wanted Moore to take over. Moore demurred, 'I can't do that, no chance. It's not fair to Bill.'

By the time Moore returned to face the Baltimore Comets on 18 July, the Sting's record was won eight, lost eight, and their hopes of making the end-of-season play-offs looked slim. However, they hit a rich vein of form and four wins in five games – including a 3-0 win in Tampa against the Rowdies, the eventual champions – meant that heading into their final match of the regular season, the Sting needed to beat the Diplomats in Washington to secure a play-off place.

The 90 minutes finished with the two sides level at 1-1. Four minutes from the end of overtime, Hill missed a penalty for the Sting that would have taken them through to the play-offs. In the shoot-out Moore failed with his spot kick, and so his season ended as it had begun, with a missed penalty. Losing 4-2 in the shoot-out meant the Sting, despite finishing second in the Central Division, missed out on the play-offs by a single point.

That was the end of his career in Chicago: 14 matches, two goals and one assist. Despite the big sell by Foulkes, the media publicity and the plush apartment on the shores of Lake Michigan, Moore hadn't been able to make the contribution to the team he had hoped for.

Moore's verdict on his playing career with the Sting is forthright:

> 'I didn't play many games there: I really struggled. The AstroTurf was bloody awful – horrible stuff, just like concrete – it ripped the skin off you if you fell over. The ball used to go about 25 feet in the air every time it came to you. It was ridiculous.
>
> 'And, of course, the surface really didn't suit my injury problems, so my "glass ankle" went again. I shouldn't have gone really. The grass at Tampa Bay would have been a better bet.'

While none of that can be denied, Moore did at least help blaze the trail for famous footballers to see out the twilight of their careers in the NASL. These included Bobby Moore, Franz Beckenbauer, Johan Cruyff and George Best. Remarkably, the latter two were also coached by Mallett during their time at Washington Diplomats and San Jose Earthquakes respectively.

Despite things not having worked out on the pitch, Moore was given an opportunity to make a new life in the States. The University of Chicago asked him if he would stay and do some coaching. It was a tempting offer but, thinking of their laundry business, he and Carol decided to return to England.

There was a final sting in the tail, perhaps mirroring the Derby County affair when Moore arguably ended up at the 'wrong' team. In the same way as Derby, not Manchester United, had gone on to win the First Division championship, history repeated itself when Tampa Bay Rowdies, whose offer Moore had respectfully declined, won their Eastern Division, the play-offs and the Soccer Bowl championship final.

So, it was back to Nottinghamshire, Moore thinking that Chicago would be his first and last overseas footballing adventure. Almost, but not quite.

No tea party in Boston

On 9 October 1978 Moore played for Tulsa Roughnecks in a friendly match at Portsmouth as a favour to the NASL team's manager, Alan Hinton, and coach Terry Hennessey. Nothing came of it, but five months later Moore received an approach from the former Coventry City manager Noel Cantwell, who was now in charge of New England Tea Men in Boston, Massachusetts. Moore knew Cantwell from his time going to watch Peterborough United when his former team-mate John Barnwell was the coach and Cantwell the manager.

A friend of Cantwell's, Arthur Smith, a former chairman of Halifax Town, phoned Moore, 'Just come over and do a few pre-season games.' Nothing ventured, nothing gained, so Moore was given permission by Burton to take time out to try his luck again in the States.

The Tea Men, so-called through association with the Boston Tea Party and their sponsorship by the Lipton Tea Company, represented the third attempt to establish a soccer franchise in Boston. This was not proving at all easy. In their first season, 1978, the club had lost the not inconsiderable sum of $1.5m. And despite signing the now-retired Eusébio as a scout, their problems were not behind them.

The team had originally planned to play in New England Patriots' Shaefer Stadium but a dispute about, of all things, ownership of the parking lot, meant they had to make use of facilities at Boston University instead. Moreover, American players were threatening an NASL-wide strike for the right to have collective bargaining rather than have their salaries determined on a team-by-team basis. When the season started in April, overseas players had to cross picket lines in order to play.

In the end, Moore's own involvement with the Tea Men started and finished in March and was limited to three pre-season, or 'exhibition', matches against clubs ranging from Minnesota Kicks to Kalmar, a touring Swedish top-division team. On the plus side, all the matches were played in balmy spring weather at the Tangerine Bowl in Orlando, Florida. Moore didn't particularly enjoy the experience and was only too happy to return to England and resume his duties with Burton.

Later that year, however, Moore would once again be dusting off his passport.

Bobby Charlton's All-Stars XI

In June 1979, out of the blue, Bobby Charlton rang Moore, 'We're taking a team of old players to South Africa for a couple of weeks to play four games, all expenses paid. Do you fancy it?' Charlton explained that he had been invited by a South African drinks company to pull together a team of mostly retired England players to help promote football across all communities. Moore thought it an interesting adventure and eagerly accepted Charlton's invitation.

Other players recruited by Charlton to his 'All-Stars XI' included his brother Jackie, Bobby Moore, Roger Hunt and Terry Paine, all from the 1966 World Cup-winning squad, defender Keith Newton from the 1970 World Cup team, and fellow international Chris Lawler.

Although apartheid-era South Africa was subject to sporting sanctions and its football association had been expelled from FIFA, the tourists were scheduled to play black and mixed-race teams, not just all-white ones as the South African government had pressured them to do. Possibly for this reason the tourists received less criticism than might otherwise have been expected from politicians and civil rights groups.

The All-Stars were, in fact, following the precedent set in 1973 when Malcolm Allison, by then the former Manchester City manager, toured the country with an earlier incarnation of British All-Stars including Geoff Hurst. They had played one game in Soweto, against a Black South Africa XI, enabling Allison to claim that they were promoting racial harmony rather than supporting apartheid. By contrast, in 1982 a tour by a 'rebel' team managed by John Barnwell and organised by *Match of the Day* presenter Jimmy Hill was roundly vilified.

In July 1979, the day after attending Martin O'Neill's wedding, Moore met up with his fellow All-Stars at Heathrow and they flew to Johannesburg. Moore was somewhat starstruck to be sitting next to his namesake on the flight but it is quite possible that Bobby wasn't paying full attention to Moore's conversation. In Johannesburg the British Airways crew would be staying at the same hotel as the team and over drinks in the bar Bobby made the acquaintance of the stewardess who would become his second wife.

The All-Stars' first match was against a Transvaal XI in Johannesburg, winning 1-0 courtesy of a Bobby Charlton goal. A few days later in Durban a Natal XI beat the tourists by the same scoreline. The quality of the football was nothing to write home about – arguably it was little credit to the South African sides that the touring team, average age mid-30s, were holding their own and even indulging in some showboating.

Nonetheless, Moore was enjoying his first trip to South Africa:

> 'Perhaps not surprisingly, when we were in Johannesburg we were told, "Don't go out at night on your own, make sure there are three or four of you." But that aside, we enjoyed meeting the locals, particularly the waiters at the restaurants: they were really nice people and you could have a good laugh with them. If you gave them a couple of quid they were absolutely over the moon because poverty was rife there.'

The third match of the tour was back in Johannesburg at the Rand Stadium against a mixed-race South African XI. The match was notable only for the sending-off of Bobby Moore after he had complained rather too vociferously about a penalty awarded against him. The former England captain was even made to appear before a South African National Soccer League disciplinary committee and was given a reprimand.

The following day the All-Stars were wheeled out for their final game of the tour against the talented Kaizer Chiefs at the Orlando Stadium in Soweto. Moore remembers the day vividly:

> 'As we drove into Soweto it was hut, after hut, after hut. All the same: small huts with a lot of people living in them. Then suddenly we came upon this huge stadium holding around 50,000. It was packed out and, to be honest, a bit intimidating at first, especially as we had an escort of big bodyguards.
>
> 'The Chiefs beat us 2-0. I couldn't believe how skilful they were. To be honest, they gave us a bit of a chasing. Although, overall, the game wasn't great it was probably a good day out for the crowd to be able to go and see a bunch of ex-England internationals play.'

Interviewed some years later, Bobby Charlton looked back on the occasion fondly, 'It was one of the nicest days I've ever had … the people were so pleased to see us. In fact, at the end they took us on their shoulders and tried to carry us off home with them. We had to fight to get our lot back on the bus.'

The tour almost ended in tragedy. With all the players enjoying a few days of sightseeing, Bobby Moore and the Charlton brothers went up country on safari. Returning to Johannesburg their light aeroplane developed a fault with the landing gear. The skill of the pilot saved the day, but it had been a close call. Bobby Charlton, a survivor of the Munich air disaster, told reporters, 'There was always a chance the undercarriage could have collapsed on impact and the aeroplane could have ripped its belly.' His brother, Jack, was more sanguine, 'Our kid was in the back and I was up front with Bobby Moore. I suppose there was a bit of a panic.'

The tour over, Moore returned to the relative obscurity of Eton Park in Burton upon Trent.

19

Something Brewing

'It was just like watching George Best – he had the wow factor.'

Burton Albion chairman Ben Robinson, on Ian Storey-Moore

Reunion

In August 1975, after his adventure in the United States, Moore rejoined Burton Albion. He was in good form but the club's fortunes took a turn for the worse, both on and off the pitch. Albion were unable to build on the previous season's fifth-placed finish, languishing in mid-table, and attendances were down.

In February 1976 manager Harry Bodle resigned, claiming he lacked the full support of the board. Within a week, two directors had also resigned, one of them stating that there was 'little hope of survival for the club'.

Albion's part-time coach, Mick Walker, a schoolteacher, was appointed to succeed Bodle. He was popular with the players and well-regarded in the game. Walker had been an apprentice with Nottingham Forest in the late 1950s and would go on, in the 1980s and '90s, to work for Howard Wilkinson at both Notts County and Leeds United, running their successful academy. He also managed County when Neil Warnock was sacked following the Magpies' relegation from the First Division in the last season before it was superseded by the Premier League.

Walker guided Albion to a tenth-placed finish in the Southern League Premier Division in 1975/76 but the following season proved to be a traumatic one for the Brewers. There was persistent press speculation about imminent bankruptcy as the team found themselves in the relegation zone. In March 1977 the newly appointed chairman, Ben Robinson, launched a public appeal to raise £5,000 to save the club. Local businesses were reluctant to contribute, however, being unconvinced that Albion deserved their money any more than other sports clubs and local charities. Robinson still has the ledger recording the donations received: £640.

Albion were unable to pay the VAT or the taxman and drastic measures were required. At the beginning of April Robinson sacked Walker, not because the manager wasn't doing a good job but because the club needed to cut costs. Phil Waller, who had made more than 250 appearances for Derby County and Mansfield Town, was appointed player-manager on a wage less than half of that of Walker's.

A couple of weeks later Albion faced a double-header against fellow strugglers Chelmsford City. Like Albion with Moore, City had their own celebrated star striker in the shape of Jimmy Greaves who, at the time, was taking a temporary sabbatical from his sad, self-confessed alcoholism. An ankle injury meant Moore missed out on a reunion with Nottingham Forest's nemesis in the first match played at City's New Writtle Street ground. True to form, Greaves opened the scoring with a first-time shot that was practically his first touch of the game and bagged a second in a 2-1 win for Chelmsford.

Before the return fixture at Eton Park, Moore and the amiable Greaves reminisced about old times. Once the match had started Greaves again gave City the lead. This time, however, Moore equalised and Waller scored Burton's last-minute winner. The attendance that afternoon was 723, rather fewer than the 55,000 who had witnessed Moore and Greaves play in the FA Cup semi-final at Hillsborough a decade earlier.

Ultimately, sharing the honours over those two games did neither Burton nor Chelmsford any favours and at the end of the 1976/77 season both clubs were relegated.

In August 1977 Moore announced – not for the first (or last) time – that he would be retiring from football:

> 'I don't think I will be playing this season because of the ankle. I am all right when the pitches are soft, but at the end of last season I was in real trouble. After the games my ankle came up like a balloon and it is no good trying to carry on like that. Burton wanted me to play in the odd game but it is a long way to travel and I am tied up with my [bookmaking] business on Saturdays. I have really enjoyed playing at Burton; they gave me a couple more years in the game.'

Albion narrowly missed promotion that year, finishing third in the Southern League Division One North.

Return to Eton Park

A couple of months into the 1978/79 season, Waller resigned, no longer able to combine being player-manager with his day job outside football. His decision may well have been influenced during a home match when he went to take a throw-in and was greeted by one of the spectators leaning over the wall and shouting at him, 'Phil, you look absolutely knackered.'

At the time, Moore was on holiday in Majorca and was mulling over an approach by Grantham Town, of the Southern League Premier Division, to become their manager. Thinking that one day he might try his hand at football management, Moore had passed his FA coaching badges. It had actually been Walter Winterbottom, England's manager before Alf Ramsey and now responsible for the FA's coaching scheme, who had encouraged Moore to do this. Moore was mindful that, a couple of years earlier, World Cup hero Geoff Hurst had become manager of another non-league team, Telford United.

Ben Robinson found out which hotel Moore was staying at and, after a series of telephone discussions, persuaded him to return to Eton Park as player-manager. Acknowledging that Moore still held out the prospect of returning to the United States to play in the NASL, Albion appointed former Derby County and Mansfield Town full-back Mick Hopkinson as his assistant.

As ever, Moore approached the challenge in a business-like manner:

> 'It will be a great challenge. I have not seen the team play, so I have got to get to know the players and sort out the problems. I shall turn out to play in matches but not until later in the season when the pitches are softer and I have settled down to the administrative part of the job.'

With Robinson and his fellow directors personally financing most of the investment, Moore started to strengthen the team by signing former Forest men Jimmy McCann and John Winfield. On 25 November 1978 Moore made his second debut for Albion, scoring in a 2-0 win against Wellingborough. Winfield netted the other goal in his first match for the Brewers.

In March 1979 Moore had his brief flirtation with New England Tea Men back in the United States. Burton finished the season in eighth place. That summer Moore further strengthened the squad by signing three more ex-Forest players – Graham Collier, Peter Hindley and Sammy Chapman – former Notts County striker John Nixon, and lower-league journeyman Neil Warnock.

In October 1979, Moore pulled off his biggest coup by signing former Derby County and England striker Kevin Hector on loan from Vancouver Whitecaps. Seven local companies stepped in to provide the sponsorship money needed to fund Hector's

£100-a-week wages, easily a record for Albion. The deal was done on the understanding that Burton would release Hector should a Football League club express an interest in signing him.

Moore's astute leadership of Burton in that first season as player-manager attracted the attention of Third Division Grimsby Town who, in the summer of 1979, were looking for a new manager. Moore's name was put forward by Forest's former assistant manager, Bill Anderson, one of the 'gang of three' who had left Moore on his own to face Clough and Taylor at the Edwalton Hotel back in 1972.

On a Sunday morning, Moore attended the interview at Blundell Park. Walking into the smoke-filled boardroom, with '12 old codgers sitting round the table', Moore found it quite an intimidating experience. A few hours later, back home in Bingham, he took the phone call from Anderson informing him that he had failed to get the job by one vote, coach and acting manager George Kerr being appointed instead. Moore simply replied, 'Fair enough. Thanks very much.'

By common consent, in 1979/80 Albion played some of their best ever football. They had a good FA Cup run through to the first round proper before losing 2-0 at home to Bury in November 1979. The match gained nationwide coverage, with Moore being interviewed by Ian St John for ITV *World of Sport*'s *On the Ball* programme and the match being covered by London Weekend Television.

Overcoming the disappointment of that cup exit, Albion's league form was good and Hector's goals helped them to a fourth-placed finish in the Northern Premier League, Moore winning a manager of the month award along the way. Shortly after his 35th birthday, Moore announced he would (once again) be hanging up his boots for good at the end of the season, the cumulative effect of ankle injuries making it impossible for him to continue playing.

The 'Battle of Anzio'

The following season, with Moore now manager rather than player-manager, Burton again reached the first round of the FA Cup, this time losing 2-1 at renowned giant-killers Blyth Spartans. Albion had actually almost fallen at the first hurdle of what turned out to be an eight-game cup run. On 13 October 1980 a 2-2 draw at home to Willenhall Town in the first qualifying round had prompted an uncharacteristic tirade from Moore, who described Albion's performance as 'absolutely terrible … a complete and utter shambles'. Only a dubiously awarded penalty in the closing stages had saved them from defeat against the West Midlands League Premier Division side.

Moore's mood wasn't improved four days later when the team assembled at Eton Park to travel to Willenhall for the replay. One of Burton's directors was a schoolteacher and had offered to drive the players and directors to the match in the school bus in return for a donation to the school. Last to arrive at the meeting point was chairman Robinson. As he got out of his car, he noticed that all the players were still sitting in theirs rather than waiting on the coach. He asked his manager what was going on. 'Ben, you need to go and have a look at that coach,' an exasperated Moore replied.

Robinson went to have a look inside: the perspex screen around the driver's seat had been replaced with plywood and all the seats had hundreds of holes in them made by schoolchildren using their pencils and fingers to burrow their way down into the foam.

Moore declared, 'It's a disgrace. We may be a non-league club, but we're playing a club that's below us in the football pyramid and we're going to turn up in a coach like that? It's not going to be very good for our image, let alone how the players are going to feel.' 'I'm sorry, Ian, we either go on the coach or we take our cars,' insisted Robinson.

Ever the pragmatist, Moore reluctantly persuaded his players to board the coach. Fortunately, the tension was broken when Sammy Chapman put his finger in one of the holes in his seat and declared, 'These holes here, they've got to be bullet holes from the Battle of Anzio!'

Albion won 2-1 but their straitened financial circumstances were in contrast with those of their hosts, the evening kick-off being played under Willenhall's new £20,000 floodlights.

Calling time at the Brewers

With the board's financial support, Moore had helped resurrect Albion's fortunes – matchday attendances would often top 1,000 compared with just 200 or 300 a couple of years earlier – but the club's momentum stalled. In October 1980, in a surprise development, First Division strugglers Derby County re-signed Hector. In the same month, Collier left for Grantham.

Four months later, following a poor run of form that culminated in a 4-0 defeat at Runcorn, Moore and Mick Hopkinson resigned. This came less than a week after they had been instructed by the board to make a 15 per cent cut to the team's wage bill. Moore was quoted as saying that the club lacked the resources to match his ambition. There was no acrimony. Robinson stated that there wasn't a financial crisis but acknowledged that Moore's ambitions exceeded the club's resources. In effect, Moore had taken Burton as far as he could.

There was another, more pressing reason for Moore's departure. Carol had been diagnosed with diabetes and it simply made sense to cut out the frequent commuting to Burton and, instead, concentrate on developing their bookmaking business in Nottinghamshire and taking some of the strain off Carol.

Moreover, it is fair to say that Moore, despite his experience and ambition, wasn't really cut out to be a football manager, being too self-deprecating and lacking in ego. For instance, when Robinson had offered him the job, Moore had accepted in a typically modest manner, 'I've never been a manager in my life, but if you're prepared to take a chance, I wouldn't mind having a go.'

Certainly, Moore, in his heart of hearts, felt he didn't have the right temperament to be a successful manager, lacking the necessary ruthlessness and willingness to stretch the truth, and not being thick-skinned enough to deal with the criticism that the job inevitably invites. He was simply too honest, too nice. By contrast, Albion made an inspired choice in appointing Moore's successor: Neil Warnock, who, according to *Burton Daily Mail* sports editor Rex Page, 'swept ... into Eton Park ... like a Sahara sandstorm – tough, gritty and abrasive'.

Moore's departure from Eton Park in February 1981 didn't, however, mark the end of his involvement in football. He spent much of the summer running coaching schools organised by former England captain Bobby Moore in Nottingham and, slightly more exotically, Sun City in South Africa.

On 4 August 1981 Moore turned out for a Scunthorpe United XI in a fundraising 'warm-up match' alongside Jack Charlton and Kevin Keegan at the Old Show Ground. The occasion was the visit of reigning European champions Liverpool to play Scunthorpe's first team in a pre-season friendly as a 'thank you' for unearthing Keegan and goalkeeper Ray Clemence. Ten years after that goalscoring debut against Forest, Keegan was still at the top of his game: the previous year he had been voted European Footballer of the Year for the second successive season, though he had been kept quiet by Kenny Burns and Larry Lloyd when his Hamburg side lost 1-0 to Forest in the European Cup Final.

Teaming up with Wignall at Shepshed

The following month Moore once again joined forces with Frank Wignall who, freshly returned from his Middle Eastern sojourn, was now manager of Shepshed Charterhouse of the Midland League. Moore was appointed coach at the Dovecote.

On 28 November 1981, despite his latest 'retirement' 18 months earlier, Moore was named in the 14-man squad when Shepshed faced the steelmakers Appleby-Frodingham in his old stomping ground of Scunthorpe. He didn't play that day, but with Shepshed being captained by Sammy Chapman, his fellow apprentice when he joined Forest in 1961, and managed by Big Frank, Moore's 20-year footballing career had come full circle.

It would be another four months before Moore made his league debut for Shepshed in a 5-1 win at Skegness on 27 March 1982. The following week, the club made its ambitions clear by signing former Leicester City, Derby and England full-back David Nish.

That season Shepshed swept all before them. They won the Midland League at the first attempt, having been promoted just the year before, adding the Leicestershire Challenge and Senior Cups, Battle of Britain Charity Cup and the Midland League Cup, beating Boston United 5-2 on aggregate over two legs.

Early in the 1982/83 season Shepshed made another star signing in the shape of Kevin Hector, following his second spell at Derby. Hector's debut on 8 October saw Shepshed beat Heanor Town 9-0, the former England international netting a hat-trick. The other scorers that day were Jeff Lissaman with two, and lightning-fast striker Dennis Jenas – father of future Nottingham Forest, Newcastle United, Tottenham Hotspur and England star Jermaine – with four goals.

On 6 November two goals from Jenas saw Shepshed beat King's Lynn 2-1 in the fourth qualifying round of the FA Cup. The attendance was 1,658. Six years earlier, before the appointment of Maurice Clayton as chairman and Dick Cooper as general manager prompted a remarkable change in the club's fortunes, such a fixture would have attracted perhaps a dozen spectators.

Shepshed's reward for reaching the first round proper of the cup was an away tie against Preston North End, the once-mighty club of Bill Shankly and Tom Finney but now struggling at the foot of the Third Division.

On Saturday, 20 November some 2,000 fans made the trip to Deepdale to witness what would be easily the biggest match in Shepshed's history. Shepshed gave a good account of themselves, but Preston's class showed as they cruised to a 5-1 win. Shepshed's vociferous travelling support were at least treated to the goal of the match (and season) after 58 minutes when Jenas collected the ball just inside Preston's half and – in a Moore-like mazy run – jinked past three defenders before firing into the roof of the net.

Hopes were high of another good cup run, this time in the FA Vase, but on 5 March 1983 Shepshed were knocked out at the quarter-final stage by Halesowen Town. The following week Wignall resigned as manager, explaining, 'My business commitments keep me occupied and prevent me from devoting sufficient time and energies needed to manage Shepshed.' In fact, he had been defrauded of the money he had invested in a garage business.

Shepshed immediately appointed Moore as manager. Two months later they completed a league and cup double for the second successive season, winning the Northern Counties East League championship and cup competitions.

The following season, Shepshed were in the running to finish top of their league for a seventh successive season until a poor run of form in the spring – culminating in a 3-0 defeat to leaders Willenhall Town – saw them trail in second place. This led to criticism of the team and its manager by a section of fans, leaving Moore distinctly unimpressed. In what – by his standards – amounted to an outburst, an exasperated Moore told the press:

> 'What surprises me is the amount of criticism considering the tremendous success the club have achieved. It's impossible for any team not to have some indifferent spells. This applies at all levels of the game whether you are Liverpool, Forest … or even Shepshed Charterhouse.
>
> 'At these times it is essential for everybody, including the fans, to pull together in order to maintain a successful club. If anyone had said, before the season started, that Shepshed

> would be one of the favourites for promotion, they would not have been believed.'

Shepshed went on to secure the runners-up spot and promotion to the Southern Premier League but by the end of May Moore had resigned as manager. As with his departure from Burton Albion three years earlier, Moore had decided that looking after his wife's health and concentrating on his business interests were paramount.

20

Gold mine

'It's a gold mine!'

Owner of launderette upon selling it to Ian Storey-Moore

Doing the laundry

Moore had seen enough former players struggle to make ends meet after hanging up their boots to know that he needed to make provision for a pension of sorts. So, in early 1972, shortly before he left Forest – and even though he was reaching what should have been his peak earning years – Moore decided to invest his savings in a launderette in Bingham. He had become acquainted with the owner who persuaded him to buy it. 'It's a gold mine!' he had been assured.

Although it allowed Moore to quip, when interviewed by *The Times*, '[At least] I won't need to sweep the roads,' the launderette turned out to be a poor investment. He reflects on the episode rather ruefully:

> 'It was the stupidest thing I ever did. It was one of those businesses where it was impossible to make money. Every time you fixed one of the washing machines another one would break, and then the next one, and so on.
>
> 'We employed a couple of ladies who did a great job running the shop and it was very busy. Customers used

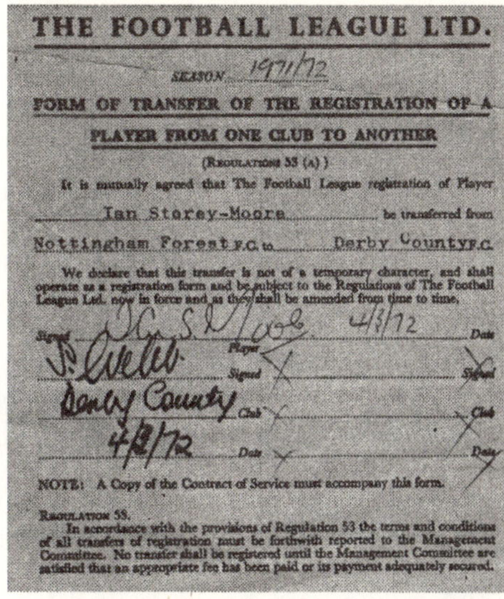

THE FOOTBALL LEAGUE LTD.

SEASON 1971/72

FORM OF TRANSFER OF THE REGISTRATION OF A PLAYER FROM ONE CLUB TO ANOTHER

(Regulations 53 (a))

It is mutually agreed that The Football League registration of Player Ian Storey-Moore be transferred from Nottingham Forest F.C. to Derby County F.C.

We declare that this transfer is not of a temporary character, and shall operate as a registration form and be subject to the Regulations of The Football League Ltd. now in force and as they shall be amended from time to time.

Signed ... 4/3/72 Date

Player

Signed ... Signed

Derby County Club ... Club

4/3/72 Date ... Date

NOTE: A Copy of the Contract of Service must accompany this form.

Regulation 53.

In accordance with the provisions of Regulation 53 the terms and conditions of all transfers of registration must be forthwith reported to the Management Committee. No transfer shall be registered until the Management Committee are satisfied that an appropriate fee has been paid or its payment adequately secured.

Behind the scenes: *Forest's manager Matt Gillies (left) invited Clough to transfer talks with Moore but vice chairman Tony Wood (right) persuaded the club's committee not to sanction the transfer. Right: The Football League transfer form signed by Moore and Derby County's secretary, Stuart Webb, but unsigned by Forest*

Signing for Manchester United: *Left: Manchester United manager Frank O'Farrell helps Moore sign on the dotted line, Monday, 6 March 1972. Right: Moore's wife Carol and pet dog Laska. Both were blamed in some quarters for the collapse of his proposed transfer to Derby County*

'Hurray up, he'll be at Everton by the weekend!': *Moore at his first Manchester United training session, Tuesday, 7 March 1972. Left to right: Martin Buchan, Alex Stepney, Denis Law (making a joke at Moore's expense), George Best, Moore, David Sadler, Francis Burns*

Instant impact: *Left: In action for Manchester United against Coventry City, 1 April 1972, when he scored for the third successive game following his debut. Right: Celebrating scoring against Derby County, 23 September 1972*

Start of final season: *Left: Pre-season photo shoot, 1 August 1972 Right: Lining up a free kick with George Best and Bobby Charlton against Ipswich Town at Old Trafford*

Going to America: *Chicago Sting squad photo for 1975 season. Moore is second left on the back row. In the middle row are franchise owner Lee Stern (first left) and head coach Bill Foulkes (fourth from left)*

The Brewers: *Burton Albion team photo from 1979/80 season. In the front row are Peter Hindley (second from left), Moore (third left) and star signing Kevin Hector (second from right)*

Shepshed Charterhouse win the double: *Manager Moore (left) with chairman Maurice Clayton (back row, right) and striker Dennis Jenas (front row, third from left) at the Dovecote, 13 May 1983*

Thank you, Scunthorpe: *Alongside Kevin Keegan and Jack Charlton for a Scunthorpe United Guest XI fund-raising match at the Old Show Ground, 4 August 1981*

Friend or foe? *A friendly match between Forest and Notts County, including local media personalities, on 2 May 1984 to raise funds for the Magpies. In his last appearance in the Garibaldi Red Moore (back row, second from left) was up against Arthur Mann (front row, third from right) whose bad tackle cost him his place in England's 1970 World Cup squad*

'Gold mine': *With Carol at their launderette, December 1973*

Behind the mic: *With Radio Trent's regional sports editor Tony Delahunty and Nottingham and England rugby star Brian Moore, promoting GEM-AM's 'Moore and Moore Delahunty' radio show*

Family tradition: *As landlord of the Wheatsheaf Inn, Bingham, Moore checks the form in the* Sporting Life, *January 1995. His step-grandfather was a publican in Tyneside*

Firm favourites: *At the Forest Legends Raceday at Nottingham Racecourse, 15 June 2015, with Des Walker, Kenny Burns, Garry Birtles, Jeff Whitefoot and John Robertson*

Promotion-winning managers *Left: With former Forest manager, Dave Bassett, July 2022. Right: With Steve Cooper for Forest's friendly against Valencia to mark the Spanish team's centenary, December 2022*

Gone for a Burton: *Moore (L), Henry Newton (R), with Burton Albion chairman, Ben Robinson, and his partner Lesley Machin, April 2023*

> to leave their clothes with us, we'd wash and dry them for collection later the same day, but all the money you took went on repairs.'

After a few years Moore was able to sell his *bête noire*, fortunately managing to recoup the money he had ploughed into it.

In the news

In the 1960s, with a view to perhaps one day emulating his hero Len Shackleton by entering the fourth estate, Moore had attended journalism evening classes. Together with David Pleat he learned shorthand and later added touch-typing to his repertoire. However, his journalistic career never got beyond penning popular articles for the *Nottingham Guardian Journal* and even this endeavour – far removed from the ghost-written, nationally syndicated articles of some of his contemporaries – was summarily terminated when he had the temerity to ask for an increase in the paltry sum he received.

So, rather than writing for newspapers, Moore eventually started selling them. In the mid-1980s he ran a newsagent's for a brief period. A friend of the family owned several them in and around Nottingham and advised Moore to 'get yourself one, it's very lucrative'. Eventually, Moore bought one on Carlton Hill, though not before the 'friend' had tried to gazump him for it.

It was a decent business but time-consuming. Moore would get up at six in the morning, drive into town to open up the shop and, after spending all morning there, head back to Bingham to work in his betting shop in the afternoon:

> 'I had some lovely staff there but it was 24/7 and very tiring. It was a bitty sort of business. We used to go to the wholesalers and come back and realise we'd forgotten the rubbers for the pencils, or the Bounty bars or Mars bars. There was so much bitty stuff. There was no money in cigarettes – you made tuppence out of a pack of 20.'

When a supermarket opened across the road, Moore could see that things would start to go downhill and after just 18 months he sold the business.

Taking a punt

A business that Moore was involved with for rather longer was one with which he had a long-standing affinity: bookmaking.

Over the years, footballers – finding themselves with spare cash and free afternoons – have always enjoyed having a flutter on a horse or two. Moore was no exception. In fact, Forest's former goalkeeper Alan Hill used to tell the story of the team getting ready before a match, all the players looking down at their boots, as the manager Matt Gillies issues his instructions and asks if there were any questions. Moore looks up, 'Who won the 2.30 at Haydock?' And he certainly wasn't alone in the Forest dressing room. The young Martin O'Neill was rarely seen without the *Sporting Life* under his arm.

At one stage Moore had taken his interest even further by buying a racehorse, Merry Music, though she never frequented the winners' enclosure.

Moore bought his first betting shop in early 1977 and kept it for almost two decades. Despite his love of going to the races – be it as a guest of Brian Clough or as Jim Baxter's chaperone – he didn't actually plan on being a bookmaker. Having retired from professional football in England and tried his luck in the United States, it was more a question of what he could do to earn a living. Notwithstanding Manchester United's generosity, Moore didn't have enough money to retire comfortably.

Moore had got to know the 'old fellow' who ran the betting shop in Long Acre, Bingham. Quite a character, he had been 'done' twice by the taxman. In those days a betting tax was levied on stakes or winnings in high street betting shops. Establishments were frequently raided by Customs & Excise to make sure the right amount of tax was being paid and collected. Customs officers would say to him, 'You know, Harold, some bookmakers even put betting slips down their shoes!' 'They don't, do they?' he would reply, feigning astonishment, while standing there with a wedge of slips in his socks.

One day, out of the blue, Harold said to Moore, 'I'm bloody fed up with this game.' Moore agreed to buy the business there and then. In April 1977 Bingham magistrates granted Moore a bookmaker's permit and betting office licence and the deal was concluded: 'I gave him £2,000 for it. It was a living.'

With the shop at Bingham being managed by Carol and an assistant, Moore went on to acquire a second betting shop, on Musters Road in West Bridgford, which had a full-time manager.

Moore's chairman at Burton Albion, Ben Robinson, recalls winning a few hundred pounds off Moore with a bet on the Lingfield Derby Trial in May 1985. He had picked up a tip on Slip Anchor, ridden by the famous American jockey, Steve Cauthen, and trained by the equally renowned Henry Cecil. The colt duly won by ten lengths before going on to record a rare start-to-finish win in the Epsom Derby the following month. Robinson felt so embarrassed at having won the bet from his friend that they spent most of it on a celebratory dinner with their wives.

In 1992 Moore expanded his betting 'empire' when he was invited by the owner of Southwell racecourse to take over the franchised operation there and improve the level of service it offered punters. Handing Moore the contract was unprecedented as it ended a 20-year duopoly enjoyed by NARBOL, the ousted operator, and the Tote over on-course betting shops around the country. Moore had been chosen because he was one of the few bookmakers who allowed customers to lay bets with tax paid on – which most punters preferred – and also offered odds on race meetings other than just Southwell. The decision was controversial and course bookies at Southwell called off a threatened strike only after taking legal advice.

Initially, the move worked out well for Moore. Long before the advent of online gambling, on-course betting could be lucrative business – on his first day at Southwell, New Year's Day 1992, Moore's operation took over £8,000, the following Monday over £6,000. Moore soon took over the betting operation at Wolverhampton racecourse as well. But within three years the owners of Southwell and Wolverhampton had put the franchises out to tender and Ladbrokes outbid Moore, leaving him to concentrate on his two high street betting shops.

Small independent bookmakers always face the risk of the big bet that comes off. Moore would mitigate the risk of potentially huge liabilities by, literally, hedging his bets with national bookmakers:

> 'You used to go through the bets all the time to see if there were any mixed bets – doubles, trebles, accumulators, Yankees, anything that included four or more horses – because if any of those kicked off with a 33/1 winner you were in trouble. You had to be really careful – it was a really stressful business and you had to know what you were doing.'

The biggest payout Moore ever made was around £8,000. On the weekend of 26 and 27 May 1990 Moore was down in London, preparing to do the radio commentary on Notts County's Third Division play-off final against Tranmere Rovers, when Carol phoned him.

'Do you want the good news or the bad news?'

'What's the bad news?'

'One of our regulars won £8,000.'

'And the good news?'

'I had a £1,000 treble that covered it.'

In 1994 a syndicate at Warwickshire County Cricket Club won £100,000 from an independent bookmaker when the Edgbaston-based side, at the time featuring Brian Lara, won the

County Championship, AXA Equity & Law Sunday League, and NatWest Trophy and only narrowly lost the final of the Benson & Hedges Cup.

No doubt inspired by Warwickshire's example, at the start of the 1995 cricket season a syndicate of Nottinghamshire County Cricket Club officials laid a bet at Moore's West Bridgford shop. For a £15 outlay per member, each of them stood to win £8,300 if Notts won the 'Grand Slam' of County Championship, Sunday League, and the two cup competitions. Fortunately for Moore, Notts finished a disappointing 11th in both the County Championship and Sunday League and in the knockout competitions didn't make it beyond the quarter-final of the Benson & Hedges Cup.

Eventually, after almost two decades as a bookmaker, Moore sold both of the shops. He still enjoys the occasional flutter, of course, and remains a regular visitor to Southwell and Nottingham racecourses in the company of friends from the footballing fraternity.

Last orders

The last business Moore ran was as landlord of the Wheatsheaf Inn on Long Acre in Bingham. This was a tenancy with Greene King rather than a free house. When Moore took it on in 1992 the pub was down on its heels, only ordering one barrel a week from the brewers.

Moore was, of course, just the latest in a very long line of former Nottingham Forest and Notts County footballers to run a pub, among them Jeff Whitefoot, Sammy Chapman, Alan Hill, John Robertson, Larry Lloyd, Willie Young and, unsurprisingly, Jim Baxter back in his beloved Glasgow.

Being a publican was, of course, another 24/7 occupation but one that Moore both enjoyed and excelled at. By 1995, towards the end of his three-year tenancy agreement, the Wheatsheaf was taking 13 barrels a week. Unfortunately, despite the mutual benefit of the success of the pub under Moore's stewardship, the landlords demanded a significant increase in the rent, at least doubling what Moore had previously been paying. Moore refused to relent, and after the brewers declined to sell him the premises, he relinquished his tenancy.

21

Behind the mic

'We've had a bit of a nasty situation in the press box.'

Ian Storey-Moore commentating on unsavoury scenes among newspaper reporters half an hour into the Hillsborough disaster

Local radio

In the late 1980s and early '90s, Moore found himself on the other side of the microphone as a football pundit and match summariser on BBC Radio Nottingham and GEM-AM, part of the independent Radio Trent group.

Nowadays, of course, football coverage saturates the airwaves, but prior to the 1988/89 season there were no live commentaries on Nottingham local radio. Stations were restricted to a handful of live updates during a game and fans would have to hope that their team's match was the one chosen for second-half commentary on BBC Radio 2's *Sport on 2* show.

When Mark Shardlow was appointed sports editor for Radio Nottingham in 1988 he set about changing this and soon the station was broadcasting second-half commentaries on Forest and County away games on alternate weeks. Also, if Forest were playing at home and for some reason Notts weren't playing that weekend, the producer would have to phone the City Ground an hour before kick-off to confirm they would be allowed to do the commentary. Broadcast rights were paid for on a match-by-match basis at a fixed rate set by the Football League.

Shardlow had, in fact, cut his teeth on football commentaries when he was a student at Trent Polytechnic. With a friend he set up the sports broadcasting service for Nottingham Hospitals radio in 1980. Unlike mainstream broadcasters, the hospital radio service was allowed to have full match commentaries. The 18-year-old student wrote to Brian Clough and was invited to the Forest manager's office to conduct an interview. Fresh from a second European Cup triumph, Clough was at the peak of his powers and an intimidating presence but put the terrified teenager at ease by pouring him a drink, saying, 'You look cold, son. This will warm you up.' Two whiskies later the interview began and provided the young reporter with an invaluable step-up in his formative career.

Fast forward to 1988 and Shardlow was presenting Radio Nottingham's Saturday afternoon sports show. The incomparable Colin Slater would commentate on Notts County, and Jeremy Nicholas on Forest. Looking for a couple of expert summarisers on the Forest games, Shardlow chose Ian Storey-Moore, still a bookmaker at the time, and Martin O'Neill, who had not long started his managerial career at Grantham Town.

Shardlow had met Moore previously and reckoned he would get on well with everyone involved in the sports show. More importantly, he knew that Forest's outstanding player of his generation would appeal to Radio Nottingham's generally slightly older audience profile.

Moore's credibility as a keen observer of the game made him an instant success as a co-commentator. Slightly less successful was his sense of direction. For the sixth round of the FA Cup that season, Forest were drawn away at Manchester United, but the commentary team nearly didn't make the match. In those days before the ubiquitous sat nav, Moore – with his intimate knowledge of Manchester – was entrusted with directing the Radio Nottingham car to Old Trafford. Unfortunately, they ended up at a deserted Maine Road. They only just managed to get to Old Trafford in time for the start of the live transmission at two o'clock. Forest won 1-0 courtesy of Garry Parker's goal. Next stop: the semi-final against Liverpool.

A Liverpudlian in Nottingham

At the same time as Radio Nottingham was expanding its sports coverage, the Radio Trent group was keen to shake things up. The station had had an up-and-down relationship with Forest ever since the popular Chris 'The Mouth' Ashley, presenter of the station's Saturday afternoon sports show in the early 1980s, had reportedly been banned from the City Ground for referring to Clough and Taylor as 'Bill and Ben'.

Now, in the late 1980s, the sporting scene in Nottingham was once again thriving. Clough had assembled another great Forest team, captained by Stuart Pearce and containing Des Walker and Neil Webb and so many other great talents. Nottinghamshire County Cricket Club had Tim Robinson, Chris Broad and Trent Bridge's favourite son, Derek Randall. Nottingham Rugby Club were still in the top flight, fielding Gary Rees and the redoubtable Brian Moore. And across the border, there was Leicestershire's cricketing star David Gower. This meant that there was plenty of scope for the commercial Radio Trent to make its mark on local sports broadcasting and the station put out an advert for the new position of regional sports editor.

Tony Delahunty, the sports editor for Pennine Radio, applied. He had made his reputation in tragic circumstances by being the radio commentator at Bradford City on 11 May 1985 when fire broke out in the main stand, killing 56 spectators and injuring hundreds more.

Delahunty's commentary brought him and the station plaudits, nationally and internationally, but also some unjustified criticism. Thus, the position at Radio Trent, a step up the broadcasting ladder, appealed to him.

His reputation got him on to the shortlist but the interview went badly. Delahunty was in no doubt he had blown his chance. As he was leaving the station's Castle Gate premises, Delahunty happened to mention that, since he was in Nottingham, he was going to see if he could get an interview with Clough. 'Good luck with that – he hasn't given us an interview for 18 months!' came the reply.

In fact, it was difficult for reporters to get interviews with anyone at Forest. Clough had discouraged his players from giving interviews by saying things like, 'Walker, I heard you on the air the other day, you're a bigger idiot than you are on the field. I'd shut up if I were you.' That said, Nigel Clough would always try and help out, as would Neil Webb and Steve Sutton.

Down at the City Ground Delahunty pressed the bell at the hatch which served as the club's reception in those days. After a long wait, none other than Forest's manager himself appeared. No sooner had Delahunty blurted out 'Hello, Mr Clough, I'm from a Yorkshire radio station' than the hatch was firmly slammed shut in his face.

A despondent Delahunty, carrying a large tape recorder, had walked back to his car when he heard a noise and turned round to see Clough standing there. 'Hey, you, you better be able to use that thing you've got under your arm or I'll stick it up your arse,' the manager said. And with that, the unlikely pair went inside to Clough's office.

This interview went little better than the one earlier in the day but – with judicious editing – was broadcast the same evening on independent radio stations around the country. Radio Trent's managing director Ron Coles and programme controller Chris Hughes heard it. Immediately they agreed to offer the job to the Liverpudlian from Pennine Radio they had interviewed – and rejected – earlier in the day.

Delahunty had the idea of presenting a sports show previewing the weekend's action. Brian Moore, as articulate off the field as he was indefatigable on it, was an obvious choice as one of the pundits, and happened to be working for a firm of solicitors next to Radio Trent's offices. Jon Holmes, the agent for Gower and Gary Lineker, suggested that Ian Storey-Moore also be approached. Quite apart from his footballing nous, Moore could also be counted on to bring his in-depth knowledge of horseracing to the show. Thus was born the *Moore and Moore Delahunty* radio show, which was broadcast for a couple of years from 6pm to 10pm on a Friday on GEM-AM. The show was a success, though Moore rarely gave out any decent racing tips.

Delahunty ensured that Radio Trent soon followed the lead taken by Radio Nottingham in broadcasting football commentaries. The rival radio stations – one reliable and respected, the other vibrant and feisty – often covered the same matches, competing head-to-head for audience numbers. Moore hedged his bets and worked for both stations.

For their commentaries, Delahunty and Moore were helped by a teenage Darren Fletcher. At the request of a friend, Delahunty had hired Fletcher to give him some work experience and found him to be hugely knowledgeable about football. On matchdays Fletcher would be back in the production room at the station feeding titbits into the headphones of the two commentators. Delahunty would say something like, 'And Gary Charles has just put in a lovely cross from the right and it's been turned into the net.' Fletcher would helpfully prompt Moore to add, 'That's the fourth time in the last five weeks he's put in the cross for a goal.' It was obvious that Fletcher loved football and, when Delahunty eventually moved on, he took over commentating duties at Radio Trent. Now, of course, he is one of the very best commentators on TV.

Delahunty quickly figured out that Clough didn't like Moore very much. Whenever Forest's manager saw the two of them on their way to do a commentary, his mouth would develop into a snarl. Even 17 years after the infamous transfer saga, Moore remained *persona non grata* in Clough's eyes.

Players' union

Although radio commentating didn't come naturally to Moore, he learned on the job and his deep knowledge of football meant his opinions were always respected. That said, Moore was always wary of criticising other players. His broadcasting colleagues could tell that, no matter what he might have been thinking, he would go out of his way to avoid saying anything live on air that could hurt anyone's feelings. That would, of course, have made him quite unsuited to modern-day commentaries where summarisers are seemingly expected to court controversy. As Delahunty reflects, 'The most negative thing I ever heard anyone say about Ian Storey-Moore is that he was too nice. I don't think they meant as a player on the football pitch, rather in his approach to life. He was almost too good to be true.'

But Moore wasn't alone in defending the 'players' union'. When Forest faced a team from London he often found himself in the commentary box alongside his namesake, Bobby, a summariser for Capital Gold Radio. Their evident mutual respect was mirrored in their unwillingness to criticise fellow footballers.

Likewise, when Delahunty left Radio Trent to go and work for LBC in London, one of his co-commentators was George Best. Delahunty would exclaim, 'That is the worst tackle I have seen for a long time and the referee isn't even reaching for a yellow. That was really, really late, wasn't it, George?' Best (who, incidentally, would talk fondly to Delahunty of his time playing with Moore) would respond, 'I'm not sure it was, Tony.' Like the two Moores, Best wouldn't say anything bad about any player if he could avoid it.

Another thing the former players had in common when doing radio commentaries was that they always took time to sign autographs and talk to fans before or after a match. Moore would often frustrate Delahunty by talking at length to fans in the car park, who wanted to know his off-air opinion about the action on the pitch and the personalities off it. Similarly, on one occasion it took Best and Delahunty almost two hours to cover the 100 yards or so through the car park at Old Trafford, such was the throng of people wanting to see their idol and such was Best's willingness to answer their every question and sign every autograph.

Hillsborough

Radio broadcasting arrangements for FA Cup ties differed from Football League matches in that Saturday afternoon programmes would be presented from grounds themselves. On such occasions there wouldn't be any backup in the studio, just an experienced technician and any number of students on work experience.

On 15 April 1989 Shardlow presented Radio Nottingham's FA Cup semi-final coverage from Hillsborough, with Jeremy Nicholas and Moore commentating and Martin Fisher a roving reporter. The programme started at two o'clock but the studio recorded every sound picked up by the commentary microphones – including off-air chat while pre-recorded interviews were being played – from half past one through to the end of transmission, originally scheduled for six o'clock.

The commentary team's description of the build-up to kick-off was standard fare, though they noted the lack of spectators on the terraces at the Leppings Lane End. As with most people in the ground that day, the first time anyone in the commentary box realised something was amiss was when fans started spilling on to the pitch at six minutes past three. Moore and his colleagues were very measured in commentating on the distressing scenes that followed. They simply described what they saw – too many fans trapped behind the fences – without speculating on the cause or number of casualties.

The studio recording picked up not only the commentary team's description of the unfolding events but also tannoy announcements and other incidental sounds. Therefore, it was an important piece of evidence and was submitted to the Taylor Inquiry and the subsequent police inquiry.

After about half an hour there was a kerfuffle in the press box. Coming four years after the Heysel Stadium disaster and at the end of a decade scarred by football hooliganism, there was a heated debate between reporters from the national press and those from Merseyside, the former seeking to apportion blame. Moore told listeners:

> 'We've had a nasty situation in the press box. There's a Merseyside reporter next to us, and national reporters behind him … He's trying to stress that there haven't been any problems with the Liverpool supporters, but he's being goaded a bit by the national press.'

Moore's contacts in the football world meant he had privileged access to certain areas of the ground, so Shardlow asked him to go down to the players' tunnel with Fisher to see if they could find out what was going on. Eventually they found Forest's coach, Moore's former team-mate Liam O'Kane, who explained what was happening and that the match had been abandoned. Forest's chairman, Maurice Roworth, agreed to give an interview.

Nearby in the commentary box was Delahunty, leading Radio Trent's broadcast. He received a message from his sister asking if he could find out whether her son, a Liverpool fan, was safe. With no backup in Radio Trent's studio back in Nottingham, he was unable to leave his commentary position. Fortunately, shortly after six o'clock, his nephew, safely evacuated, was able to call home from a phone box a mile or so from the ground.

Both commentary teams knew that Forest supporters' families would be concerned and kept stressing that the incident was taking place at the opposite end of the ground and that Forest fans weren't directly involved. Once the game had been abandoned, they told listeners that Forest fans were slowly, but safely, leaving the ground. Of course, people had started leaving much earlier, the sight of fellow football supporters being given mouth-to-mouth resuscitation on the pitch forever etched in their memory. Many Forest fans who had parked on the surrounding suburban streets were invited in by local residents to have a consoling cup of tea and to phone their families to let them know they were safe – acts of kindness to Nottingham folk by the good people of Sheffield that are, sadly, sometimes forgotten in the occasionally hostile rivalry between football fans in the two proud cities.

By the time the two Nottingham-based radio stations finished broadcasting from Hillsborough, the official death toll was in the 20s. Their reporters left to attend the press conference arranged by the police. Radio Nottingham's broadcast subsequently won the prestigious New York Radio Festival award for live coverage of a breaking news story.

1991 and all that

Moore was Radio Trent's summariser when Forest got to the FA Cup Final two years later. Like pretty much everyone else who saw it, he remains baffled how Spurs' Paul Gascoigne wasn't sent off for his violent assaults on Garry Parker and Gary Charles:

> 'I've never seen tackles like it! Unbelievable how he ever stayed on the pitch. That's not to say he wasn't a very good player, of course he was, but that day it was just blatantly obvious he should have been sent off.'

Of course, Forest lost 2-1 after extra time, and the final word belongs to Clough who, when interviewed by Radio Nottingham's Shardlow shortly after the final whistle, simply said, 'Thank you for coming.'

22

Heroes and Villans

'An absolute joke!'

Ian Storey-Moore's view on the decision by Forest's board of directors to sell Kevin Campbell in July 1998

Return from exile

Just two years after that cup final heartbreak, Nottingham Forest were relegated and Clough retired. European Cup winner Frank Clark was appointed as manager and asked Alan Hill, the club's youth team coach, to be his assistant and chief scout.

Hill approached Moore, his friend and former team-mate, to make a long-overdue return to the City Ground. Initially looking after the under-13 and under-16 teams, Moore was fortunate to be able to coach talented youngsters such as Jermaine Jenas, Andy Reid and Shaun Wright-Phillips. Jenas's father Dennis, who had played for Moore at Shepshed Charterhouse, was now also a coach at Forest's youth academy. Ultimately Wright-Phillips slipped through the net when Forest released him – an infamous piece of bad judgement by the club – but in Moore's defence it hadn't been his decision as he wasn't in overall charge of the youth setup.

Under Clark, Forest enjoyed three successful seasons: promotion in 1994, a third-placed finish in what is now the Premier League – no newly promoted team has finished higher

– and the quarter-final of the UEFA Cup in 1996. But they struggled after the sale of Stan Collymore and in December 1996 Clark was sacked. A few weeks later he was appointed manager at Manchester City and took Hill with him. Forest now needed a chief scout.

Irving Korn, who had recently replaced Fred Reacher as chairman, asked Moore, 'Do you fancy doing a bit of scouting?' 'I've never done it before, but if you want me to, yes,' was Moore's typically diffident response. Before formally accepting the job Moore, true to form, had the decency to speak with his predecessor, telling the press:

> 'I wanted to do the job, of course, but Alan's seat was still warm and we are good friends, so I didn't want it to look like I'd jumped into his grave.
>
> 'Typically of Hilly there was no ill feeling. He just told me to go ahead and make the most of it and told me that I could do the job no problem.'

He continued confidently:

> 'I've no doubts that I'm up to it. I know a lot of people in the game and I've played it at the highest level. Those things are important and it helps you when you have to go to another club and mix with other coaches and scouts. That's when you pick up little snippets about players and what they are planning to do. Those that could be looking for a move and what they might be asking for in wages. These are the sort of circles I will be moving in and hopefully picking up some useful information.'

Moore's appointment as chief scout came immediately after Stuart Pearce agreed to become player-manager until the end of the season. The *Nottingham Evening Post* noted the end of

Moore's long exile from the City Ground, headlining with 'Spy Moore in from the cold'. Moore told the newspaper:

> 'Basically, Stuart has told me to organise the whole scouting network. He's got plans for the future and wants me to keep an eye on possibilities as well as provide information on teams. This is something that I've always wanted to do.
>
> 'It's a great opportunity for me to use my knowledge of the game and contacts that I've made over the years to put something back into Forest.'

Moore was responsible for scouting for players, of course, but also watching opposition teams before they were due to play Forest. He had to prepare match reports, describing tactics, set pieces, etc., a time-consuming part of his job that involved hours typing away on the computer. Whereas most clubs employed someone alongside the chief scout to do match reports, Moore had to do both. Fortunately the shorthand and touch-typing skills he had learned at evening classes back in the 1960s came in handy.

Drawing on his extensive network of contacts, Moore enlisted Joe Mallett, the man who had taken him on as an apprentice way back in 1961, to do some scouting for Forest. Mallett now lived on the south coast and would watch matches in London and the south-east and report back to Moore.

Strikers

In the event, one of Moore's first transfer targets was at the opposite end of the country, in Scotland. He made several visits to Glasgow to watch Pierre van Hooijdonk score at will for Celtic. In March 1997 Dave Bassett was appointed general manager and assistant to Pearce and was instrumental in ensuring that van Hooijdonk signed for Forest that same month.

After a winless run-in at the end of the season confirmed Forest's relegation, Bassett succeeded Pearce. Normally, new managers bring their own backroom staff with them but Bassett wanted Moore to stay on as chief scout. He was impressed by the new boss's work ethic, always being willing to attend matches to watch players Moore had been keeping an eye on. The pair soon formed a friendship that endures to this day.

On the pitch, things couldn't have gone better in the following 1997/98 season. Despite strong competition from teams such as Middlesbrough, Sunderland, Charlton Athletic and Ipswich Town, Forest won the First Division (now the Championship) thanks in no small measure to van Hooijdonk and Kevin Campbell scoring over 50 goals between them.

Once back in the top flight, however, everything quickly unravelled after the notorious decision by Forest's board of directors to sell Campbell, which prompted van Hooijdonk to go on strike. 'An absolute joke!' reflects Moore bitterly a quarter of a century later on one of the worst decisions in the club's history. Without the goalscoring partnership that had been so successful the season before, Forest were abject and Bassett was sacked in January 1999.

The interim appointment of Ron Atkinson didn't go down well with the City Ground faithful. Moore actually got on well with Atkinson, finding him affable and a good person to work with, and being impressed that he would join in the training sessions, though relegation inevitably followed.

In July 1999 Nottinghamshire businessman and lifelong Forest fan Nigel Doughty invested £12m in Forest, saving the club from administration. At the time he was chairman of Umbro and used his football contacts to identify a new manager. The appointment of David Platt was initially met with indifference by fans and Moore found him to be something of a mixed bag.

While disappointed that the new manager wasn't interested in going on scouting missions, Moore was pleased at least to be consulted on the loan signing of John Terry from Chelsea for a six-game spell in the Garibaldi Red. However, presumably influenced by having spent four seasons playing in Serie A, Platt signed several Italian players Moore had never heard of. Moore knew that the final decision on transfers always lay, quite rightly, with the manager, but the Italians weren't a success, to say the least.

It should be said, however, that Platt treated the backroom team well, such as when he generously invited them all down to London for an end-of-season, all-expenses-paid weekend.

Two successive mid-table finishes in the First Division and the lure of the England under-21 manager's job saw the end of Platt's time at the City Ground. The much-maligned Forest hierarchy then made one of their best ever decisions, the inspired appointment of Paul Hart, director of Forest's youth academy, as manager in July 2001.

Like Bassett, Hart had a great work ethic and would unhesitatingly go on scouting missions with Moore. Above all he was a brilliant coach – as good as any Moore had ever worked with – who brought the likes of Jenas, Reid, Michael Dawson and Gareth Williams through the youth ranks and into the first team.

One of the most successful signings that Moore instigated – and one that has had far-reaching implications for the club – was that of Ipswich striker David Johnson, in January 2001. Johnson's son, Brennan, was born in Nottingham four months later. Although DJ's career at Forest started slowly, it took off in 2002/03 when his 27 goals helped propel the team to the play-offs, only for the Reds to be knocked out by Sheffield United after losing a two-goal advantage with just 20 minutes of the semi-final second leg remaining.

A kick in the teeth

Despite the huge disappointment, Hart and Moore knew that with two or three new signings everything would be in place for a renewed promotion challenge the following season. Unfortunately, chairman Nigel Doughty had other plans, as Moore ruefully reflects:

> 'After the play-offs we said to the chairman that we should keep the squad together, try and get two or three more players in like Darren Huckerby, who we had on loan from Manchester City, and we would be there or thereabouts next season. We were under the impression he agreed and over the summer we made plans accordingly.
>
> 'Then just a couple of weeks before the new season started, the chief executive, Mark Arthur, came in and said, "No, sorry, the better players have got to go, he wants to sell them and you can only sign free transfers." So we had to sell the likes of Jenas, Dawson, Reid and Riccardo Scimeca and were left with absolutely nothing. We scrambled around to get some free transfers in and they were absolutely useless.
>
> 'I'm convinced Nigel Doughty had the best interests of the club at heart and, to be fair, he invested a huge amount of his own money to keep it afloat financially. But it was such a shame – it really was a tragedy, a ridiculous decision from a football perspective. Paul and I were fuming about it. We were absolutely gutted and, on reflection, we should have both resigned. It was a real kick in the teeth and ended up costing Paul his job.'

Within a year, Doughty had sacked Hart and appointed Joe Kinnear in his place, apparently on the basis that he had won more manager of the month awards than any other manager available at the time. Although he guided Forest out of the First Division relegation zone to a mid-table finish, Kinnear soon proved to be even more unpopular with the fans than Platt.

It was an unhappy time for Moore:

> 'To be honest, I hated it after Paul was sacked. I really disliked working there. I fell out with Doughty – I told him what I thought. It seemed that every time we got a decent side together it was dismantled for one reason or another.'

From Moore's point of view, the only good thing to come out of Kinnear's time at Forest was that he brought Mick Harford with him – 'a great coach and a good guy' – with whom Moore really enjoyed working. When Kinnear was sacked after a poor start to the 2004/05 season, Harford was temporarily put in charge. To Moore's surprise, Harford wasn't given the job on a permanent basis despite having the backing of the players and backroom staff. Instead, Doughty appointed Gary Megson, yet another manager who sorely tried the patience of the City Ground faithful.

Like Platt and Kinnear before him, Megson showed no interest in Moore's scouting missions, preferring to do his own transfer deals. Moore looks back on this period despondently:

> 'Megson said to me, "The only way we'll get out of this division is if we boot it from back to front." After working with Paul Hart, I thought blimey, what a waste.'

Megson's approach to football was never likely to go down well on Trentside and just over a year later, in February 2006, he had departed 'by mutual consent'. Unfortunately, Forest's financial difficulties had not gone away and a cost-saving redundancy programme saw the departures of over 30 back-office staff, coaches Liam O'Kane and Ian Bowyer, and Moore:

> 'I knew I was going to have to go because I had made my views clear to Doughty. I wasn't very happy at first but we got back on good terms and he started inviting me to come to games again. And to be fair to Doughty he acknowledged that he had made mistakes and later resigned as chairman when his appointment of Steve McClaren ended in failure.'

Doughty intimated to Moore that he would like him to return to work at the City Ground at some point, but in the event Moore wasn't out of work for long.

Villans

After a tremendously successful period managing Leicester City and Celtic, Martin O'Neill had taken time out to care for his wife, Geraldine, who was battling cancer. During that period he told Moore, 'The next job I get I want you to come with me.' Moore's friend and former team-mate was true to his word. When O'Neill took the manager's job at Premier League Aston Villa in August 2006, with John Robertson as his assistant, he appointed Moore chief scout with a clear remit:

> 'We always said from day one that it was the manager's decision as to whether we should buy a player. I said, "That's absolutely fine, Martin, I agree with that." And I still agree with that.
>
> 'If I really liked a player and he didn't fancy him, that was fair enough. And, conversely, if I didn't fancy a player but Martin still went ahead and bought him, we would support him in that decision because he was the manager.'

Almost immediately Villa's long-standing chairman and owner, 'Deadly' Doug Ellis, sold the club to New Yorker Randy Lerner, a credit card tycoon who owned the Cleveland Browns American football team. His ambition matched O'Neill's and the two struck up a good rapport.

One of the new management team's first – and best – signings was Ashley Young from Watford in January 2007, as Moore recalls:

> 'We all liked him and saw he had some ability. I watched him and sent different scouts to watch him. I told Martin he would cost about £5m and that although he wouldn't go straight in the first team he definitely had something about him. Then West Ham came in and the price went up: first £6m, then £7m, and finally £8m. But Martin stuck to his guns and bought him. He didn't start particularly well

> but he got better and better and later that year got into the England side.'

In that first season, 2006/07, Villa finished 11th in the league, unremarkable perhaps but five places higher than the season before. The 2007/08 season saw Villa finish sixth and at the start of the following season they signed James Milner from Newcastle for £12m and achieved another sixth-placed finish.

Moore was impressed, but not surprised, by O'Neill's work ethic; he would always go and watch players if Moore asked him to – there was no delegating of that to others or secretly doing his own deals as Moore had experienced with some of the managers at Forest. Moore remembers one hard-working weekend in particular:

> 'We were looking at West Ham's centre-half James Collins. They were playing on the Sunday. On the Saturday I went up to Blackburn because Villa were due to play them shortly. So, I picked Martin up at the training ground on the Saturday, drove up to Blackburn from Birmingham, then back down. Martin drove home to Beaconsfield. Next morning I drove from Bingham, picked him up at Watford and we went on to West Ham to watch Collins in the afternoon. After the game Martin drove straight up to Liverpool to meet up with the Villa team. His work ethic was second to none.'

O'Neill's commitment and support meant that Moore was, for the first time in many years, enjoying being a scout again. That is not to say there weren't irritations in the job. The workload was hectic and – more so than at Forest because Villa had more money to spend – involved a lot of overseas travel which often frustrated Moore:

> 'There were hundreds of overseas agents trying to sell players, trying to make a living. They used to send videos but I never relied on them, I had to go and see the players for myself.
>
> 'When we went abroad we used to take in two or three games if we could manage it. Sometimes we would watch players we'd seen on videos – where they looked like world-beaters – and they turned out to be bloody useless, completely different in the flesh. After ten minutes I'd think, "What on earth am I doing here?" There were so many occasions you went abroad and had a wasted trip but it was something you had to do.'

The same was often true for scouting missions in this country:

> 'You could drive up to watch Liverpool in midweek – it might be a miserable winter's night – then you'd have to leave ten minutes before the end to beat the traffic and think, "That was bloody awful, why have I come here?"'

Some light relief would be afforded, though, on the regular occasions when Villa's former manager, Moore's Scunthorpe Boys team-mate Graham Taylor, visited him at Villa Park for an afternoon cup of tea.

In September 2009 Villa signed Collins from West Ham along with Richard Dunne from Manchester City. The pair formed a formidable defensive partnership and that season only three teams conceded fewer goals in the Premier League as Villa finished sixth for the third time in a row. In addition, Villa got to Wembley twice – unluckily losing to Manchester United in the League Cup Final and being beaten by Chelsea in the semi-final of the FA Cup. Quite understandably, O'Neill and Lerner wanted to push further and get the Villans into the Champions League. However, the close-season proved to be quite tumultuous.

With Manchester City in strong pursuit of Milner, who had indicated his desire to move to Eastlands, and Tottenham Hotspur reportedly interested in Ashley Young, Moore was looking for reinforcements for Villa's midfield.

Possible transfer targets would be bandied around all the time. For instance, O'Neill and Moore were keen to prise Scott Parker away from West Ham. Another player Moore kept tabs on for a long time was Belgian international Moussa Dembélé. Ostensibly a centre-forward, he was playing for AZ Alkmaar, champions of the Dutch Eredivisie.

O'Neill had travelled with Moore to watch Dembélé play in the Netherlands and they concluded that he would fit in well in Villa's midfield. A few weeks before the start of the 2010/11 season Moore took a call from the player's agent. He suggested that, if Villa were still interested, he would be available for around £3m.

Things came to a head in early August 2010 during discussions between O'Neill and the club's hierarchy. In four years Villa had spent £179m on new players, £90m net after taking account of players sold. Although the three successive sixth-placed finishes arguably justified that investment – certainly it was a remarkable run that would nowadays be the envy of most clubs – no agreement could be reached on the availability of transfer funds. Despite previous indications to the contrary, it now became clear that Villa wouldn't be signing Dembélé or Parker to replace Milner. Assistant manager Robertson broke the news to Moore, 'Sorry, Ian, it looks like they're going to put the block on everything.'

Five days before the start of the season O'Neill, assistants Robertson and Steve Walford, and chief scout Moore left Villa. At the age of 65 Moore decided to put the days of traipsing all over the country and the continent behind him and retired from his long, remarkable career in football.

23
Epilogue

Ahead of Moore lay long-postponed overseas holidays with Carol, entertaining days at the races, enjoyable – if at times frustrating – afternoons and evenings watching Forest or Burton, amiable Thursday get-togethers with fellow Reds legends, leisurely hours in coffee shops with family and friends, and frequent requests for interviews and appearances from the media and supporters alike.

Behind him were well over 100 top-flight goals, full international recognition with England, a starring role alongside all-time greats in George Best, Denis Law and Bobby Charlton, a place among the European pioneers helping to popularise the game in the US, and a decade dedicated to non-league football.

Not to mention at least two fan clubs, numerous Trent End chants in his honour, regular appearances in fans' all-time Forest XIs and scoring arguably the greatest goal ever by a Garibaldi Red.

Not bad for a 'nearly man'.

24

Immortalised in song

'You can hear the Trent End sing!'

No tribute to Ian Storey-Moore would be complete without acknowledging the many and varied ways he has been celebrated in song by the Forest faithful. More than half a dozen chants (some still sung with gusto more than half a century later) were devoted solely or in part to him. No other Forest player comes close and there cannot be many footballers at any club, in any era, with so many chants in their honour.

The song we chose for the title of this book is as succinct a summary of Moore's huge value to the team as you could wish for: 'Give it to Moore, give it to Moore – he will score, he will score!' This is based on 'Give It To Me (All Your Love)' by the Troggs.

Moore is celebrated in the Trent End's take on another late 1960s pop song:

Ian Moore running down the wing,
You can hear the Trent End sing –
A sensation! A sensation! A sensation!
Hear what I say now –
Ian Moore, viva Ian Moore!
Ian Moore, viva Ian Moore!
Viva! Viva! Viva Ian Moore! Viva!

Based on 'Viva Bobby Joe' by The Equals

The Trent End cast their (goal) net wide when it came to songs to adapt, taking in folk songs:

Singing aye-aye Ian Storey-Moore,
Singing aye-aye Ian Storey-Moore,
Singing aye-aye Ian,
Aye-aye Ian,
Aye-aye Ian Storey-Moore!

Based on 'She'll Be Coming Round The Mountain' – traditional, arranged by the Trent End

And even French *chansons*:

Come on and cheer again,
Come on and cheer again,
For we are here again to see the Forest win!
Come on and score again
With Ian Moore again,
For we are sure again we're gonna win today!

Based on 'Milord', most famously performed by Edith Piaf

As Moore generously insists, Forest's successes were very much a team effort and here he twice shares top billing with some of his team-mates:

Those were the days, my friend,
We thought they'd never end,
We'd sing and dance for ever and a day.
We'd see Joe Baker score
And Ian Storey-Moore!
Those were the days,
Oh yes, those were the days.

Based on 'Those Were the Days' by Mary Hopkin

I'm going to tell you how it's going to be –
Derby nil and Forest three!
I'm going to tell you who's gonna score –
Wignall, Baker, Storey-Moore!

Based on 'Not Fade Away' by Buddy Holly & the Crickets, the Rolling Stones, and others

When Moore and Henry Newton were in the preliminary England squad for the 1970 World Cup, the Trent End soon came up with the goods:

Heigh ho, heigh ho,
It's off to Mexico
With Ian Moore and Hen-er-y
Heigh ho, heigh ho, heigh ho, heigh ho!

Based on 'Heigh Ho' from Disney's Snow White and the Seven Dwarfs

Finally, and needing little introduction to present-day Reds supporters, a forthright comparison of Moore with Derby County striker and Moore's one-time Burton Albion teammate, Kevin Hector:

When Derby go down again, again, we'll sing, we'll sing,
When Derby go down again, again, we'll sing, we'll sing!
When Ian Moore scores a goal
You can shove your Hector up your hole
And we'll all go mad when Derby go down again!

Based on the American Civil War song 'When Johnny Comes Marching Home'

Career statistics

Milestones

- 31 January 1945: Born in Ipswich
- May 1962: Signs professional terms with Nottingham Forest
- 10 May 1963: Makes first-team debut against Ipswich Town and provides assist in Forest's 2-1 win
- 26 December 1963: Scores in second appearance, a 3-3 draw with Sheffield United at the City Ground
- 1 March 1967: Makes England under-23 debut in 3-1 defeat by Scotland
- 8 April 1967: Scores hat-trick in 3-2 FA Cup quarter-final win against Everton, with Sir Alf Ramsey in attendance
- 13 May 1967: Forest finish second in the First Division, at the time their highest ever placing
- 8 January 1968: Marries Carol Ann Griffiths
- 2 December 1969: Selected, with Henry Newton, for England's squad of 30 for pre-World Cup training, medicals and internationals
- 14 January 1970: Makes England full international debut in friendly against the Netherlands at Wembley
- 27 December 1971: Scores what is widely considered to be the greatest ever goal at the City Ground in 1-1 draw with Arsenal
- 4 March 1972: Paraded at the Baseball Ground as Derby County's new 'British record signing'
- 6 March 1972: Signs for Manchester United for £200,000 after Forest's committee refuses to sanction transfer to Derby

- 11 March 1972: Scores on Manchester United debut in 2-0 win against Huddersfield Town
- 15 September 1973: Scores in final game for Manchester United, a 3-1 win against West Ham United at Old Trafford
- December 1973: Retires from English professional football because of recurring injuries
- April 1975: Signs for NASL team Chicago Sting
- 1975–81: In three separate spells with Burton Albion, first as player then player-manager, scores 52 goals in 157 appearances
- 1981–84: Player-manager of Shepshed Charterhouse, winning the Northern Counties East league and cup double

118 goals for Forest or 119?

When dealing with events of half a century or more ago, recollections may, of course, vary. We have done our best to get our facts right but any mistakes are ours and ours alone.

One area where we have taken a different tack to other writers on Forest's history is the number of goals Moore scored for the Garibaldi Reds. This is generally quoted as 118. We have opted for 119. We think the extra goal comes from including the Texaco Cup tie against Airdrieonians on 14 September 1970 when Moore scored in a 2-2 draw at the City Ground. The competition later became the Anglo-Scottish Cup and, as such, was the first trophy won by Nottingham Forest under Clough and Taylor. So, we think that match counts, as does Moore's goal. Hence, our figure is 119.

Goalscoring feats

- Moore scored more top-flight goals (105) for Nottingham Forest than any other player since the First World War
- Moore was the leading scorer in five out of his last six seasons at Forest, averaging a goal every 2.2 games
- His 119 goals for Forest represented one in every three goals scored by the team in the matches in which he played

- Moore scored two hat-tricks for Forest: against Everton in the FA Cup quarter-final in April 1967 and against Crystal Palace in the First Division in March 1971
- Moore scored in each of his first three games for Manchester United
- He scored against every First Division team he faced
- His 132 league and cup goals for Forest and United were scored against the following opposition:
  - 10: West Bromwich Albion
  - 9: Southampton
  - 8: Newcastle United
  - 7: Sheffield United, West Ham United
  - 6: Everton, Stoke City
  - 5: Chelsea, Coventry City, Derby County, Ipswich Town, Leicester City, Liverpool
  - 4: Arsenal, Blackpool, Crystal Palace
  - 3: Burnley, Fulham, Manchester City, Sunderland, Tottenham Hotspur, Wolverhampton Wanderers
  - 2: Aston Villa, Huddersfield Town
  - 1: Airdrieonians, Bari, Barrow, Birmingham City, Leeds United, Leyton Orient, Manchester United, Mansfield Town, Northampton Town, Norwich City, Notts County, Oxford United, Scunthorpe United, Sheffield Wednesday, FC Zürich
- Based on newspaper reports of the matches in which he played, Moore also made 55 assists.

Professional Matches in England and United States

Key:
Ⓖ = goal
Ⓐ = assist

International and representative appearances

England

1	Friendly 14 Jan 70	H	The Netherlands	D	0-0	75,000

England Under-23

1	Friendly 1 Mar 67	H	Scotland	L	1-3	21,860
2	Friendly 10 May 67	H	Austria	W	3-0	20,043

English Football League XI

1	Friendly 23 Sep 70	H	Irish League	W	5-0	20,743
2	Friendly 17 Mar 71	A	Scottish League	W	1-0	17,657

First-Team Appearances by Season

Key:
Ⓖ = goal
Ⓐ = assist

Nottingham Forest

1962/63

1	Div 1	10 May	A	Ipswich Town	W	2-1	13,055	Ⓐ

1963/64

2	Div 1	26 Dec	H	Sheffield United	D	3-3	23,938	Ⓖ
				25-yard volley (17)				
3	Div 1	28 Dec	A	Sheffield United	W	2-1	24,865	ⒼⒼ
				First-time shot (56); dribbled past two defenders & beat keeper (59)				
4	FAC-3	4 Jan	H	Preston North End	D	0-0	26,906	
5	Div 1	11 Jan	A	Wolverhampton Wanderers	W	3-2	15,468	Ⓐ
6	FAC-3	13 Jan	A	Preston North End	L	0-1	29,374	
7	Div 1	18 Jan	H	Stoke City	D	0-0	17,995	
8	Div 1	15 Feb	H	Blackpool	L	0-1	17,008	
9	Div 1	21 Mar	H	Sheffield Wednesday	W	3-2	17,749	ⒶⒶ
10	Div 1	28 Mar	A	Ipswich Town	L	3-4	12,017	ⒼⒼⒶ
				Volley from a partially cleared corner (35); tap-in after keeper saved Barnwell's shot (57)				
11	Div 1	30 Mar	A	Chelsea	L	0-1	26,086	
12	Div 1	4 Apr	H	Birmingham City	W	4-0	13,897	Ⓖ
				Clinical finish after Hinton laid the ball back (79)				
13	Div 1	11 Apr	A	West Bromwich Albion	W	3-2	14,442	

14	CoCup*	14 Apr	A	Notts County	W	5-1	14,501
15	Div 1	18 Apr	H	Burnley	L	1-3	19,005
16	Div 1	25 Apr	A	Manchester United	L	1-3	32,786

Games – goals – assists	*League*	*FA Cup*	*CoCup*	*Total*
Season	12 – 6 – 4	2 – 0 – 0	1 – 0 – 0	15 – 6 – 4
Cumulative	13 – 6 – 5	2 – 0 – 0	1 – 0 – 0	16 – 6 – 5

Wins – draws – losses	*League*	*FA Cup*	*CoCup*	*Total*
Season	5 – 2 – 5	0 – 1 – 1	1 – 0 – 0	6 – 3 – 6
Cumulative	6 – 2 – 5	0 – 1 – 1	1 – 0 – 0	7 – 3 – 6

Also played and scored in an 8-0 friendly win against a New Zealand XI on 20 April 1964 at the City Ground.

* CoCup = Nottinghamshire FA County Cup

1964/65

17	Div 1	19 Dec	H	West Ham	W	3-2	20,009	
18	FAC-3	9 Jan	H	Norwich City	W	1-0	28,574	
19	Div 1	16 Jan	H	Manchester United	D	2-2	43,009	
20	Div 1	23 Jan	A	Fulham	L	1-4	15,827	Ⓐ
21	Div 1	13 Feb	H	Stoke City	W	3-1	21,829	Ⓖ
				Poacher's goal after goalmouth scramble (66)				
22	FAC-5	20 Feb	A	Crystal Palace	L	1-3	41,167	
23	Div 1	22 Feb	A	Chelsea	W	1-0	29,038	
24	Div 1	27 Feb	H	Leicester City	W	2-1	32,985	Ⓖ
				Chested down Crowe's left-wing cross and beat Gordon Banks from narrow angle (66)				
25	Div 1	6 Mar	A	Sunderland	L	0-4	34,990	
26	Div 1	13 Mar	H	Arsenal	W	3-0	24,497	
27	Div 1	20 Mar	A	Aston Villa	L	1-2	14,433	
28	Div 1	1 Apr	H	Liverpool	D	2-2	23,926	ⒼⒶ
				Header from Hinton's left-wing cross (10)				

29	Div 1	3 Apr	A	Sheffield Wednesday	D	0-0	17,784	
30	Div 1	10 Apr	H	Blackpool	W	2-0	16,595	Ⓖ
				Played through by Addison and beat keeper from 10 yards (24)				
31	Div 1	19 Apr	H	Sheffield United	D	0-0	16,924	
32	CoCup	8 May	H	Mansfield Town	W	5-0	9,074	Ⓖ
				Dribbled past four defenders then slotted ball past keeper (57)				

Games – goals – assists	*League*	*FA Cup*	*CoCup*	*Total*
Season	13 – 4 – 2	2 – 0 – 0	1 – 1 – 0	16 – 5 – 2
Cumulative	26 – 10 – 7	4 – 0 – 0	2 – 1 – 0	32 – 11 – 7

Wins – draws – losses	*League*	*FA Cup*	*CoCup*	*Total*
Season	6 – 4 – 3	1 – 0 – 1	1 – 0 – 0	8 – 4 – 4
Cumulative	12 – 6 – 8	1 – 1 – 2	2 – 0 – 0	15 – 7 – 10

Also played in a friendly against a Combined XI at Field Mill to raise funds for the widow of Ralph Hunt (Chesterfield) and in four of Forest's end-of-season tour matches in North America. In total: five games, six goals.

1965/66

33	Div 1	7 Sep	H	Arsenal	L	0-1	30,540	
34	Div 1	9 Oct	H	West Ham United	W	5-0	19,262	Ⓖ
				First-time shot from Hindley's cut-back from the right (44)				
35	Div 1	16 Oct	A	Sunderland	L	2-3	31,987	Ⓐ
36	Div 1	23 Oct	H	Aston Villa	L	1-2	20,833	
37	Div 1	30 Oct	A	Liverpool	L	0-4	38,418	
38	Div 1	6 Nov	H	Tottenham Hotspur	W	1-0	29,611	
39	Div 1	13 Nov	A	Fulham	D	1-1	13,863	
40	Div 1	20 Nov	H	Blackpool	W	2-1	19,549	
41	Div 1	27 Nov	A	Blackburn	L	0-5	9,834	
42	Div 1	19 Feb	A	Leeds United	L	0-4	26,283	
43	Div 1	8 Mar	H	Burnley	W	1-0	28,246	Ⓖ
				Scored with a deflected shot from Barnwell's right-wing cross (83)				
44	Div 1	12 Mar	A	Northampton Town	D	3-3	18,670	ⒼⒶ
				Low shot across the keeper following Baker's quickly taken throw-in (60)				

45	Div 1	15 Mar	A	Everton	L	0-3	37,455	
46	Div 1	19 Mar	H	Stoke City	W	4-3	21,175	Ⓖ
	Poacher's goal after Hindley's shot, after a run from the halfway line, was blocked (60)							
47	Div 1	26 Mar	A	Burnley	L	1-4	10,027	
48	Div 1	2 Apr	A	Tottenham Hotspur	W	3-2	27,593	
49	Div 1	11 Apr	A	Chelsea	L	0-1	39,380	
50	Div 1	12 Apr	H	Chelsea	L	1-2	29,569	
51	Div 1	16 Apr	A	Blackpool	W	3-0	10,354	
52	Div 1	23 Apr	H	Blackburn	L	0-3	17,742	
53	Div 1	26 Apr	H	Fulham	L	1-2	19,733	
54	Div 1	30 Apr	A	Leicester City	L	1-2	18,485	
55	Div 1	7 May	H	Sheffield Wednesday	W	2-1	16,413	
56	Div 1	10 May	H	Liverpool	D	1-1	22,105	Ⓖ
	Rounded keeper to score following Baker's through ball (60)							

Games – goals – assists	*League*	*FA Cup*	*CoCup*	*Total*
Season	24 – 5 – 2	0	0	24 – 5 – 2
Cumulative	50 – 15 – 9	4 – 0 – 0	2 – 1 – 0	56 – 16 – 9

Wins – draws – losses	*League*	*FA Cup*	*CoCup*	*Total*
Season	8 – 3 – 13	0	0	8 – 3 – 13
Cumulative	20 – 9 – 21	1 – 1 – 2	2 – 0 – 0	23 – 10 – 23

Also played in friendlies against Doncaster Rovers and Nuneaton Borough to mark the official switching-on of new floodlights; a friendly at Crystal Palace, and in two of Forest's three end-of-season tour matches in Belgium and France. In total: five games, one goal.

1966/67

57	Div 1	20 Aug	H	Stoke City	L	1-2	21,848	Ⓐ
58	Div 1	24 Aug	A	Chelsea	L	1-2	27,501	Ⓖ
	Headed home right-wing cross from Hinton (73)							
59	Div 1	27 Aug	A	Sheffield United	W	2-1	16,047	ⒼⒶ
	Brought down cross from Barnwell to score (43)							
60	Div 1	30 Aug	H	Chelsea	D	0-0	22,199	

61	Div 1	3 Sep	H	West Bromwich Albion	W	2-1	21,871	Ⓖ
								Scored from Baker's left-wing cross (8)
62	Div 1	6 Sep	H	Fulham	W	2-1	22,135	ⒼⒼ
								Blistering volley from narrow angle (27); header from Baker's cross (88)
63	Div 1	10 Sep	A	Leeds United	D	1-1	35,634	
64	LC-1	13 Sep	H	Birmingham City	D	1-1	19,271	
65	Div 1	17 Sep	H	Newcastle United	W	3-0	21,732	Ⓖ
								Beat keeper after being put through by Barnwell's quickly taken free kick (63)
66	LC-1R	20 Sep	A	Birmingham City	L	1-2	21,510	
67	Div 1	24 Sep	A	Tottenham Hotspur	L	1-2	34,405	Ⓐ
68	Div 1	1 Oct	H	Manchester United	W	4-1	41,854	
69	Div 1	8 Oct	A	Leicester City	L	0-3	39,970	
70	Div 1	15 Oct	A	Liverpool	D	1-1	32,887	Ⓐ
71	Div 1	26 Oct	A	West Ham United	L	1-3	22,982	Ⓖ
								Close-range conversion of Hinton's left-wing cross (86)
72	Div 1	29 Oct	H	Blackpool	W	2-0	22,083	Ⓖ
								Close-range header after Wignall had headed on Newton's free kick (1)
73	Div 1	5 Nov	A	Liverpool	L	0-4	40,534	
74	Div 1	12 Nov	H	Sunderland	W	3-1	24,962	Ⓖ
								Collected pass from Newton and beat Montgomery with sharp turn and shot (23)
75	Div 1	19 Nov	A	Aston Villa	D	1-1	18,165	Ⓐ
76	Div 1	26 Nov	H	Arsenal	W	2-1	20,482	Ⓖ
								Deflected shot after being set up by Baker (13)
77	Div 1	10 Dec	H	Sheffield Wednesday	D	1-1	22,540	
78	Div 1	17 Dec	A	Stoke City	W	2-1	23,312	
79	Div 1	23 Dec	A	Everton	W	1-0	34,084	Ⓖ
								Scored from narrow angle from McKinlay's free kick (21)
80	Div 1	26 Dec	H	Everton	W	1-0	36,227	
81	Div 1	31 Dec	H	Sheffield United	W	3-1	27,683	ⒼⒶ
								Goalmouth scramble after Lyons' shot had been saved (64)
82	Div 1	7 Jan	H	West Bromwich Albion	W	2-1	21,975	Ⓖ
								Shot into the roof of the net after being put through by Newton (80)

83	Div 1	14 Jan	H	Leeds United	W	1-0	43,849	Ⓖ
Scored in off the post after Sprake had touched Wignall's header on to the bar (21)								
84	Div 1	11 Feb	A	Manchester United	L	0-1	62,727	
85	FAC-4	18 Feb	H	Newcastle United	W	3-0	45,962	ⒶⒶⒶ
86	Div 1	25 Feb	H	Leicester City	W	1-0	47,188	Ⓖ
Poacher's goal to beat Banks following pass by Barnwell (84)								
87	Div 1	4 Mar	A	Blackpool	D	1-1	14,003	Ⓖ
Scored with last kick of the game after solo run and deflected shot (90)								
88	FAC-5	11 Mar	H	Swindon Town	D	0-0	45,878	
89	FAC-5R	14 Mar	A	Swindon Town	D	1-1	28,008	
90	Div 1	18 Mar	H	West Ham United	W	1-0	31,426	
91	FAC-5R2	20 Mar	N	Swindon Town	W	3-0	52,596	
92	Div 1	25 Mar	A	Sheffield Wednesday	W	2-0	42,213	Ⓖ
Shot from the edge of the box after being set up by Newton (21)								
93	Div 1	27 Mar	H	Burnley	W	4-2	41,586	
94	Div 1	28 Mar	A	Burnley	W	2-0	17,695	
95	Div 1	1 Apr	H	Southampton	W	3-1	37,731	ⒼⒶ
Scored penalty after his header had been handled (73)								
96	FAC-6	8 Apr	H	Everton	W	3-2	47,510	ⒼⒼⒼ
Scored from eight yards after Rankin had saved Wignall's shot (65); left-footed shot from edge of the area after being set up by Wignall (68); headed hat-trick goal at fourth attempt after first shot blocked, second shot saved and first header hit crossbar (89)								
97	Div 1	15 Apr	H	Aston Villa	W	3-0	41,468	ⒼⒼ
Scored both goals from close in after being set up by headers by Wignall (65, 85)								
98	Div 1	19 Apr	A	Sunderland	L	0-1	26,215	
99	Div 1	22 Apr	H	Arsenal	D	1-1	36,196	Ⓖ
Volley from narrow angle (48)								
100	FAC-SF	29 Apr	N	Tottenham Hotspur	L	1-2	55,000	
101	Div 1	2 May	H	Manchester City	W	2-0	33,352	Ⓐ
102	Div 1	6 May	A	Southampton	L	1-2	25,305	
103	Div 1	13 May	A	Fulham	W	3-2	20,417	

Games – goals – assists	*League*	*FA Cup*	*FL Cup*	*CoCup*	*Total*
Season	39 – 21 – 8	6 – 3 – 3	2 – 0 – 0	0	47 – 24 – 11
Cumulative	89 – 36 – 17	10 – 3 – 3	2 – 0 – 0	2 – 1 – 0	103 – 40 – 20

Wins – draws – losses	*League*	*FA Cup*	*FL Cup*	*CoCup*	*Total*
Season	23 – 7 – 9	3 – 2 – 1	0 – 1 – 1	0	26 – 10 – 11
Cumulative	43 – 16 – 30	4 – 3 – 3	0 – 1 – 1	2 – 0 – 0	49 – 20 – 34

Also played in two end-of-season friendlies in Spain, against Barcelona at the Camp Nou (attendance 45,000) and Valencia in the Mestalla Stadium. In total: two matches, no goals.

1967/68

104	Div 1	19 Aug	A	Sheffield United	W	3-1	29,223	Ⓖ
				Rounded keeper and scored from narrow angle after being put through by Newton (78)				
105	Div 1	22 Aug	H	Coventry City	D	3-3	44,950	Ⓖ
				Penalty after Baker had been fouled (53)				
106	Div 1	29 Aug	A	Coventry City	W	3-1	41,212	Ⓖ
				Beat the offside trap to score past stranded keeper (41)				
107	Div 1	2 Sep	A	Manchester City	L	0-2	29,547	
108	Div 1	5 Sep	H	Liverpool	L	0-1	39,352	
109	Div 1	9 Sep	H	Newcastle United	W	4-0	30,151	ⒼⒶ
				Hammered a fine shot into the roof of the net following Lyons' cross (64)				
110	LC-2	13 Sep	A	Scunthorpe United	W	1-0	13,235	Ⓖ
				Rounded the keeper to score after being set up by McKinlay (81)				
111	Div 1	16 Sep	A	West Bromwich Albion	L	1-2	21,136	Ⓖ
				Hammered shot past keeper after lay-off by Wignall (77)				
112	ICFC-1*	20 Sep	A	Eintracht Frankfurt	W	1-0	4,500	
113	Div 1	23 Sep	H	Chelsea	W	3-0	34,871	Ⓖ
				Low shot under keeper Bonetti following right-wing run and cross by Hindley (59)				
114	Div 1	30 Sep	A	Southampton	L	1-2	26,724	
115	Div 1	7 Oct	A	Burnley	D	1-1	18,400	
116	LC-3	10 Oct	A	Burnley	L	0-3	14,421	

117	Div 1	14 Oct	H	Sheffield Wednesday	D	0-0	37,983	
118	ICFC-1	17 Oct	H	Eintracht Frankfurt	W	4-0	27,090	ⒶⒶ
119	Div 1	25 Oct	A	Tottenham Hotspur	D	1-1	40,928	
120	Div 1	28 Oct	H	Manchester United	W	3-1	49,946	Ⓐ
121	ICFC-2	31 Oct	H	FC Zürich	W	2-1	32,896	Ⓖ
Scored from penalty spot after Swiss defender had handled a left-wing cross (71)								
122	Div 1	4 Nov	A	Sunderland	L	0-1	29,158	
123	Div 1	18 Nov	A	Fulham	L	0-2	22,413	
124	Div 1	2 Dec	A	Everton	L	0-1	44,765	
125	Div 1	3 Feb	A	Chelsea	L	0-1	33,483	
126	Div 1	10 Feb	H	Southampton	D	2-2	27,318	Ⓖ
Swept the ball into the net from Winfield's left-wing cross (82)								
127	FAC-4	17 Feb	A	Leeds United	L	1-2	51,739	
128	Div 1	24 Feb	H	Burnley	W	1-0	21,305	
129	Div 1	13 Mar	A	Leeds United	D	1-1	32,508	
130	Div 1	30 Mar	H	Sunderland	L	0-3	24,543	
131	Div 1	12 Apr	H	West Ham United	L	0-3	36,589	
132	Div 1	13 Apr	H	Fulham	D	2-2	20,658	Ⓖ
Header following free kick by Hennessey (7)								
133	Div 1	16 Apr	H	West Ham United	D	1-1	22,189	
134	Div 1	20 Apr	A	Sheffield Wednesday	D	0-0	28,805	
135	Div 1	22 Apr	H	Everton	W	1-0	23,809	Ⓖ
Header from corner (57)								
136	Div 1	4 May	A	Leicester City	L	2-4	25,605	Ⓖ
Breakaway goal, running from halfway line to beat Shilton (4)								
137	Div 1	11 May	A	Liverpool	L	1-6	38,850	
138	CoCup	14 May	H	Notts County	W	3-0	14,042	Ⓖ
Penalty after foul on Hilley (7)								

Games – goals – assists	*League*	*FA Cup*	*FL Cup*	*Europe*	*CoCup*	*Total*
Season	28 – 10 – 2	1 – 0 – 0	2 – 1 – 0	3 – 1 – 2	1 – 1 – 0	35 – 13 – 4
Cumulative	117 – 46 – 19	11 – 3 – 3	4 – 1 – 0	3 – 1 – 2	3 – 2 – 0	138 – 53 – 24

Wins – draws – losses	*League*	*FA Cup*	*FL Cup*	*Europe*	*CoCup*	*Total*
Season	7 – 9 – 12	0 – 0 – 1	1 – 0 – 1	3 – 0 – 0	1 – 0 – 0	12 – 9 – 14
Cumulative	50 – 25 – 42	4 – 3 – 4	1 – 1 – 2	3 – 0 – 0	3 – 0 – 0	61 – 29 – 48

* Inter-Cities Fairs Cup

1968/69

139	Div 1	10 Aug	H	Burnley	D	2-2	30,298	
140	Div 1	14 Aug	A	Chelsea	D	1-1	36,515	Ⓖ
				Prodded home after being set up by Baxter (26)				
141	Div 1	17 Aug	H	West Ham United	L	0-1	31,114	
142	Div 1	20 Aug	H	Sheffield Wednesday	D	0-0	27,819	
143	Div 1	28 Aug	A	Newcastle United	D	1-1	34,613	Ⓖ
				Scored penalty after Frank Clark handled on the line (80)				
144	Div 1	31 Aug	A	Everton	L	1-2	45,951	
145	LC-2	3 Sep	H	West Bromwich Albion	L	2-3	23,970	Ⓖ
				Beat three defenders before firing unstoppable shot into top corner (63)				
146	Div 1	7 Sep	A	West Bromwich Albion	W	5-2	23,377	ⒼⒼⒶ
				Fired into roof of net after being set up by Baker (19); brilliant run and shot (88)				
147	Div 1	14 Sep	H	Coventry City	D	0-0	22,260	
148	Div 1	21 Sep	A	Tottenham Hotspur	L	1-2	37,386	Ⓖ
				Shot into far corner past Jennings after being set up by Baker (82)				
149	Div 1	5 Oct	H	Stoke City	D	3-3	21,519	ⒼⒼ
				Beat Banks with two headers from crosses by Lyons (25) and Baxter (33)				
150	Div 1	8 Oct	H	Newcastle United	L	2-4	17,651	ⒼⒼ
				Header from Lyons' cross (56); fierce shot after being put through by Newton (60)				
151	Div 1	12 Oct	A	Sunderland	L	1-3	25,575	Ⓖ
				Right-footed shot into far corner from edge of penalty area (11)				

152	Div 1	19 Oct	H	Ipswich Town	L	1-2	21,148	Ⓖ
				Calmly rolled the ball home after right-wing cross by Hall (10)				
153	Div 1	26 Oct	A	Manchester City	D	3-3	32,937	Ⓖ
				Beat keeper after being played through by Chapman (56)				
154	Div 1	2 Nov	H	Wolverhampton Wanderers	D	0-0	19,490	
155	Div 1	9 Nov	A	Leicester City	D	2-2	26,828	Ⓖ
				Beat Shilton after exchanging passes with Chapman (63)				
156	Div 1	16 Nov	H	Arsenal	L	0-2	24,550	
157	Div 1	23 Nov	A	Queens Park Rangers	L	1-2	18,857	
158	Div 1	30 Nov	H	Liverpool	L	0-1	25,175	
159	Div 1	7 Dec	A	Southampton	D	1-1	17,957	
160	Div 1	14 Dec	H	Sunderland	W	1-0	18,007	Ⓖ
				Controlled Hennessey's shot to beat Montgomery (17)				
161	Div 1	21 Dec	A	Ipswich Town	W	3-2	18,739	Ⓖ
				Forced ball over the line after goalmouth scramble (51)				
162	Div 1	26 Dec	A	Stoke City	L	1-3	20,452	Ⓖ
				Beat Banks after being put through by Baker (18)				
163	FAC-3	4 Jan	A	Preston North End	L	0-3	20,008	
164	Div 1	11 Jan	A	Wolverhampton Wanderers	L	0-1	24,659	
165	Div 1	18 Jan	H	Leicester City	D	0-0	27,776	
166	Div 1	19 Apr	A	Coventry City	D	1-1	37,772	Ⓖ
				Dribbled past three players before driving the ball home from just inside penalty area (8)				

Games – goals – assists	*League*	*FA Cup*	*FL Cup*	*Europe*	*CoCup*	*Total*
Season	26 – 17 – 1	1 – 0 – 0	1 – 1 – 0	0	0	28 – 18 – 1
Cumulative	143 – 63 – 20	12 – 3 – 3	5 – 2 – 0	3 – 1 – 2	3 – 2 – 0	166 – 71 – 25

Wins – draws – losses	*League*	*FA Cup*	*FL Cup*	*Europe*	*CoCup*	*Total*
Season	3 – 12 – 11	0 – 0 – 1	0 – 0 – 1	0	0	3 – 12 – 13
Cumulative	53 – 37 – 53	4 – 3 – 5	1 – 1 – 3	3 – 0 – 0	3 – 0 – 0	64 – 41 – 61

Also played in a pre-season tour match against Werder Bremen in West Germany, the home match against Leeds United abandoned when the Main Stand fire broke out; and in a friendly against a Bristol XI in a testimonial for Bristol Rovers forward Alfie Biggs. In total: two full games, no goals.

1969/70

No.	Comp	Date	Venue	Opponent	Result	Score	Attendance	
167	Div 1	9 Aug	A	Ipswich	D	0-0	19,310	
168	Div 1	12 Aug	H	Stoke City	D	0-0	22,740	
169	Div 1	16 Aug	A	Leeds United	L	1-4	34,290	
170	Div 1	20 Aug	A	Stoke City	D	1-1	20,028	
171	Div 1	23 Aug	A	Arsenal	L	1-2	30,290	Ⓖ
				30-yard shot past Wilson following short free kick taken by Barnwell (57)				
172	Div 1	26 Aug	H	West Bromwich Albion	W	1-0	22,924	Ⓖ
				Beat keeper with 30-yard shot along the ground (2)				
173	Div 1	30 Aug	H	West Ham United	W	1-0	27,097	Ⓐ
174	LC-2	3 Sep	A	Barrow	W	2-1	8,919	Ⓖ
				Injury-time winner slammed home from O'Kane's pass (90)				
175	Div 1	13 Sep	H	Southampton	W	2-1	23,200	ⒼⒼ
				Diving header from Rees's cross (59); scored direct from free kick (62)				
176	Div 1	16 Sep	A	Coventry City	L	2-3	26,038	Ⓐ
177	Div 1	20 Sep	A	Sunderland	L	1-2	16,044	
178	LC-3	23 Sep	H	West Ham United	W	1-0	20,939	
179	Div 1	27 Sep	H	Crystal Palace	D	0-0	23,394	
180	Div 1	4 Oct	A	Liverpool	D	1-1	44,859	Ⓐ
181	Div 1	11 Oct	H	Manchester City	D	2-2	30,037	ⒼⒶ
				Header past Corrigan from Chapman's cross (36)				
182	LC-4	15 Oct	A	Oxford United	L	0-1	20,734	
183	Div 1	18 Oct	A	Manchester United	D	1-1	53,702	Ⓖ
				Sent Stepney wrong way from penalty spot after Hilley brought down in the area (17)				
184	Div 1	25 Oct	H	Burnley	D	1-1	19,771	Ⓐ
185	Div 1	29 Oct	A	Leeds United	L	1-6	29,636	
186	Div 1	1 Nov	A	Everton	L	0-1	49,610	
187	Div 1	8 Nov	H	Tottenham Hotspur	D	2-2	24,034	Ⓖ
				Beat Jennings from 20 yards following short free kick by Newton (66)				
188	Div 1	15 Nov	A	Newcastle United	L	1-3	24,307	
189	Div 1	22 Nov	H	Chelsea	D	1-1	23,808	
190	Div 1	29 Nov	A	Derby County	W	2-0	38,225	ⒼⒶ
				Header from Hall's corner (27)				

191	Div 1	6 Dec	H	Sheffield Wednesday	W	2-1	19,039	
192	Div 1	13 Dec	A	Southampton	W	2-1	20,153	Ⓖ Ⓐ
				From Winfield's short free kick, swerved past Channon before scoring from 25 yards (48)				
193	Div 1	20 Dec	H	Wolverhampton Wanderers	W	4-2	15,921	Ⓖ Ⓐ
				Fierce drive into the net after being set up by Hilley (71)				
194	Div 1	26 Dec	H	Arsenal	D	1-1	38,915	
195	Div 1	27 Dec	A	West Ham United	D	1-1	31,829	Ⓖ
				Tap-in after keeper missed McCaffrey's right-wing cross (80)				
196	FAC-3	3 Jan	H	Carlisle United	D	0-0	23,419	
197	FAC-R	6 Jan	A	Carlisle United	L	1-2	12,840	Ⓐ
198	Div 1	17 Jan	A	Crystal Palace	D	1-1	22,531	
199	Div 1	24 Jan	H	Sunderland	W	2-1	19,544	Ⓐ
200	Div 1	31 Jan	H	Liverpool	W	1-0	30,838	
201	Div 1	7 Feb	A	Manchester City	D	1-1	27,077	

Games – goals – assists	*League*	*FA Cup*	*FL Cup*	*Europe*	*CoCup*	*Total*
Season	30 – 11 – 9	2 – 0 – 1	3 – 1 – 0	0	0	35 – 12 – 10
Cumulative	173 – 74 – 29	14 – 3 – 4	8 – 3 – 0	3 – 1 – 2	3 – 2 – 0	201 – 83 – 35

Wins – draws – losses	*League*	*FA Cup*	*FL Cup*	*Europe*	*CoCup*	*Total*
Season	9 – 14 – 7	0 – 1 – 1	2 – 0 – 1	0	0	11 – 15 – 9
Cumulative	62 – 51 – 60	4 – 4 – 6	3 – 1 – 4	3 – 0 – 0	3 – 0 – 0	75 – 56 – 70

Also played in two pre-season tour matches against Maastricht in the Netherlands and Rot-Weiss Essen in West Germany, and in a return friendly at the City Ground against Rot-Weiss Essen; three games, no goals.

1970/71

202	Div 1	15 Aug	H	Coventry City	W	2-0	25,317	Ⓖ
				Header after keeper had saved Rees's shot (30)				
203	Div 1	18 Aug	H	West Bromwich Albion	D	3-3	24,423	Ⓐ Ⓐ Ⓐ
204	Div 1	22 Aug	A	Ipswich Town	D	0-0	19,150	
205	Div 1	26 Aug	A	Newcastle United	D	1-1	35,132	Ⓖ
				Unstoppable 30-yard right-foot shot (29)				

No.	Comp	Date	H/A	Opponent	Res	Score	Att	Goals
206	Div 1	29 Aug	H	Wolverhampton Wanderers	W	4-1	24,343	Ⓖ
				Scored from penalty spot after Ingram had been fouled (60)				
207	Div 1	2 Sep	A	Stoke City	D	0-0	13,951	
208	Div 1	5 Sep	A	Crystal Palace	L	0-2	26,510	
209	LC-2	9 Sep	A	Huddersfield Town	D	0-0	18,165	
210	Div 1	12 Sep	H	Manchester City	L	0-1	28,896	
211	Tex	14 Sep	H	Airdrieonians	D	2-2	13,177	Ⓖ
				Scored from rebound after keeper saved shot by Rees (70)				
212	Div 1	19 Sep	A	Liverpool	L	0-3	40,676	
213	LC-R	21 Sep	H	Huddersfield Town	W	2-0	15,818	Ⓖ
				Header from Hilley's cross (85)				
214	Div 1	21 Nov	A	Burnley	L	1-2	13,013	Ⓖ
				Powerful cross-shot from the edge of the area after quick breakaway (52)				
215	Div 1	28 Nov	H	Derby County	L	2-4	30,539	Ⓖ
				Header from a narrow angle from Lyons' right-wing cross (33)				
216	Div 1	5 Dec	A	Southampton	L	1-4	19,016	
217	Div 1	12 Dec	H	Chelsea	D	1-1	20,060	Ⓖ
				Header following cross from the left by Rees (44)				
218	Div 1	19 Dec	H	Ipswich	L	0-1	14,085	
219	FAC-3	2 Jan	H	Luton Town	D	1-1	23,230	
220	Div 1	9 Jan	A	West Bromwich Albion	W	1-0	20,015	Ⓖ
				Scored from ten yards after goalmouth scramble following corner (54)				
221	Div 1	16 Jan	H	Newcastle United	W	2-0	21,798	ⒼⒼ
				Scored from eight yards (8) and with header (40), both from crosses by Rees				
222	FAC-4	23 Jan	H	Leyton Orient	D	1-1	25,349	Ⓖ
				Penalty following foul on Cormack (44)				
223	FAC-R	1 Feb	A	Leyton Orient	W	1-0	18,530	
224	Div 1	6 Feb	H	Southampton	W	2-0	18,009	Ⓖ
				Scored from close range after Collier's header had been blocked on the line (63)				
225	FAC-5	13 Feb	A	Tottenham Hotspur	L	1-2	46,336	Ⓖ
				Penalty following foul on Cormack (68)				

226	Div 1	17 Feb	A	Chelsea	L	0-2	19,339	
227	Div 1	20 Feb	H	Burnley	W	1-0	20,873	Ⓖ
				Scored from six yards after being set up by Martin's header (28)				
228	Div 1	24 Feb	A	West Ham United	L	0-2	35,601	
229	Div 1	6 Mar	H	Huddersfield Town	L	1-3	15,798	
230	Div 1	13 Mar	A	Manchester United	L	0-2	39,339	
231	Div 1	20 Mar	H	Everton	W	3-2	21,643	Ⓖ
				Prodded the ball home after keeper saved Cormack's shot (6)				
232	Div 1	27 Mar	H	Crystal Palace	W	3-1	16,507	ⒼⒼⒼ
				Header from Lyons' right-wing cross (8); penalty after Martin pulled down by keeper (52); rising shot after goalmouth scramble (69)				
233	Div 1	31 Mar	A	Derby County	W	2-1	34,857	Ⓖ
				Header from Cormack's right-wing cross (82)				
234	Div 1	3 Apr	A	Wolverhampton Wanderers	L	0-4	20,531	
235	Div 1	9 Apr	A	Manchester City	W	3-1	33,772	
236	Div 1	10 Apr	H	West Ham United	W	1-0	23,032	Ⓖ
				Rounded the keeper to score after being put through by Martin (44)				
237	Div 1	13 Apr	A	Arsenal	L	0-3	40,692	
238	Div 1	17 Apr	A	Blackpool	W	3-2	10,028	Ⓖ
				Shot past keeper from ten yards out following Cormack's left-wing cross (82)				
239	Div 1	24 Apr	H	Liverpool	L	0-1	20,678	
240	Div 1	27 Apr	H	Stoke City	D	0-0	13,502	
241	Div 1	1 May	A	Leeds United	L	0-2	43,083	

Games – goals – assists	*League*	*FA Cup*	*FL Cup*	*Europe*	*Other*	*Total*
Season	33 – 18 – 3	4 – 2 – 0	2 – 1 – 0	0	1 – 1 – 0	40 – 22 – 3
Cumulative	206 – 92 – 32	18 – 5 – 4	10 – 4 – 0	3 – 1 – 2	4 – 3 – 0	241 – 105 – 38

Wins – draws – losses	*League*	*FA Cup*	*FL Cup*	*Europe*	*Other*	*Total*
Season	12 – 6 – 15	1 – 2 – 1	1 – 1 – 0	0	0 – 1 – 0	14 – 10 – 16
Cumulative	74 – 57 – 75	5 – 6 – 7	4 – 2 – 4	3 – 0 – 0	3 – 1 – 0	89 – 66 – 86

Also played in three pre-season tour matches in Sweden, scoring a hat-trick against Landskrona.

1971/72

242	Div 1	14 Aug	A	Liverpool	L	1-3	51,427	Ⓖ
				Penalty after Martin brought down by Clemence (38)				
243	Div 1	18 Aug	A	Leicester City	L	1-2	32,079	
244	Div 1	21 Aug	H	West Ham United	W	1-0	17,185	Ⓖ
				Penalty after Rees fouled (44)				
245	Div 1	24 Aug	H	Southampton	L	2-3	14,350	ⒼⒶ
				Direct free kick from just outside the area (53)				
246	Div 1	28 Aug	A	Crystal Palace	D	1-1	17,699	
247	Div 1	31 Aug	H	Stoke City	D	0-0	19,017	
248	Div 1	4 Sep	H	Sheffield United	L	2-3	27,041	Ⓖ
				Lobbed keeper after chasing long clearance (32)				
249	LC-2	7 Sep	H	Aldershot	W	5-1	8,380	
250	Div 1	11 Sep	A	Coventry City	D	1-1	20,380	
251	Div 1	18 Sep	H	Manchester City	D	2-2	21,488	ⒼⒶ
				Penalty after Martin fouled (77)				
252	Div 1	25 Sep	A	Wolverhampton Wanderers	L	2-4	20,631	ⒼⒶ
				Left-foot shot from 20 yards following pass by Jackson (5)				
253	Div 1	2 Oct	H	Huddersfield Town	L	1-2	15,693	
254	LC-3	6 Oct	H	Chelsea	D	1-1	16,811	
255	Div 1	9 Oct	A	Ipswich Town	D	1-1	16,285	Ⓖ
				Glancing header from Lyons' cross from the right (14)				
256	LC-R	11 Oct	A	Chelsea	L	1-2	24,817	Ⓖ
				Long-range shot by Richardson deflected off Moore's heel past Bonetti (24)				
257	Div 1	16 Oct	H	Liverpool	L	2-3	20,945	ⒼⒼ
				Scored 100th league goal with 20-yard shot past Clemence after wrong-footing Liverpool defence (12); played through by Robertson for second goal (85)				
258	Div 1	23 Oct	A	Tottenham Hotspur	L	1-6	35,846	Ⓐ
259	Div 1	26 Oct	H	Huddersfield Town	W	1-0	9,459	
260	Div 1	30 Oct	H	Derby County	L	0-2	37,170	
261	Div 1	6 Nov	A	Chelsea	L	0-2	25,812	
262	Div 1	13 Nov	H	West Bromwich Albion	W	4-1	20,024	ⒼⒶ
				Cut in from the left past two tackles to score from edge of the penalty area (87)				

263	Div 1	20 Nov	A	Newcastle United	L	1-2	24,583	
264	Div 1	27 Nov	H	Leeds United	L	0-2	29,463	
265	Div 1	4 Dec	A	Manchester United	L	2-3	45,048	Ⓐ
266	Div 1	11 Dec	H	Everton	W	1-0	18,639	
267	Div 1	18 Dec	A	Sheffield United	L	1-2	27,663	
268	Div 1	27 Dec	H	Arsenal	D	1-1	42,750	Ⓖ
				74-yard run, beating three defenders before shooting past Wilson (15)				
269	Div 1	1 Jan	A	Manchester City	D	2-2	38,777	
270	Div 1	8 Jan	H	Crystal Palace	L	0-1	19,033	
271	FAC-3	15 Jan	A	Millwall	L	1-3	17,940	
272	Div 1	22 Jan	H	Leicester City	L	1-2	27,250	Ⓖ
				Scored from eight yards after Shilton failed to hold Fraser's right-wing cross (30)				
273	Div 1	29 Jan	A	Southampton	L	1-4	17,043	Ⓖ
				Scored from 12 yards from McIntosh centre after initial shot had been saved (12)				
274	Div 1	12 Feb	H	Tottenham Hotspur	L	0-1	20,209	
275	Div 1	19 Feb	A	Derby County	L	0-4	31,801	

Games – goals – assists	*League*	*FA Cup*	*FL Cup*	*Europe*	*Other*	*Total*
Season	30 – 13 – 6	1 – 0 – 0	3 – 1 – 0	0	0	34 – 14 – 6
Cumulative	236 – 105 – 38	19 – 5 – 4	13 – 5 – 0	3 – 1 – 2	4 – 3 – 0	275 – 119 – 44

Wins – draws – losses	*League*	*FA Cup*	*FL Cup*	*Europe*	*Other*	*Total*
Season	4 – 7 – 19	0 – 0 – 1	1 – 1 – 1	0	0	5 – 8 – 21
Cumulative	78 – 64 – 94	5 – 6 – 8	5 – 3 – 5	3 – 0 – 0	3 – 1 – 0	94 – 74 – 107

Also played in two pre-season tour games against Kaiserslautern and Hannover 96 in West Germany, in the return friendly against Hannover 96 at the City Ground, and in a friendly against Notts County. In total: four games, two goals.

Manchester United

1971/72

1	Div 1	11 Mar	H	Huddersfield Town	W	2-0	53,581	Ⓖ
								Scored with header after Best's shot saved by keeper (62)
2	Div 1	25 Mar	H	Crystal Palace	W	4-0	41,550	Ⓖ
								Fierce shot into roof of the net after his free kick was blocked (62)
3	Div 1	1 Apr	A	Coventry City	W	3-2	37,901	ⒼⒶⒶ
								Burst clear of two defenders to shoot home from 25 yards (20)
4	Div 1	3 Apr	H	Liverpool	L	0-3	53,826	
5	Div 1	4 Apr	A	Sheffield United	D	1-1	45,045	
6	Div 1	8 Apr	A	Leicester City	L	0-2	35,970	
7	Div 1	12 Apr	H	Manchester City	L	1-3	56,362	
8	Div 1	15 Apr	H	Southampton	W	3-2	38,437	Ⓖ
								Close-range effort (32)
9	Div 1	22 Apr	A	Nottingham Forest	D	0-0	35,063	
10	Div 1	25 Apr	A	Arsenal	L	0-3	49,125	
11	Div 1	29 Apr	H	Stoke City	W	3-0	34,959	ⒼⒶ
								Set up by Law to finish from ten yards after neat exchange of passes (16)

Games – goals – assists	*League*
Season	11 – 5 – 3

Wins – draws – losses	*League*
Season	5 – 2 – 4

1972/73

12	Div 1	12 Aug	H	Ipswich Town	L	1-2	51,459	Ⓐ
13	Div 1	15 Aug	A	Liverpool	L	0-2	54,799	
14	Div 1	19 Aug	A	Everton	L	0-2	52,348	
15	Div 1	23 Aug	H	Leicester City	D	1-1	40,067	Ⓐ
16	Div 1	26 Aug	H	Arsenal	D	0-0	48,108	
17	Div 1	30 Aug	H	Chelsea	D	0-0	44,482	

18	Div 1	2 Sep	A	West Ham United	D	2-2	31,939	Ⓖ
Scored from the rebound after Law's shot was blocked (77)								
19	LC-2	6 Sep	A	Oxford United	D	2-2	16,560	
20	Div 1	9 Sep	H	Coventry City	L	0-1	37,073	
21	LC-R	12 Sep	H	Oxford United	W	3-1	21,486	ⒼⒶⒶ
Dribbled past several defenders to score from 16 yards (35)								
22	Div 1	16 Sep	A	Wolverhampton Wanderers	L	0-2	34,049	
23	Div 1	23 Sep	H	Derby County	W	3-0	48,255	Ⓖ
Headed Best's cross across goal beyond the keeper (33)								
24	Div 1	30 Sep	A	Sheffield United	L	0-1	37,347	
25	LC-3	3 Oct	A	Bristol Rovers	D	1-1	33,957	
26	Div 1	7 Oct	A	West Bromwich Albion	D	2-2	39,209	ⒼⒶ
Headed Best's corner in off the bar (76)								
27	LC-R	11 Oct	H	Bristol Rovers	L	1-2	29,349	
28	Div 1	14 Oct	H	Birmingham City	W	1-0	52,104	
29	Div 1	21 Oct	A	Newcastle United	L	1-2	38.170	
30	Div 1	4 Nov	A	Leicester City	D	2-2	32,575	Ⓐ
31	Div 1	11 Nov	H	Liverpool	W	2-0	53,944	
32	Div 1	18 Nov	A	Manchester City	L	0-3	52,050	
33	Div 1	25 Nov	H	Southampton	W	2-1	36,073	
34	Div 1	2 Dec	A	Norwich City	W	2-0	35,910	ⒼⒶ
MacDougall chased a long through ball and crossed for Moore to score (13)								
35	Div 1	9 Dec	H	Stoke City	L	0-2	41,347	
36	Div 1	16 Dec	A	Crystal Palace	L	0-5	39,484	
37	Div 1	23 Dec	H	Leeds United	D	1-1	46,382	
38	Div 1	26 Dec	A	Derby County	L	1-3	35,098	Ⓖ
Header from Kidd's cross, followed by double V-sign for Derby fans (61)								
39	Div 1	6 Jan	A	Arsenal	L	1-3	51,194	Ⓐ
40	Div 1	3 Mar	H	West Bromwich Albion	W	2-1	46,735	
41	Div 1	10 Mar	A	Birmingham City	L	1-3	51,278	
42	AngIta	4 Apr	H	Bari	W	3-1	14,303	Ⓖ
Scored from close range after being set up by Law's header (30)								

Games – goals – assists	*League*	*FL Cup*	*Europe*	*Total*
Season	26 – 5 – 6	4 – 1 – 2	1 – 1 – 0	31 – 7 – 8
Cumulative	37 – 10 – 9	4 – 1 – 2	1 – 1 – 0	42 – 12 – 11

Wins – draws – losses	*League*	*FL Cup*	*Europe*	*Total*
Season	6 – 7 – 13	1 – 2 – 1	1 – 0 – 0	8 – 9 – 14
Cumulative	11 – 9 – 17	1 – 2 – 1	1 – 0 – 0	13 – 11 – 18

1973/74

43	Div 1	12 Sep	H	Leicester City	L	1-2	40,793	
44	Div 1	15 Sep	H	West Ham United	W	3-1	44,757	Ⓖ

Easy finish after George Buchan dummied the keeper (83)

Games – goals – assists	*League*	*FL Cup*	*Europe*	*Total*
Season	2 – 1 – 0	0	0	2 – 1 – 0
Cumulative	39 – 11 – 9	4 – 1 – 2	1 – 1 – 0	44 – 13 – 11

Wins – draws – losses	*League*	*FL Cup*	*Europe*	*Total*
Season	1 – 0 – 1	0	0	1 – 0 – 1
Cumulative	12 – 9 – 18	1 – 2 – 1	1 – 0 – 0	14 – 11 – 19

Nottingham Forest and Manchester United Combined

Games – goals – assists	*League*	*FA Cup*	*FL Cup*	*Europe*	*Other*	*Total*
Nottingham Forest	236 – 105 – 38	19 – 5 – 4	13 – 5 – 0	3 – 1 – 2	4 – 3 – 0	275 – 119 – 44
Manchester United	39 – 11 – 9	0	4 – 1 – 2	1 – 1 – 0	0	44 – 13 – 11
Total	275 – 116 – 47	19 – 5 – 4	17 – 6 – 2	4 – 2 – 2	4 – 3 – 0	319 – 132 – 55

Wins – draws – losses	*League*	*FA Cup*	*FL Cup*	*Europe*	*Other*	*Total*
Nottingham Forest	78 – 64 – 94	5 – 6 – 8	5 – 3 – 5	3 – 0 – 0	3 – 1 – 0	94 – 74 – 107
Manchester United	12 – 9 – 18	0	1 – 2 – 1	1 – 0 – 0	0	14 – 11 – 19
Total	90 – 73 – 112	5 – 6 – 8	6 – 5 – 6	4 – 0 – 0	3 – 1 – 0	108 – 85 – 126

Chicago Sting
1975

1	NASL	2 May	H	Denver Dynamos	L	0-2	4,536	
2	NASL	9 May	H	Dallas Tornado	W	3-2	4,264	Ⓖ
				Diving header from Gordon Hill's cross to give the Sting their first ever win (85)				
3	NASL	16 May	H	Los Angeles Aztecs	W	1-0	4,117	
4	NASL	21 May	A	San Antonio Thunder	W	2-1	3,711	
5	NASL	23 May	H	San Jose Earthquakes	L	2-2*	4,081	
6	NASL	30 May	A	Portland Timbers	L	0-1	9,526	
7	NASL	1 Jun	A	Seattle Sounders	L	1-2	16,366	Ⓖ
				Scored with 20-yard shot (85)				
8	NASL	6 Jun	H	Denver Dynamos	W	1-0	4,094	
9	NASL	8 Jun	A	St Louis Stars	L	0-1	6,832	
10	NASL	20 Jun	H	Philadelphia Atoms	W	6-2	3,984	
11	NASL	18 Jul	H	Baltimore Comets	W	4-1	5,183	
12	NASL	23 Jul	A	Denver Dynamos	W	3-2	3,443	
13	NASL	25 Jul	H	San Antonio Thunder	W	1-1*	6,412	
14	NASL	10 Aug	A	Washington Diplomats	L	1-1*	3,519	

* Result decided by penalty shoot-out
Official NASL statistics credited Moore with one assist.

Acknowledgements

The authors would like to thank, first and foremost, Ian Storey-Moore for agreeing to work with us on this book. He willingly endured numerous interviews by us, unerringly recalling events from a lifetime ago, and patiently, good-naturedly answered what must have seemed like an endless list of inane and obscure questions. In addition to trusting us to faithfully tell the story of his life and career, he entrusted us with the care of the precious scrapbooks, compiled by his proud father, which are full of faded newspaper clippings, magazine articles and other mementoes that trace his footballing journey from the playing fields of Scunthorpe to Wembley.

We would like to thank Ian's wife, Carol, his sister, Anne, and his team-mate and good friend, Henry Newton, for helping us to piece the jigsaw together. The same applies to Ben Robinson, the long-standing chairman of Burton Albion, for shining a light on Ian's time in non-league football, and to peerless broadcasters Tony Delahunty and Mark Shardlow for lifting the veil on what goes on behind the microphone. They were all only too happy to help and were generous with their time and encouragement.

We are grateful to the remarkable Martin O'Neill, who we reckon must be the Hardest Working Person in Football. Fresh from writing his splendid, best-selling autobiography – and despite seemingly spending an inordinate amount of time on planes, trains and automobiles – Martin jumped at the chance to pen a vivid and entertaining foreword in praise of Ian.

Various talented individuals generously and willingly contributed their work to the book. Thank you Bob Bond, Norman Giller, Gerry Murray and Matt Wilkinson.

Thank you also to those who helped source the photographs and images that do so much to bring Ian's story to life. Trevor Wood of Fotomargo, providers of professional photographic services in West Bridgford, Nottingham, expertly restored old images from Ian's scrapbooks, especially what were two very damaged pictures of his parents, Vic and Lily. Natalie Jones and the archive team at Reach Licensing dealt patiently and efficiently with many requests to search through the photographic archive of Nottingham's newspapers from the 1960s and 1970s and went beyond the call of duty by finding many images that were unpublished at the time. Tony Graham and his colleagues painstakingly trawled through Colorsport's archive for photographs of Ian. Thank you also to Marc Cutler and the archive team at News Licensing and to Rebecca Lucas of the North Lincolnshire Museum for her assistance in sourcing the image of Lincoln Gardens in the 1950s.

We are grateful also to the staff at Bingham Library and the team at Costa Coffee in Bingham for hosting our meetings with Ian.

Finally, thank you to Jane Camillin and everyone at Pitch Publishing for helping realise our long-held ambition to see Ian's story in print.

Image credits

Front cover

1.	1971/72 season photocall	Colorsport

Dust jacket front panel

2.	Rogues' Gallery portrait Matt Wilkinson, www.rogues.gallery	
3.	Victor Storey-Moore	Ian Storey-Moore
4.	Lilian Storey-Moore	Ian Storey-Moore
5.	Aerial view of Lincoln Gardens	North Lincolnshire Council
6.	In the garden at 107 Lincoln Gardens	Ian Storey-Moore
7.	Whitefoot, McKinlay and Burkitt	Mirrorpix
8.	With David Pleat	Colorsport
9.	With Sammy Chapman and David Wilson	Colorsport
10.	Forest first-team squad 1964/65	Colorsport
11.	Pre-season photocall, August 1966	Colorsport
12.	In front of Main Stand, 1966/67	Ian Storey-Moore
13.	The 1966/67 'Nearly Men'	Alamy
14.	Shooting vs Manchester United	Mirrorpix
15.	Johnny Carey signing autographs	Mirrorpix
16.	Signing autographs for young fans	Mirrorpix
17.	Joe Baker injury	Colorsport
18.	First goal against Everton	Mirrorpix
19.	Bridgford End crowd reaction	Colorsport
20.	Second goal against Everton	Mirrorpix
21.	Hat-trick goal against Everton	Mirrorpix
22.	Forest 3 Everton 2 cartoon	Bob Bond, www.footballershappen.com
23.	Reading the newspaper	Getty Images
24.	Listening to the FA Cup semi-final draw	Mirrorpix

25. Wedding photo with Forest team — Ian & Carol Storey-Moore
26. Wedding photo in limousine — Ian & Carol Storey-Moore
27. With Henry Newton — Mirrorpix
28. Wearing international caps — Ian Storey-Moore
29. Shooting vs Derby County — Mirrorpix
30. In Forest's classic away kit — Alamy
31. Pre-season photocall 1970/71 — Colorsport
32. Cartoon strip from *Tiger Comic* — Tiger © Copyright Rebellion Publishing IP Ltd. All rights reserved
33. Scoring against Arsenal — Mirrorpix
34. With Alan Ball — Mirrorpix
35. With fan club — Mirrorpix
36. Final goal at the City Ground — Mirrorpix
37. With Brian Clough at Baseball Ground — Alamy
38. With Peter Taylor — Mirrorpix
39. Matt Gillies and Tony Wood — Paul Popper/ Popperfoto/Getty Images
40. Derby County transfer form — Sunday Express/Mirrorpix
41. Signing for Manchester United — Mirrorpix
42. Carol and Laska Gerry Murray, www.gerrymurrayphotos.com
43. Denis Law cracks a joke — Alamy
44. In action against Coventry City — Colorsport
45. Celebrating against Derby County — Bob Thomas Sports/Getty Images
46. Pre-season photocall 1972 — Colorsport
47. With George Best and Bobby Charlton — Alamy
48. Chicago Sting squad photo 1975 — Stuart Humphreys
49. Burton Albion — Ian Storey-Moore
50. Shepshed Charterhouse — Mirrorpix
51. Scunthorpe United Guest XI — Ian Storey-Moore
52. Forest versus Notts County friendly — Mirrorpix
53. Ian & Carol at launderette — News Licensing (JS776394)
54. With Tony Delahunty and Brian Moore — Mirrorpix
55. Publican at Wheatsheaf Inn — Robert Rathbone, www.robertrathbone.co.uk
56. Forest Legends Raceday — Mirrorpix

Bibliography

Books

Baxter, J., *The Party's Over* (Cornerstone, 1984)

Brindley, J., *20 Legends: Nottingham Forest* (Vertical Editions, 2016)

Broughton, C., *Forest Ever Forest* (Tricky Red Publications, 2001)

Dickinson, M., *Bobby Moore – The Man in Full* (Yellow Jersey Press, 2014)

Dolloway, A.S., *Nottingham Forest in the Sixties – The Forgotten Decade* (Mad Max Publishing, 2015)

Dolloway, A.S., *Those Were The Days: Nottingham Forest in the 60s – Extra Time* (Max Media Publishing, 2019)

Donnelly, J., *Jimmy The Weed – Inside The Quality Street Gang: My Life in the Manchester Underworld* (Milo Books, 2011)

Horner, M., *He Shot, He Scored: The Official Biography of Peter Ward* (Sea View Media, 2009)

Hurst, G., *1966 and All That: My Autobiography by Geoff Hurst* (Headline Publishing Group, 2002)

Marples, D., *The History Boys – Thirty Iconic Goals in the History of Nottingham Forest* (Pitch Publishing, 2018)

Matthews, T., *The Forest Who's Who* (Britespot Publishing, 2004)

McVay, D., *Forest's Cult Heroes* (Know The Score Books, 2007)

O'Neill, M., *On Days Like These* (Macmillan, 2022)

Page, R., *Burton Albion: The Complete History* (The Derby Books Publishing Company, 2010)

Robertson, J., *Supertramp* (Mainstream Publishing, 2011)

Smales, K., *Forest: The First 125 Years – The Official Statistical Record of the Nottingham Forest Football Club* (Temple Printing, 1991)

Soar, P., *The Official History of Nottingham Forest* (Polar, 1998)

Taylor, D., *Deep into the Forest* (The Breedon Books Publishing Company, 2009)

Taylor, P. and Langley, M., *With Clough, By Taylor* (Sidgwick & Jackson, 1980)

Annual handbooks

Chicago Sting, *Media Guide*, 1975
Nottingham Football Post, *Post Football Guide*, 1963 to 1972
Nottingham Forest, *Official Handbook*, 1961/62 to 1971/72

Matchday programmes

Aston Villa
Burton Albion
England under-23 and full international matches
Football League Review
Manchester City
Manchester United
Nottingham Forest
Sheffield Wednesday
Stoke City

Magazines, fanzines and comics

Backpass
Bandy & Shinty
Goal
Soccer Star
Shoot!
Tiger

Newspapers (in print and via digital archives at britishnewspaperarchive.com, newspapers.com and pressreader.com)

Local newspapers:
Birmingham Sunday Mercury
Burton Daily Mail
Coventry Evening Telegraph
Derby Evening Telegraph
Liverpool Echo
Manchester Evening News
Newcastle Evening Chronicle
Nottingham Evening Post

Nottingham Evening News
Nottingham Football Post
Nottingham Guardian Journal
Scunthorpe Evening Telegraph
South London Press

National newspapers:
Daily Express
Daily Mail
Daily Mirror
Daily Sketch
Daily Telegraph
Financial Times
News of the World
The Observer
Sporting Life
The Sun
Sunday Express
Sunday Mirror
Sunday Observer
Sunday People
Sunday Telegraph
The Times
Weekly News

US newspapers:
Boston Globe (Massachusetts)
Chicago Tribune (Illinois)
Daily Herald (Illinois)
Edwardsville Intelligencer (Illinois)
Elk Grove Herald (Illinois)
Fort Collins Coloradoan (Colorado)
Mt. Vernon Register-News (Illinois)
North Adams Transcript (Massachusetts)
San Antonio Express (Texas)
Statesman Journal (Oregon)

Websites

General:
wikipedia.org

British football statistics and related information:
11v11.com
englandstats.com
fchd.info
mufcinfo.com
punditarena.com
thecityground.com
vintagefootballers.com

US soccer statistics and related information:
nasljerseys.com
soccerhistoryusa.org
soccerstats.us
statscrew.com
ussoccerplayers.com
unitedfactsbook.com

Nottingham in the 1960s and early 1970s:
leftlion.co.uk
nottinghampost.com
nottstalgia.com

Grainy clips of Ian Storey-Moore playing for Nottingham Forest, Manchester United and Chicago Sting:
youtube.com

Index